CATASTROPHE
the violent earth

CATASTROPHE
the violent earth

Tony Waltham

Crown Publishers, Inc. New York

The publishers would like to thank the following for supplying illustration material:

Alabama Geological Survey 45; Associated Press 20, 41; Bristol United Press 48; Camera Press 5 (and back jacket) photo by Delaney/Hacker, 8, 12, 14 photo by Filipiniana Press, 15 (and front jacket) photo by Astor Magnusson, 16 photo by Astor Magnusson, 17 (and back jacket) photo by U.S. Navy, 31, 35, 39, 44; Hawaiian Observatory 18; Illustrated London News 1; Keystone Press Agency 2, 6 (and back jacket), 7, 11, 23, 32, 33; Frank W. Lane 3, 27 photo by *Montreal Gazette*, 28 photo by Alberta Government, 34; Popperfoto 26, 42, 43, 47, 52 (and back jacket), 54; Press Association 22, 25, 37, 49, 56; *San Francisco Examiner* 29; Syndication International 36; *The Times* 24; U.S. Geological Survey 4, 9, 10, 13, 40, 46.

All other material supplied by the author.

Line maps by R & B Art.

Map on p. 6 redrawn courtesy Penguin Books Ltd (from *Volcanoes* by Peter Francis, 1976).

First published in the USA 1978 by Crown Publishers, Inc., New York

Library of Congress Cataloging in Publication Data

Waltham, Tony.
   Catastrophe: The Violent Earth
   1. Natural Disasters.   I. Title
GB5018.W34   1978   904'.5   78.8756
ISBN   0-517-532093

Printed in Great Britain

CONTENTS

PREFACE

There are dozens of books on geology and earth processes. There are dozens of books on disasters and the heart-rending human stories which spring from them. Why then this book? Quite simply, to bridge the gap – to bring together the catastrophes to mankind and their geological causes, and to balance man's responsibilities against seemingly unavoidable natural events.

All three thousand million of us in the world live on the ground, and we tend to regard that ground as something solid and reliable. When it fails us – by shaking or exploding, collapsing or sliding away – we are left feeling vulnerable. For too many of us this is either a direct or a veiled threat, yet in many cases the threat is due to man's own folly, and is therefore avoidable. This book considers the possibilities of avoiding such disasters, looks at the geology of the situations in non-technical terms, and so gives the non-geologist a little more understanding of the fascinating but sometimes hazardous world in which we live.

The original idea for the book developed from a series of lectures given to civil engineering students at Trent Polytechnic. These students were not specialists in geology, but they had to appreciate how civil engineers could either precipitate or magnify the effects of natural disasters – or with care minimise the effects. Researching for those lectures I discovered the need for such a book. In pursuing many of the case-histories given here, I found a mass of information concerning some and a haze of devious comments on others. Bringing all these cases together in a book which has no great academic pretensions has, I hope, produced something of interest to many laymen, but still also relevant to those students.

In some cases it has proved impossible to avoid introducing obscure geological concepts, where these are at the root of a particular catastrophe. For these instances a glossary is appended, but geological jargon has been avoided as far as possible wherever the situation can be correctly described in plain English. Similarly, the book can be understood without reference to other works, and a basic bibliography is appended only for those who want to go further into the more specialised literature.

If the end result of this book is a greater understanding of our environment, then it will have been worth the undertaking.

TONY WALTHAM
Nottingham 1978

EARTHQUAKES

Just before midday on 1 September 1923, a suburban train was on its way from Tokyo to Yokohama. Suddenly the train lurched violently from side to side, and the passengers clung to their seats as it made an emergency stop. Looking from the coach windows, the travellers saw with horror the stone face of a cutting explode on to the railway tracks. Tiles and even entire roofs were torn from houses and a four-storey concrete building disintegrated in a cloud of dust.

Tokyo and Yokohama had just been hit by a terrible earthquake. 'Quake' is exactly what the earth does: it heaves and sways, rocks about, and even splits open. The movement may last only for seconds, or at the most for a few minutes, but in that time the effect can be catastrophic. Earthquakes vary enormously in intensity. There may be only mild shaking movements which will disturb people and make lights swing around, but will do hardly any structural damage to buildings. They may be so slight that they can be detected only by instrument – small earth vibrations on this scale occur in some parts of the world every few minutes.

Certain regions in the world are recognised as earthquake belts, notably around the perimeter of the Pacific Ocean and across central Asia to the Mediterranean Sea. Outside these and many other lesser belts, the chance of severe damage from an earthquake is small – Britain, for example, can be regarded as safe. But within the belts, earthquakes may strike in almost any place and at any time. When the shaken region is an unpopulated mountain or desert, the effect may be slight: even a strong earthquake in the empty wastes of Siberia may become little more than a scientific record, but the same earthquake in an urban region can cause terrifying destruction. Tokyo, Lisbon, Skopje, Guatemala City, Managua and San Francisco are just some of the cities that have been almost wiped out by earthquakes.

Strictly speaking, earthquakes are ground movements caused by shock waves. The geological forces which are active within the earth's interior are inconceivably vast – vast enough to move entire continents, albeit very slowly, for geological time is on a slow scale. The movements which take place result in stress building up in the rocks which form the crust of the Earth. These stresses can go on building up until they are greater than the strength of the rocks themselves; then the rocks break and move, in order to release the build-up of stress. They may move only a few feet, but the energy released by billions of tons of rock moving just that far is immense, and it is dissipated by shock waves which shake the rocks and the ground above.

But rock movement and shock waves are not the only features of earthquakes. The actual displacement of rock which causes the earthquake is only rarely seen at the surface – more commonly it is completely underground, often at a depth of many miles. In this case the vibration of the ground has many secondary consequences. In urban areas much of the destruction of buildings is due directly to their being shaken so much that they just fall apart, and such damage frequently leads to fires from broken gas mains and shorted electrical circuits. When the water mains have also been broken by the ground movement, a town may burn almost unchecked. The ground itself may also break up with the shaking. Soft sediments are particularly likely to slump and subside and open up in great cracks; in hill regions the landslides frequently triggered by earthquakes can lead to vast destruction in their own right. An additional hazard in coastal areas is the effect of the ground movements on the sea: gigantic waves, known as tsunamis, may sweep over quake-flattened towns or even travel across seas and oceans to cause havoc thousands of miles away.

Near the south-east end of the island of Jamaica, overlooked by the towering Blue Mountains, there is a large sheltered bay with a long sand spit projecting right into it. Inside the sand spit, known as the Palisadoes, is a perfect natural harbour; it is now known as Kingston Harbour, for the port and capital city of Jamaica has grown up on its inland rim. But Kingston has not always been the site of the port. An earlier settlement was at Port Royal, right at the end of the eight mile long Palisadoes spit. It was a fine defensive site, and with the harbour tucked inside it Port Royal grew in importance during the seventeenth century. It was the centre of the buccaneering world of the Caribbean and was known, after the most notorious pirate, as Henry Morgan's capital. Though Port Royal was built only on sand and gravel, it contained two heavily defended forts and a church overlooking houses, shops and warehouses, many built of wood and mostly clustered around the harbour side. The town was a hive of activity, the commercial centre for a large area.

But all this came to an end just before midday on 7 June 1692, when Port Royal was hit by an earthquake. Contemporary accounts tell how the earth heaved and swelled, how houses were shaken and shattered, how the bells of St Paul's church first rang but then were silenced as the tower collapsed, and how the brick buildings crumpled into piles of debris. Great cracks opened and closed in the ground, as the sand and gravel on which the town was built slumped into the sea: two-thirds of the town slid beneath water. The ground vibrations set up great waves in the harbour and many ships were overturned, though some were swept on land and their crews saved. The greatest wave was formed as the sea swept out of the harbour; when it came crashing back in, it flooded forever all of the town not already below sea level. Within three minutes, 2000 people had died, and Port Royal was lost – never again to become more than the fishing village it is today.

The focus – the source from which the shock waves emanated – of the Port Royal earthquake is not known; it could have been many miles away. Many of the buildings were shaken and broken by the ground vibrations, which also caused the great waves in the harbour, but the reason Port Royal suffered so badly was because of its inadequate foundations. The sand and gravel of the Palisadoes is loose and unconsolidated, besides which parts of the town had been built on badly laid fill just dumped into sea. Strong vibration of all this sediment made it extremely unstable and it moved only too easily. The great cracks which opened up across the town, and which actually swallowed some of the fleeing inhabitants, were nothing to do with the rock movements that caused the earthquake but were the result of the sand slumping into the sea. Vibrating a sand bank such as the Palisadoes is like tamping down a jar of sugar – the loose material will move down the slightest gradient. The

1692 earthquake created just that effect, causing the sand and the town to slide massively and disappear into the harbour. Had Port Royal been built on a rock headland, it might have been damaged in the earthquake, but it is unlikely that it would have been so completely destroyed.

Earthquake waves and ground movement

The most damaging effect of the majority of earthquakes is the actual vibration of the ground by the shock waves themselves. There are four different types of earthquake waves which each have their own individual characteristics and travel at contrasting speeds. First to arrive at any point are the two types of waves which travel very fast through the rock. These are the primary P waves which are of a compressional wave form (like the bumping of trucks in a shunting goods train), and the secondary S waves, which are shear waves (as in a shaken skipping-rope). In most cases both the P and S waves are of such small amplitude that they can only be detected instrumentally, on seismographs; but they do have another significance. Though the actual speed of the waves depends on the rock type through which they are travelling, the P wave moving at 4–5 miles per second is always about twice as fast as the S wave, and the difference in arrival time at a seismograph station can therefore be used to determine the distance to the source, or focus, of the earthquake. Much slower than both these 'through-the-rock' waves are the surface waves. The speed of these is about half that of the S waves, but they have the greatest amplitude and cause most damage, making the ground visibly quake.

Though earthquakes are often described as instantaneous events and on a geological time-scale they are – they do last for a measurable length of time. The different waves arrive at different times, but only the surface waves are significant in terms of damage. Normally the surface movement will last for less than a minute: at San Francisco in 1906 the earthquake lasted about 40 seconds, although the great earthquake of Alaska in 1964 lasted five times as long. After this the waves just damp down, but then come the aftershocks. These are the extra pulses of wave motion which emanate from further rock movements at or near the same point as the original disturbance; they can last for many days and may be only instrumentally detectable, or they may be major events in their own right. In the twenty-four hours after the 1964 Alaska earthquake there were 28 aftershocks, 10 of which were significantly large. Aftershocks commonly make the clearing-up operation after an earthquake both hazardous and ineffectual.

The dramatic nature of earthquakes tends to lead to embellishment and exaggeration in eye-witness accounts, and in most cases, earthquake waves are felt merely as strong and violent ground movements. Nevertheless groundwaves – literally waves moving across the ground just as in a lake – do occur and some accounts can be taken as reliable. In the Californian earthquake of 1906 groundwaves up to 3 feet high were described in some places, and elsewhere waves a third of that height with a wavelength of 60 feet were seen moving across the ground. A much shorter wavelength, of 6–12 feet, was ascribed to groundwaves in the 1934 earthquake in the Ganges Valley of India, and in the same country the great Assam earthquake of 1897 set up waves which moved 'faster than a man could walk but slower than he could run'.

The scale of an earthquake is normally described by either its intensity or its magnitude. The magnitude of a quake is measured on a scale named after the man who developed it, the Richter scale. This defines the magnitude as the logarithm of the amplitude (measured in thousandths of a millimetre) of the largest wave recorded on a standard seismograph 100 kilometres from the epicentre (the point on the surface directly above the focus or origin of the quake). Magnitude is therefore accurately measurable for any earthquake, and each division on the scale, from 1–9, represents an order of magnitude: magnitude 5 would be 10 times the energy released in a quake of magnitude 4. In contrast the intensity of an earthquake is a qualitative measure of the effect at any particular point. It is recorded on the modified Mercalli scale which runs from I to XII (always in roman numerals to avoid confusion with magnitude), and the divisions are based on observed movement and the extent of damage. The intensity of an earthquake, of course, falls off with increasing distance from the epicentre. An intensity of VII will be experienced near the epicentre of an earthquake of magnitude 5, which is the weakest earthquake to cause extensive damage to buildings, though properly built earthquake-proofed buildings should survive. Major earthquakes are those with a magnitude of 6.5 or more, where extensive damage corresponds to IX on the intensity scale. The worst earthquakes, such as the San Francisco one of 1906 with a magnitude of 8.3, result in almost total damage equivalent to XI or XII on the intensity scale.

Earthquake waves, like any other wave form, can be damped, or amplified, or can even resonate due to differing ground conditions. Consequently the intensity of earthquake damage depends not only on the quake magnitude but also on the local geology. The most marked geological contrast in earthquake behaviour is between solid rocks and unconsolidated sediments. Far from having any cushioning effect against earthquake vibration, uncemented sediments provide the worst possible foundation material.

The 1967 earthquake in Venezuela's capital city, Caracas, was, with a magnitude of 6.5, not especially strong, but four high-rise buildings collapsed like pancakes, with a death toll of 200. All four buildings stood on alluvium: the sediment became almost totally incoherent when vibrated and the earthquake waves were freely amplified; and in addition the wave frequency in the alluvium was the same as the natural frequency of the buildings so that an undulating harmonic motion developed, destroying them completely. In complete contrast was the much stronger earthquake which struck southern California in 1952. Within the damage zone lay Crystal Cave, in which a party of tourists, surrounded by solid limestone, had felt nothing. These geological differences have significant implications in the science of earthquake zoning, and particularly so when the many side-effects of earthquake vibration of sediments are taken into account.

Faults and earthquakes

It has long been realised that earthquakes are closely related to faults, but until around the turn of the last century it was thought that faults were caused by earthquakes. This was founded on simple observation of surface faulting, but a more systematic study of larger-scale and deeper faults showed that the opposite is true.

In many parts of the Earth's crust there are differential forces which result in slow elastic deformation of the rocks. These stresses can go on building up strain in the crust which eventually surpasses what the rocks can endure. The rocks break, and movement takes place along the fracture until the strain in the rock is partly or wholly relieved. This sudden movement and release of energy establishes the shock waves which form an earthquake – an explanation of earthquake origins known as the Elastic Rebound Theory. Earthquake aftershocks, which normally do not originate from precisely the same spot as the main shock, are caused by the transfer of strain to adjacent blocks of rock themselves already partially strained. Each movement triggers more movements until the whole effect dies out.

The slow build-up of strain in rocks is shown in the way faults can move by slow creep, independent of sudden failure and earthquakes. In the famous 1906 earthquake at San Francisco, the Pacific Ocean floor moved about 20 feet northwards past the American landmass, but in the previous fifty years there had been additional movement totalling over half that distance without any earthquakes. The same fault zone is still moving, and buildings and sidewalks in Hollister, further south in California, are actually being slowly torn apart sideways. A weakness in the Elastic Rebound Theory is that at depths of more than three miles the pressure and temperature are so high that rock does not break but deforms plastically. If, however, water seeps in it will reduce friction along crack boundaries enough to allow sudden movement. This inflow of water indicates that the cracks in the rock must be enlarging under the increasing stress, which has given this hypothesis the name of the Dilatational Source Theory. The theory is not yet completely understood, but the dilating of the rock and the subsequent water movement can be inferred from measured shock-wave velocities, so it must provide at least some of the answer in some cases.

Many small faults seen to move at the surface, particularly those in layers of soft sediments, are the result of earthquakes. They are mainly caused by settling of the sediment due to the shock-wave vibration, and are the exceptions to the rule of fault origins for earthquakes. Usually the fault movement of an earthquake is entirely at depth, but in some cases it is seen at the surface. The 1959 earthquake in Montana, USA, was associated with a fault which developed a scarp 14 miles long and up to 14 feet high. In Alaska's 1964 earthquake the fault was not seen at the surface, but surveying revealed that 100,000 square miles of land and sea-floor had been displaced. Almost half the area had moved up and half down, and the maximum total relative movement was 38 feet. In the 1923 Tokyo earthquake, it was claimed that parts of the bed of Sagami Bay had moved up or down by hundreds of feet, but this seems hard to believe and one must question the reliability of the submarine surveys. The greatest undisputed vertical movement in an earthquake was recorded in 1899 at Yakatut Bay, Alaska, when parts of the shoreline were uplifted by 47.5 feet.

Clearly, the worldwide distribution of earthquakes must be related to the distribution of faults, especially active faults – and these do have an easily recognisable pattern. The outer crust of the Earth consists of a layer averaging 40 miles in thickness, consisting of about a dozen major plates which are themselves relatively rigid. These plates, however, move about on the more plastic inner layers of the Earth which are in almost perpetual very slow motion due to convection currents rising from the hot centre. The boundaries between the plates are therefore

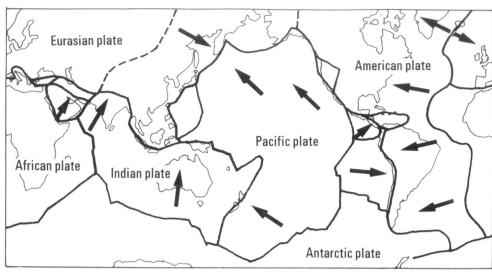

The major plates which make up the Earth's crust, with the plate boundaries marking the belts of instability commonly expressed as earthquakes and volcanoes.

the geologically active parts of the world. The movement on the plate boundaries can be of contrasting types: some plates are moving towards each other, with consequent overriding, some are tearing apart, and others have a purely sideways slip. Each movement gives rise to its own variety of faulting, but all result in earthquakes. In contrast to these earthquake belts, the plates themselves are stable and normally free of major deep-seated earthquakes. Among the rare exceptions were the 1811 earthquakes of New Madrid in a stable plate area of the eastern United States.

Two-thirds of the world's significantly large earthquakes have occurred in the Circum-Pacific Belt. This most active of the earthquake zones lies along a number of plate boundaries, and to people living in this belt earthquakes are almost a way of life. The second great earthquake belt lies along the plate boundaries from the East Indies, along the Himalayas and down the axis of the Mediterranean. Though it does not equal the Pacific for total numbers of earthquakes, 75 per cent of the world's earthquake deaths during the twenty years up to 1970 were in this belt – due largely to the higher population densities within it.

Japan suffers appallingly from earthquakes, due to its position near the boundary of three major plates. On 1 September 1923 an earthquake of intensity 8.3 was centred in Sagami Bay. The result was widespread destruction in both Tokyo and the port of Yokohama, but even worse were the fires which started during the earthquake and, because the water mains were broken and useless, raged unchecked through the many wooden buildings. Over half the city of Tokyo was burned to the ground, as well as practically the whole of Yokohama. The death toll was horrific: 40,000 people crowded into a city park in an attempt to escape from the burning buildings, and all but 2000 of them died, mostly of smoke asphyxiation. In all, 142,800 people died as the result of that one earthquake – still Japan's worst ever. The Pacific earthquake belt continues to move. Though Japan has not been

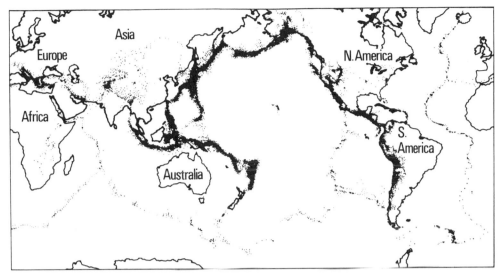

World distribution of earthquakes. Comparison with the map opposite shows clearly the relationship between earthquakes and plate boundaries.

hit in recent years, the toll continues elsewhere in the belt – Peru in 1970, California in 1971, Nicaragua in 1972, Guatemala in 1973 and the Philippines in 1976. At the same time, the Himalaya–Mediterranean belt has continued to be active, with Turkey being the worst hit.

Straddling the great Himalaya–Mediterranean earthquake belt, Turkey is typical of a country which has lived with earthquakes throughout its history. In 1939, 40,000 people died when the city of Erzincan was largely destroyed by a quake of magnitude 7.9. Since then there have been twenty more earthquakes in Turkey involving loss of life, in which nearly 20,000 more people have died. The most recent was on 24 November 1976 at Muradiye near Lake Van; it had a magnitude of 7.6 and effectively flattened the town of Muradiye. In addition, dozens of villages were almost totally destroyed; the poorly constructed stone houses with their heavy timber and stone roofs collapsed all too easily. The death toll ran to over 4000, and rescue work was severely hampered by numerous aftershocks. The remoteness of the area and sub-zero temperatures added to the misery of the thousands of homeless villagers.

The distribution of Turkey's earthquakes shows a definite pattern. Half of the recent major quakes lie on a curved east–west line which traces that of the Anatolian Fault Zone. This major fracture line represents the boundary between the enormous Eurasian plate to the north, and the Turkish plate which is one of the smaller plates in the broken zone between Eurasia and the large plate on which Africa lies. Current movement on the Anatolian Fault is horizontal, with the southern block moving to the west by about four inches a year, and this great line of disturbance can be traced westwards into the Aegean and Balkan areas and eastwards into the earthquake belts of Iran. Not all Turkey's earthquakes lie right on this line. The two most recent and most disastrous quakes at the eastern end of the country, at Lice (1975) and Muradiye, both had their epicentres just off the line of the main fault but they were close enough to be considered a feature of the same plate boundary. Rather different was the catastrophic earthquake at Gediz in 1970. This and a number of other nearby quakes of lesser severity occurred well south of the Anatolian Fault. However, most of the earthquakes in the Gediz area have originated on major faults around the Menderes structural block, and they appear to be due to strain building up within the Turkish block itself and then being relieved by movement on pre-existing faults. The initial strain can probably be traced back to movement on the Anatolian Fault.

A feature of the Anatolian Fault Zone is that ground breakage occurs along most of its length. Some of the breakage has been due to slow continuous movement, and in other parts the movement was erratic enough to cause the various earthquakes. But the distribution along the fault zone of breakage during this century shows two gaps, where it would seem reasonable to infer that the rocks must now have a considerable strain accumulated within them – perhaps soon to overcome the resistance of the rocks and cause more earthquakes. The western gap is in the region of a number of earthquakes towards the end of the last century, so perhaps that part of the fault zone was relieved of stress then, but the eastern gap appears to be potentially the most dangerous zone along the fault. Meanwhile, thousands of people rebuild their villages after each earthquake, for it would be impossible to evacuate the entire zone. Memories are short, and people either forget or accept the hazards: they continue to live on the Anatolian Fault – including that section between Erzincan and Varto where the signs are so ominous.

The San Andreas Fault is probably the best known in the world, because it is spectacularly active and passes through two of the world's largest and richest urban areas – San Fancisco and Los Angeles. The line of the fault is northwest–southeast almost along the coast of southern California, and it is a massive tear fault essentially formed by the Pacific Ocean floor and a tiny coastal strip, moving northwards past the American continent at a rate of 2.5 inches a year. It is not just a single clean break but a zone with many branches. Most significant are the inland branches near San Francisco which pass through Oakland and Berkeley, and the complex pattern of faults behind Los Angeles where the Garlock Fault along the southern edge of the Sierra Nevada massif is a major fracture in its own right. It is the continued movement in many of the faults which has caused California's numerous earthquakes.

Side-effects: landslides, subsidence and tsunamis

Earthquakes have many alarming side-effects, which may add enormously to the immediate panic – and to the death toll. Perhaps the most frequently described and over-dramatised phenomena are earth fissures, or ground cracks, which are variously claimed to have swallowed men, animals, even houses and complete villages. As with so many popular misconceptions there is a grain of truth in these descriptions, though their actual scale may be less spectacular. Ground cracks can occur along the line of the break in the rocks which actually causes the earthquake, but such cracks are rare, usually limited in extent, and seldom gaping. The yawning fissures of earthquake accounts are likely to be secondary features formed by movement in generally unconsolidated surface sediments; they are usually

8

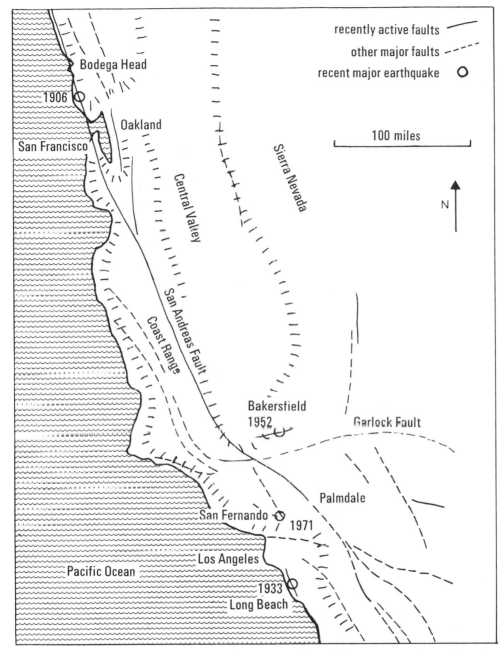

The San Andreas fault system of southern California and the recent major earthquakes which have originated on it.

associated with subsidence and landslide movement occurring when earthquake vibrations cause the sediments to lose cohesion and strength. Some spectacular fissures developed on Turnagain Heights in the 1964 Alaska earthquake; many long fissures over 3 feet wide and 10 feet deep were reported in the Mississippi Valley earthquake of 1811; Italy's 1783 earthquake in Calabria was the scene of huge numbers of fissures, some up to 225 feet deep, associated with extensive and disastrous landslides; and fissures were a major cause of damage both in Jamaica's 1692 earthquake at Port Royal and in that at Pegu, Burma, in 1930. In all these cases the fissures developed in thick layers of unconsolidated' surface sediments, giving yet another example of the inadequacy of sediment for foundations in earthquake-prone regions.

Vertical land movement, either uplift or subsidence, must be a common feature in earthquakes but is rarely great enough to be noticed without accurate surveying. The exception to this is the effect of subsidence in low-lying areas, where the result may be immediate inundation. The most famous side-effect of the 1811 New Madrid earthquake in the Mississippi Valley was the extensive subsidence and the formation of the 'sunken lands'. Vertical movement of over 20 feet was recorded, and as the subsided areas lay along the lines of river valleys they rapidly filled with water, and a whole series of elongate lakes was formed. The new Lake St Francis was 40 miles long, and Reelfoot Lake, though much shorter, was up to 4 miles wide. While many areas subsided others were uplifted or tilted, and in some places the tilting caused river channels to reverse their flow. The subsidence in this earthquake appeared to have two modes of origin: some, together with the tilting and uplifting, was due to the large-scale crustal warping which caused the earthquake, and this was then amplified by the settlement due to vibration of the river valley alluvium.

Alaska's 'Good Friday Earthquake' of 27 March 1964 was one of the largest known to man – it had a magnitude of about 8.5. Had it occurred in a more heavily populated area it would have ranked among the greatest disasters of all time. The epicentre of the main earthquake was almost midway between the cities of Anchorage and Valdez, and it caused serious damage over more than 25,000 square miles. Crustal displacement extended over an even greater area, right out to Kodiak Island nearly 500 miles to the south-west, as the floor of the Pacific Ocean moved in a sudden jerk in and underneath Alaska. Even in such a thinly populated area, over 100 people died and damage ran to over $300 million. Around the epicentre at Prince William Sound roads and railways were cut, and villages were either shaken to the ground or overrun by gigantic sea waves. Mines, railway tunnels and oil wells, all of which were relatively near to the earthquake's epicentre but cut in solid rock, suffered minimal damage, but the cities of Anchorage and Valdez about 80 miles away, built as they were on convenient coastal plains of unconsolidated sediments, were both heavily damaged.

Turnagain Heights is one of a number of low plateaux in and around Anchorage, occupied by a pleasant residential development. The plateau stands about 70 feet high and on the north-west side is bounded by cliffs overlooking the sea. Geologically it is very simple: horizontal glaciofluvial gravels about 5–20 feet thick rest on the lacustrine clays and silts of the Bootlegger Cove Clay which extend well below sea-level. When the earthquake struck, the houses suffered little from direct vibration, and for about a minute the ground held them firm. But the 1964 quake was unusual in that it lasted nearly four minutes, and within that time the entire structure of Turnagain Heights failed. A massive landslide developed as the clays and gravels moved on almost horizontal slip surfaces out in the direction of the sea cliffs. In some places the high-water mark was pushed back half a mile by the slide; behind the slide the ground broke up, subsided erratically, and was torn apart by

1 (above) *The scene of destruction near Uyeno station in Tokyo, with houses reduced to rubble by the fire which followed the 1923 earthquake.* 2 (below) *Structural damage caused by the unusually strong ground vibration in Tokyo's disastrous earthquake of 1923, which killed over 140,000 people.*

3 (above) *Debris from Huascaran's ice avalanche in 1962 swept down the Llanganuco valley on to the village of Ranrahirca. The ridge (arrowed) kept the debris clear of Yungay, off the left of the picture.* 4 (below) *In 1970 another landslide from Huascaran, triggered by the earthquake in Peru, swept over the arrowed col (see also above and map on p. 13) and buried Yungay beneath the rubble in the foreground.*

5 *A villager stands forlornly amid the rubble after the Persian earthquake of 1965, in which so many houses were completely destroyed because of their adobe construction.*

6 *The earthquake at San Fernando in 1971 demolished this freeway interchange, built to a design which was quite inadequate for an earthquake-prone area.*

7 (above) *A rare photograph taken from a train window of the havoc at a railway station after the 1976 earthquake at Tangshan, China.*   8 (below) *In 1976 the entire population of Peking spent many days and nights sitting in the streets, waiting for a predicted earthquake which never materialised.*

9 *One of the many spectacular effects of the famous San Francisco earthquake in 1906. Most of the houses in this street ended up at similarly crazy angles.*

10 (above) *The San Andreas Fault stretches from top to bottom of this photograph, just right of the highway. The housing estates between the road and the hills straddle the fault zone.* 11 (below) *The Olive View Hospital after the 1971 San Fernando earthquake, when the staircase blocks fell off the ends of each wing of the building.*

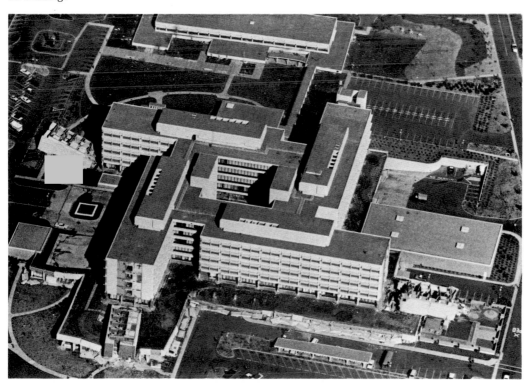

12 (above) *Earthquake vibrations amplified in the poor foundation material of this concrete multi-storey building in Caracas caused it to pancake, leaving only the floors intact.* 13 (below) *The school on Government Hill at Anchorage suffered severe damage in the 1964 earthquake through sliding of the conglomerate and clay on which it was built.*

huge tension fissures. Dozens of houses were wrecked, and many more were severely damaged by ground cracks beneath them. One man described standing in his front drive seeing his own house move rapidly away from him and then his neighbour's house slide into a great fissure.

This massive slide at Turnagain Heights, together with other comparable slides in similar geological situations in the city, was due to the complete failure of sensitive layers within the Bootlegger Cave Clay. Sensitive clays are those which, if disturbed and remoulded without any loss of interstitial water content, lose practically all their strength. When the individual clay grains are separated from each other by water, the whole material acts almost as a liquid. The prolonged vibration by the 1964 earthquake was enough to eliminate any strength that these clays had, and consequently they behaved as layers of lubricant on which rested the remaining clays and overlying gravels. With the free face of the sea cliffs on the nothern side offering no resistance to any such movement, a massive complex landslide moved on the failed clays in that direction. The overlying gravels played no part in the initial failure, but once the clay had spread out to the north, the more resistant gravel beds not only subsided but broke and tilted irregularly.

The most worrying thing about the failure of Turnagain Heights is that it was predictable. Many small old landslips were recognisable before 1964 around the edge of the plateau, and gravels on top of clays are well known to be prone to slip; what is more, Anchorage is known to be in an active earthquake belt, and even though the 1964 quake was an exceptionally large one, earthquakes are notorious triggers of movement on unstable slopes. The sensitivity of clay can easily be determined in a laboratory experiment, and the US Geological Survey's report on the Anchorage region, published in 1959, described both the extremely low strength of the Bootlegger Cove Clay and the likelihood of earthquakes disturbing it. Incredibly, the city planners, engineers and builders, together responsible for siting the residential suburbs on Turnagain Heights, either did not know of this report, or ignored it. Maybe the dramatic scale of the landslide was not predictable, but there can be no excuse for any future development in such a situation.

The most spectacular effect of earthquakes on sediment occurs when the vibration makes very porous saturated sands compact. The compaction is caused by better packing of the sand grains and a consequent decrease of space between them, and the result is an upward movement of the water squeezed out of these voids. The water movement then tends to support the grains and the result is liquefaction of the sand – turning it into a quicksand. The Japanese coastal city of Niigata was built on a plain of porous, undercompacted sand, which unfortunately liquefied extensively during an earthquake in June 1964. The results were dramatic. Houses sank gently into the liquid sediment: one house-owner 'lost' his ground floor, for when the earthquake ceased and the ground restabilised his front door porch had its roof at the new ground level. Parked vehicles sank into the ground, and a buried sewage tank floated to the surface. Several apartment blocks suffered damage in a most unusual way. Because Niigata was known to be in an earthquake belt, as is the whole of Japan, the blocks had been built to withstand earthquake vibrations. Indeed, they did not fail in 1964, but a building is only as strong as its foundations, and instead of collapsing the buildings just lost their balance on the liquefied ground and tilted over. Some moved only a little, but one block lay right over on its side, with hardly a crack in its reinforced concrete structure. The movement was slow as the sand had still been very viscous, and a woman on top of a block at the time of the earthquake rode safely down on the tilting building and stepped off at ground level.

As the water escapes from and 'blows' up out of a liquefying sand it can form geysers or mud spouts on the surface. In the San Francisco quake of 1906 the geysers reached heights of 20 feet, and when they subsided they left conical craters surrounded by small heaps of sand and mud. Another side-effect is seiches – waves formed by ground movement in lakes and rivers which can result in water being slopped over lake rims or dams – though few cases of serious damage have been reported. There is considerable debate on the audio-visual effects of earthquakes. Certainly some earthquake waves have vibration frequencies which make them audible to man, and many more can be heard by animals. Various descriptions have likened earthquake sounds to high winds, express trains, distant rumbles of gunfire, and even explosions. Such reports may be exaggerated because of the not surprisingly stressed state of the people giving them, but it is acceptable that earthquake sounds exist. There is more doubt about claims of flashes of light associated with earthquakes, which are frequently described by witnesses. Some may be ascribed to lightning in the disturbed atmosphere, or to the shorting of electrical appliances in populated areas; others are not easily explained but could be related to the barely understood build-up of static electricity through ground movement.

Landslides are among the most destructive earthquake effects. The vibration and disturbance due to an earthquake results in a temporary, very marked reduction in the critical angle at which a slope of any given material will fail. Again the most disastrous effects are on unconsolidated sediments. In California's 1971 earthquake a landslide developed in San Fernando and moved on a slope of less than 2°, whereas a 10° slope is normally regarded as safe in almost any sediment. The December 1920 earthquake in the Kansu region of northern China is best known for the enormous landslides which it triggered. Kansu is in the great basin of the Hwang Ho River where the dominant landscape is of a broad dissected plateau of loess, a fine wind-blown silt, uncemented and with a very low internal cohesion. When vibrated it failed dramatically, and hundreds of slides developed: one was large enough to move a road over half a mile. More tragic was the loss of life. Many of the peasant population of the area lived in cave houses which they had carved into the sides of the loess hills; the sediment was ideal for this purpose, as it could be worked by hand tools yet would hold firm over quite large rooms – until disturbed by vibration or slide movements. The cave homes were instantly destroyed, and the toll of human life approached 100,000. During the famous 1923 earthquake in Japan, a landslide of red loam soil met a mountain stream above Sagami Bay. The combination resulted in a great mudflow 50 feet deep which swept down the valley and took houses, a road, a railway station and a train containing 200 passengers into the sea, without a single survivor. Again, in Italy's 1783 earthquake in Calabria, thick clay layers and soils slipped *en masse* off the bedrock granite of the mountains, and many of the 30,000 deaths in this disaster were caused by landslides and mudflows.

All four of these earthquake-triggered landslides developed in unconsolidated sediments, and they show clearly the hazards of sediment as opposed to solid rock in earthquake belts. At the same time they demonstrate the inability of any planning or engineering design to prevent such disasters – short of the totally impractical step of depopulating all sloping regions in earthquake belts. Besides, solid rock too can fail under earthquake stresses. The 1959 earthquake in Montana, USA, triggered a huge landslide near Hebgen Lake. The slide was in weathered and jointed rock, and as well as burying a holiday camping-ground it blocked the Madison River valley and formed a temporary lake. Even more destructive were the landslides caused by the 1970 earthquake in Peru.

On the afternoon of 31 May 1970, all but one of a sixteen-man team of Czechoslovakian mountaineers were killed when an avalanche of snow and ice hit their camp on Nevados Huascaran, one of the highest mountains in the Peruvian Andes. The avalanche was triggered by an earthquake – and elsewhere in Peru the effects of the earthquake were far more devastating. The epicentre of the quake was 15 miles out beneath the floor of the Pacific: it struck without any warning, with a magnitude of 7.7. The nearest town was Chimbote, built on the coastal plain, which suffered extensive damage when the vibration caused compaction and spreading of the plain sediments. Some areas were heavily fissured and others sank below the water-table to become permanently flooded. Many modern concrete buildings survived, but nearly all the traditionally built adobe houses crumbled to the ground. As the shocks began people ran into the streets, and only a few were killed.

In complete contrast, 30 miles inland in the heavily populated Huaylas valley, immediately west of the highest mountains, the death toll was horrific. Situated in the crowded valley, the main city of Huaraz could not spread out like Chimbote on its wide plain; its houses were mostly two or three storeys high, lining both sides of narrow streets. Though the earthquake was weaker here it lasted 30 seconds, and half that time was enough to see the collapse of most of the stone-built houses. With their heavy tiled roofs they almost burst into the streets, and most roads ended up 10 feet deep in rubble. The people had no chance, and 10,000 of them – half the population – died in Huaraz alone.

Further down the Huaylas valley there were dozens of landslides on the steep slopes of the recently uplifted mountains. Numerous terrace slopes in alluvium and glaciofluvial gravels failed, and in addition many snow avalanches were caused by the earthquake which then triggered larger landslides and mudflows. Two slides blocked rivers and formed dangerously unstable lakes until trenches could be cut through the debris dams. Worst of all was the avalanche on the steep and unstable Nevados Huascaran. From near the summit of this 21,860 foot mountain, a half-mile-long chunk of snow cornice crashed down the near-vertical western face. It fell 3000 feet to the foot of the face, where it pulverised – partially melted due to frictional heat, and mixed with millions of tons of broken rock and moraine debris – and continued down the mountain. It was an enormous avalanche of debris, looser than a landslide, flowing like a mudflow, and in its next 8 miles it had a vertical descent of 10,000 feet. It moved at up to 250 mph – so fast that in places it rode on an air cushion, right over bushes and vegetation which it left untouched. Hurtling down a side valley it aimed for the floor of the main Huaylas valley. At the junction lay the village of Ranrahirca: it was annihilated. The speed of the avalanche was such that rocks 20 feet across were thrown into the air, landing hundreds of yards beyond the flow, and the main flow rode clean over low hills.

One lobe of the avalanche hurtled over a 500 foot high ridge and swept down on to the town of Yungay. When the earthquake had initially shaken, and half destroyed Yungay, the inhabitants had heard and seen the avalanche starting high up on

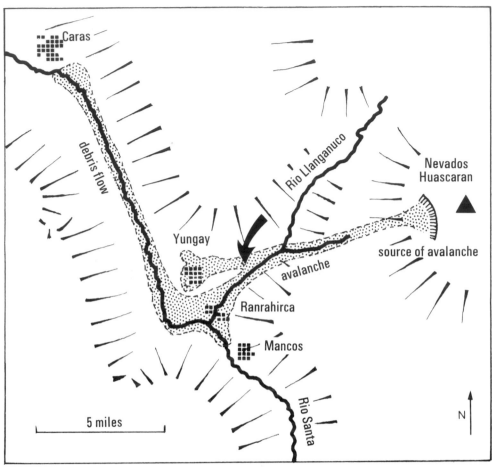

The course of the destructive avalanche from Huascaran which was set off by the great Peru earthquake of 1970.

Huascaran. They had started running, aiming for high ground – a hill with the cemetery on it was the nearest to the centre of the town. Two minutes later the avalanche arrived, almost like a breaking wave with its front wall of mud and debris higher than most of the buildings. The people were still running. Ninety-two of them made it to the safety of the cemetery hill. Most of the rest died. Figures varying from 10,000 to 20,000 have been quoted as the death toll in the town of Yungay, buried for ever in the avalanche debris: either way it was a terrifying disaster.

There was no warning of the 1970 earthquake, and the possibility of a repeat has to be lived with in Peru. But there were important lessons to be learned, and certain changes that could be made after the event. It was safe to rebuild Chimbote where it was, avoiding a few low-lying areas on weak ground. Huaraz could be rebuilt but with wider streets, for it was mainly the density of buildings which had caused the high death toll there. The village of Ranrahirca had to be resited out of range of the avalanche threat; (it had already been half destroyed in 1962 by a smaller avalanche from Huascaran, not started by an earthquake; after that it had been rebuilt on the same site – only a second disaster rammed the message home). On the other hand Yungay, protected by a ridge from any but the very largest of avalanche slides, was as well situated there as anywhere else, given the hazards of any earthquake-prone mountain region.

One of the more terrifying side-effects of earthquakes peculiar to coastal regions is inundation by tsunamis. Tsunami is a Japanese term for an unusually large sea wave, commonly misnamed 'tidal wave'. Most tsunamis have an earthquake origin, being masses of water physically impelled by a fault movement on the seabed, though they can also originate from submarine landslides or volcanic activity. Seismic tsunamis are usually formed where submarine faults have a significant vertical movement, and faults of this type most commonly occur along the coasts of Japan, the Aleutian Islands and South America, making the Pacific Ocean the home of most tsunamis. Horizontal fault movements, such as along the Californian coast, do not result in tsunamis, and while this makes the Californian coast relatively safe, statistics show that the east coast of Honshu, Japan, can expect a locally destructive tsunami on average every ten years.

In the open ocean tsunamis normally have a barely detectable amplitude and a very long wavelength, with successive waves anything from five minutes to an hour apart. They travel at speeds of around 400 mph, but the speed is proportional to depth, so that in coastal areas the waves slow down and build up in height, rushing ashore as highly destructive breakers which have been known to run up on land to heights of nearly 100 feet above normal sea-level. The most destructive tsunami known was on the densely populated Bengal coast of northern India in 1876 when over 200,000 people died. Twenty years later Japan's worst ever tsunami hit the earthquake-prone Sanriku coast of northern Honshu. The epicentre of the earthquake was 93 miles out to sea, and the mild shocks felt on land caused little alarm. Fishermen working out in the epicentral region did not notice the tsunami because of its low amplitude in the deep water. But when they returned to port they found a scene of terrible devastation. Whole villages had been flattened, and being high summer the beaches had been crowded when the tsunami struck: over 27,000 people were killed. In March 1933 the same area was again hit by a tsunami, and this time 3000 people died. In both cases the maximum run-up of the waves, over 80 feet, had been in the heads of narrow inlets where the waves had been laterally constrained and so had built up in height – and where lay many fishing villages.

The destructive force of a tsunami is immense. If the wave is breaking as it crosses the shore it can smash houses merely by the weight of water, and even more effectively when debris and boats are hurled inland too. A steady rise in water causes buildings to float away, and it also generates the destructive uplift of ground sediments through the rise in pressure of the groundwater. When the town of Concepción in Chile was hit by its third major tsunami, in 1835, the sea just rose very calmly to 30 feet above its normal level, but the resultant backwash was violently destructive, carrying many buildings out to sea. On 1 April 1946 a tsunami which originated near the Aleutian Islands struck the town of Hilo on Hawaii. A barely noticeable rise in sea-level was followed by the water retreating from the foreshore. Many people walked out on to the new 'beach', but they should have known better, for the retreat was soon followed by the first wave crest. When the tsunami hit the harbour it was a 12 foot high wave sweeping inshore at over 20 mph, behind which the sea was almost flat. There were eight waves altogether, and crests built up to heights of over 50 feet in some tapering inlets.

15

The 1946 tsunami at Hilo killed 159 people, but it also prompted the establishment of the Pacific Tsunami Warning System. This is a communications network covering all the countries bordering the Pacific Ocean, designed to give advance warning of dangerous tsunamis. Clearly the PTWS can do nothing to warn of tsunamis very close to the earthquake epicentres which are their origin, but as, for example, the waves take ten hours to travel from Japan to Hawaii, the system does have a significant value.

The problem is estimating how destructive any tsunami will be when it arrives on a particular coast, and deciding whether to organise massive coastal evacuation and risk a false alarm, or merely to prepare for a smaller wave. Tsunamis are strongest in the direction of the seabed movement which caused them, but on a smaller scale the amount of damage will always depend on the shape of the local coastline. Immediately after the 1964 Alaska earthquake a tsunami warning was sent to Crescent City in northern California. Many inhabitants moved out of the seafront areas before the waves struck, but after two waves had arrived some of the people returned, only to be drowned by the larger third and fourth waves. One bizarre and unforeseen result of the television bulletins issuing warnings of the tsunamis was that thousands of people flocked to the beaches around San Francisco 'to watch the waves', which fortunately were not serious in that area.

Recent research on tsunamis in the Pacific has shown that the atmosphere is disturbed by the same forces that cause the sea waves, and that the soundwaves, which are detectable by instruments, travel faster than the tsunamis. The seismic airwaves arrived two and a half hours ahead of the tsunami at Crescent City in 1964, and there is hope that these airwaves could provide a warning system for the future. In the same way, the ionosphere is disturbed by tsunami earthquakes, and variations in reflected radio waves could offer yet more warning.

However, beyond gaining a few hours' warning there is little that can be done to avoid tsunami disasters. In the rebuilding of Hilo after 1946 some foreshore zones were left undeveloped, and the danger of villages at the head of some narrow bays has been recognised, but short of depopulating half the Pacific coast the hazards of tsunamis in this area must be accepted as a part of life.

Earthquake belts and stable areas

As we have already seen, the most active earthquake belts extend around the rim of the Pacific Ocean and along the Himalaya–Mediterranean line. The activity of the latter belt means that Europe can be divided into two regions of contrasting seismic character. The northern part is essentially stable and not prone to major earthquakes, while the southern part, around the Mediterranean, presents a very different picture. Though the Mediterranean area does not compare with the Pacific fringes for the frequency of its earthquakes, it is distinguished by being the site of one of the world's largest known shocks.

In the year 1755 there were no instruments to measure accurately the scale of earthquakes, but it is now generally accepted that the quake which hit the Portugese capital of Lisbon on 1 November of that year would have had a magnitude of about 8.9. There is probably a maximum limit to the magnitude of earthquakes, dictated by the amount of strain that can accumulate in rocks at any depth before their failure, and the evidence suggests that the Lisbon earthquake was near that limit. The shock was felt over an enormous area – including the whole of Europe and all along the length of the Mediterranean. In Lisbon itself the destruction was appalling. There was no warning of the earthquake until 9:30 in the morning, when a sound like underground thunder was heard, accompanied by the first of three major shocks spread over about six minutes. Whole sections of the city collapsed in heaps of rubble, and fires started to rage through the broken houses. It was All Saint's Day, and many hundreds of people celebrating Mass died in the churches as crumbling masonry rained down on them. It is estimated that about 60,000 people died in the Lisbon earthquake – most in that first six minutes. There were many aftershocks, and over an hour after the main earthquake the sea retreated leaving the foreshore dry, only to sweep back in again in a series of disastrous tsunamis. The long delay in arrival of the tsunamis suggests that they may have been associated with the aftershocks, and it is thought that most of the shock waves originated from epicentres out to sea. There was an unfortunate side-effect to the delayed tsunamis. During the morning many people tried to escape the crumbling and burning city by taking boats across the River Tagus to the south. At 11:00 over 100 people were gathered on a brand-new marble quay on the banks of the Tagus when a tsunami swept in and drowned every one of them. Watchers from boats saw quay and people disappear beneath the wave, and when the water retreated there was no sign of the massive stone quay. Contemporary accounts describe it as being 'swallowed by a fissure in the earth', but it is most likely that it just completely subsided into its sand foundations which would have liquefied due to the rise in groundwater pressure associated with the tsunamis.

Twenty-eight years after the Lisbon disaster, in 1783, the Calabria region of southern Italy was hit by a major earthquake, the main damage being due to the triggering of dozens of landslides on the steep sides of the valleys. The same area suffered another terrible earthquake in 1908 when over 100,000 people died. The city of Reggio, in Calabria, and its twin port in Sicily, Messina, were extensively damaged, firstly due to collapse of poorly made buildings and then by tsunamis which swept both shores of the Straits of Messina. And so the Mediterranean earthquake belt has continued to shake itself at irregular intervals. In 1926 a quake of magnitude 8.3 was centred near the island of Rhodes in the seismically very active Aegean Sea. The southern side of the Mediterranean suffered twice, in 1954 and 1960. In the former, thousands of people died around Orleansville in Algeria, and the disaster was made worse when the Lamartine Dam collapsed during the earthquake and over 200 people were drowned in the floodwaters. The earthquake of 1960 at Agadir in Morocco was particularly disturbing because it was in a region thought to be free of major earthquakes. There had not been one in that area since 1731, but in the 1960 earthquake the town of Agadir was so heavily damaged that the area was afterwards just bulldozed flat and abandoned.

The 1963 earthquake in Skopje, Yugoslavia, destroyed about 75 per cent of the buildings in the city. Over 1200 people died, but this was actually a surprisingly low figure for the magnitude of the quake and was largely due to the fact that no major fire broke out in the rubble of the town, for the shock came early on a summer morning when few houses had any fires going, and the electricity was promptly turned off at the main supply. In Sicily a series of earthquakes in 1968 destroyed a number of villages. The first shocks were not the strongest, though they disturbed the villagers enough to make them leave their homes; the sixth and seventh shocks destroyed most of the houses. Most of the 281 people who died were in the village of Montevago, where the earlier shocks had not been so strongly felt and most people had stayed in their houses. A warning by minor foreshocks probably saved many lives in the Friuli earthquake in northern Italy in May 1976 – even though the death toll did rise to 966. At 8:55 in the evening a sharp tremor rattled pictures and crockery in the houses, followed five minutes later by a stronger shock which caused no damage but resulted in people running into the streets in panic. It was another two minutes before the main shock, which lasted 55 seconds and reached a magnitude of 6.8. Whole villages crumbled into ruins, and many people were saved by not being indoors.

The British Isles provide the perfect contrast to the seismic zone of the Mediterranean. They lie safely on a plate, in a stable area – there is no record of an earthquake whose centre lay beneath Ireland. England, Wales and Scotland have had earthquakes, but they were very minor. During 1975–7 there were dozens of small disturbances in the Stoke-on-Trent area. These are now known to have originated mostly on small existing faults deep within the Coal Measures, which have moved when stressed by the migrating subsidence-waves caused by coal mining. There may also have been some disturbances on old faults in the basement rocks below the Coal Measures, for small deep-seated movements on this scale can occur anywhere, even well away from the active plate boundaries of the world, but rarely cause much damage. Some television sets fell from their stands in the November 1976 tremor at Warrington, and a parrot was reported to have fallen from its perch in the Hereford earthquake earlier in the same year! A series of tremors in the coalfield north of Nottingham in 1974 and 1975 had similar origins to the disturbances around Stoke-on-Trent; many people were disturbed by noises in the night, and some felt the vibrations, but reports of damage were rare.

The Colchester earthquake of 22 April 1884 was probably the strongest ever felt in Britain. The village church at Langenhoe was wrecked when the roof caved in, but the tower fortunately stood firm. Some earth fissures opened up in sediments on Mersea Island, and in the village of Wivenhoe many chimneys fell and house roofs caved in. The shock caused what is probably Britain's only earthquake fatality, when masonry fell down a house chimney in the village of Rowhedge and killed a child sitting on the kitchen floor. The 1884 event was unusual for Britain and has been dubbed 'the great English earthquake', but it hardly compares with earthquakes elsewhere in the world.

One of the most massive earthquakes, for which California is famous, was the one of magnitude 8.3 which had its epicentre just north of San Francisco on 19 April 1906. It was the San Andreas Fault itself which moved, and its displacement could be seen along a length of 275 miles. The greatest movement was 21 feet horizontally, spectacularly demonstrated by a single-storey timber-frame building which survived the shaking but ended up with its front garden path nowhere near its front door. There were three separate shocks lasting over a minute, and the damage was appalling. Whole areas of the city were rased to the ground, and on the outskirts a train was thrown bodily off its tracks by the violent shaking. The most serious damage was in the dock areas around the shore of the bay where buildings founded only on soft alluvium suffered far worse, amplified, vibrations than houses built on the solid rock of higher ground. But worse was to come when fire broke out, for the mainly wooden buildings of the city burned all too easily. Water mains were fractured and useless, and little could be done – even dynamiting firebreaks proved futile, and the fire raged for three days. In the end, 500 blocks of the city were completely destroyed, but the death toll of about 700 was surprisingly low. It was perhaps fortunate that the skyscrapers so typical of American cities had not really caught on in San Francisco – which makes the thought of a repeat quake in the future all the more terrifying.

There have been many other earthquakes in California before and since that one of 1906, but perhaps the most important was not the largest. At 6:00 am on 9 February 1971, a quake of magnitude 6.6 hit San Fernando, a suburb of Los Angeles. It is significant because it was in a densely populated region and was so intensively recorded and studied that it taught many lessons about potential earthquake damage in an urban area. The origin of the quake was on a previously unmapped fault beneath Magic Mountain six miles north of the main populated valley, and the shocks lasted a full minute. Both gas and electricity supplies were knocked out at source, and this must have been partly responsible for the lack of fire after the quake. Most houses in the area were wood frame and they survived well, though many brick chimneys fell, and it was probably the early hour of the event that saved many people from being killed by masonry falling in the streets. As it was, only 65 died in all, even though old, unreinforced buildings were damaged as far away as downtown Los Angeles.

There were about a thousand landslides in the hills behind San Fernando, though all were either shallow surface slides or rockfalls in some of the canyons. The more serious ground disturbance was on the alluvial plains around the mountains, and here a number of highways were badly damaged as the unconsolidated ground was thrust and compressed. A major highway interchange, including some very high flyover viaducts which had just been completed, collapsed as the reinforced concrete slabs fell from the relatively thin support towers. It is questionable whether such elaborate and high overpasses could really be considered acceptable design in such an earthquake-prone area. But the value of reinforced concrete was demonstrated by the damage to two hospitals. The forty-year-old Sylmar Veteran's Hospital with its unreinforced buildings collapsed almost completely and took with it forty-four lives. In contrast, the modern reinforced concrete of the Olive View Hospital withstood the tremors, except for the falling away of the staircase housings which were tagged on to the ends of the main buildings. However, the two-storey administrative block pancaked, as the upper floor descended intact and crushed the ground floor. It was a serious design failure, and had the shock not been at 6 am the death toll could have been much higher.

It was fortunate that so many lessons were learned from the San Fernando earthquake at such a low cost in lives. The other incredible piece of luck was that the waterlevel in the Lower Van Norman Reservoir had been lowered for maintenance reasons just before the earthquake. The earth dam had been cheaply constructed by a method which left inadequately consolidated, saturated sediment in its core, and with the vibrations from the quake it developed a massive slip failure in its upstream face. The water ended up only just short of overtopping the failed dam, and 80,000 people had to be evacuated from their homes until the reservoir could be drained out. The lesson on dam design in earthquake regions had very nearly been learned at catastrophic expense.

The East–West communication gap means that little is known about the large-scale structural geology of China, but we do know that there have been many earthquakes along a belt from Yunnan to Peking and north-eastwards into Manchuria, and this probably marks the line of some form of plate boundary. The east coast and Taiwan lie along the active plate boundary around the Pacific, but the south-east provinces are almost aseismic. There has been a scatter of quite large earthquakes in the western part of the country. The Yunnan–Peking belt has included both of China's worst earthquakes, which appear to have been the two most destructive in the world.

On 28 July 1976 an earthquake occurred about 100 miles south-east of Peking in the heavily populated region of north-east China. Not only was the earthquake very powerful, with a magnitude of 8.2, but its epicentre was right in the great industrial city of Tangshan. The result was death and destruction on an almost unprecedented scale. Homes, shops, office blocks and factories all crumbled into rubble, and practically the whole city was flattened. Parts were built on unconsolidated sediments which settled and fissured badly during the earthquake. An entire hospital and a crowded train were both reported to have completely disappeared in fissures, though there were reports that these were related to the collapse of old and shallow coal-mine workings. Tangshan had a population of one and a half million, and it is thought that few can have escaped some injury during the destruction of the city. Being in China, no official report of the disaster emerged, but a very reliable though unofficial report via a Hong Kong newspaper quoted a death toll of 655,237, though this included deaths in areas outside Tangshan, as far away even as Tientsin and Peking. A significant and cheering feature of this appalling death toll was that it apparently did not include any of the 10,000 miners who were in the eight deep coal mines beneath the city at the time of the earthquake. As the mines were cut in solid rock, the miners suffered none of the amplified shock waves experienced in swaying buildings or on surface sediments. Although there was some rock fall and flooding all the miners escaped – and six months later all but two of the mines were again operative.

China's worst ever earthquake, on 23 January 1556, was centred at Hsian, in Shensu province. Hsian is on the banks of th great Hwang Ho River and the region affected by the earthquake consisted only of soft sediment plains between low hills of loess silt. Contemporary reports of the quake describe whole towns sinking into the ground, into sediments liquefied by the vibrations, and thousands of cave houses which were carved into the soft loess hills collapsing within seconds. As the shock arrived at 5 o'clock in the morning, most families were still in their homes, and this undoubtedly contributed to the exceptionally high death toll of 830,000 – the only fatality figure higher than the Tangshan disaster.

Shock waves from the Tangshan disturbance reached as far as Peking and did considerable damage in China's capital city. The Chinese seismologists then predicted more earthquakes, so after the shock on 28 July most of the seven million inhabitants camped out in the city streets, much of the time in heavy rain. The people were advised to evacuate all buildings and keep clear of any construction; buildings more than five storeys high were placed out of bounds, and all large stores were closed. There was a major aftershock on 2 August, which caused more damage, and some deaths among rescue workers in the previously ruined buildings. Still the people of Peking camped out in the rain, but there were no more major tremors, and on 15 August the authorities considered the danger to be over and the people returned to their homes. Clearly a safe line had been taken in this mass emptying of the city's buildings, and it raises the question of just how much earthquakes can be predicted.

The prediction and inducement of earthquakes

Earthquake prediction has always been a popular topic, but it is only in the last ten years or so that it has moved from the hands of soothsayers and religious fanatics into the scientific world. Unfortunately it is still a difficult subject. The Chinese claim to have predicted 18 out of 31 recent earthquakes, but they admit to also having had some false alarms. Monitoring by Californian seismologists over the last few years revealed 25 sets of 'earthquake indications', but only 15 of them were followed by major tremors. Though progress is clearly being made, such success rates are not good enough. Earthquake warnings do not yet have adequate credibility with the general public, and in America at least the chaos and inconvenience that would follow a major false alarm would be likely to produce enough law suits to deter the most dedicated predictor.

One obvious way of predicting earthquakes is by examining foreshocks, even though significant build-up of foreshocks to a main event is the exception rather than the rule. The shocks can be detected with seismographs, or by studying animal behaviour. Immediately before the 1835 earthquake on the coast of Chile, all the seagulls flew inland, and dogs evacuated the town of Takahuana. People commented on how the city's dogs howled through the night before the 1906 earthquake in San Francisco, and the Chinese have noted that snakes leave their burrows and rats emerge from buildings just before a quake. Clearly animals can detect far smaller vibrations than are felt by man; in careful tests the Japanese have found that pheasants are the most sensitive of all and furthermore are able to distinguish minute earthquake tremors from vibrations due to passing traffic. Anomalous animal behaviour will only foretell earthquakes which have some foreshocks, but the Chinese relied heavily on this method in one of the most successful earthquake predictions to date. Throughout 1974 animal behaviour in the area of Haicheng in Manchuria was seen by many non-professional observers to be erratic, and the signs increased markedly on 28 January 1975. At 2 pm on 4 February a warning was issued of a major quake to be expected inside two days. The local population moved out of their homes, and open-air film shows were laid on 'to entice the masses out'. At 7.30 pm on the same day there was an earthquake of magnitude 7.3 which flattened 90 per cent of the town but caused 'minimal loss of life'.

Some rather vague prediction methods have been based on the occurrence of natural events which can trigger off an earthquake. The tidal pull at a new or full moon can be just enough to push strained rocks beyond their elastic limits, and earthquakes tend to be more common in the Himalayan regions during the monsoon flooding. 'Earthquake weather' – notably thin trails of high wispy cloud – is formed in decreasing atmospheric pressure, which may also act as a trigger. Patterns in earthquake activity are even more dubious prediction factors. Lisbon has had major quakes in the years 1344, 1531 and 1755 which suggests another is

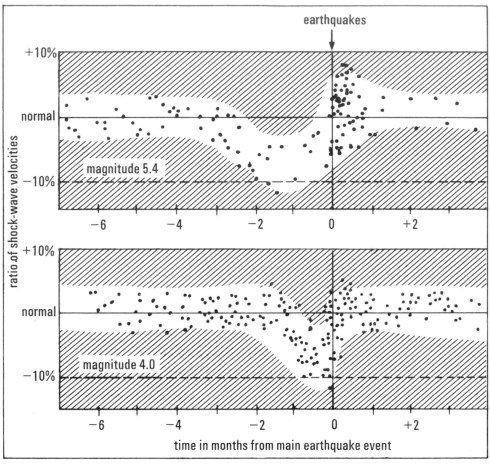

Variations in seismic wave velocities preceding two Russian earthquakes which could have been predicted from the temporary anomalies.

due now, but prediction on a 200-year cycle is useless in practical terms. The Anatolian Fault Zone has suffered recent movement along nearly its whole length in Turkey – except in one zone near Erzincan. This section of the fault may therefore be temporarily locked, with the rocks stressed and ready to fail, but an accurate time-indicator of any expected quake is not forthcoming. On similar grounds, and backed by much better instrumentation, it was predicted in 1973 that a section of 'locked' San Andreas Fault near Hollister in California would develop an earthquake within six months – but nothing happened.

The most exciting advance in earthquake prediction was recently made by the Russians, and is explained in terms of the properties of rock changing as it undergoes dilation under stress immediately prior to failing and producing an earthquake. Most important is the variation in seismic wave velocity. The P waves slow down due to the rock fracturing, during dilation, but then speed up again as water fills the fractures just before the earthquake. This means that the seismologist merely has to record the shock waves from minor tremors, which take place almost continually, and wait until he notices a velocity change. From this he can both tell that an earthquake is due and predict its timing, as it will take place when the wave velocities return to normal. This can be seen on the recordings of shock waves before two Russian earthquakes. (In practice the ratio of the P and S wave velocities is measured and this drops 5–10 per cent before a major quake.) On the upper recording the ratio dropped steadily for two months; then it started to rise again, and so the earthquake could have been predicted for another two months' time. Even more useful is that the period of time covered by these changes indicates the size of the earthquake that can be expected. The first Russian quake was of magnitude 5.4 after four months of lowered velocities. The warning period was only two months for the quake of magnitude 4, and if the period of changes lasted for fourteen years it would indicate a potentially catastrophic earthquake of magnitude 7. Since the Russians discovered this phenomenon, American, Japanese and Chinese seismologists have verified it and even made successful prediction in areas where a dense enough net of seismographs is established. Also, side-effects of the rock dilation include other complex factors such as decrease in electrical resistivity of the rock, change in magnetic susceptibility, and increase in the radon content of groundwater – and monitoring these factors simultaneously with wave velocities can add weight to any predictions.

Japanese seismologists have preferred to base their earthquake predictions on surface deformation as revealed by very accurate surveying, and particularly by measuring slow tilting of the ground near a fault, but time predictions are not so easy by this method. Around Palmdale, near Los Angeles, an area of over 5000 square miles has very gently risen over the period 1959–74, the centre having lifted by eighteen inches. The domed area straddles the San Andreas Fault which locally has not moved since 1932, and it is thought that the ground rise is an effect of rock dilation which usually precedes an earthquake – a theory backed up by a measured drop in seismic wave velocities in the area. But since 1974 the 'Palmdale Bulge' has stopped rising, and nobody yet knows exactly what this means.

Now that earthquake mechanisms themselves are better understood it is tempting to look at the possibility of actually controlling quakes. Unfortunately there is no way in which man can stop an earthquake, but he might be capable of inducing earth movements before the rock stresses build up to dangerously high levels. The most obvious earthquake trigger is a large explosion: a nuclear device exploded underground in Nevada in 1968 itself caused a shock of magnitude 6.3, followed by a related series of earthquakes of up to magnitude 5.0. Another way of inducing stress artificially is by constructing large reservoirs, which then not only overload the rocks by the weight of water but also increase groundwater pressure and therefore reduce frictional stability within the rocks. When Lake Mead was first filled in Arizona in 1935 there were 600 shocks up to magnitude 5.0 in ten years, in an area previously aseismic. The Koyna Reservoir, near Bombay, was first filled in 1967 and triggered many earthquakes, including a disastrously large one of magnitude 6.5 which destroyed houses and caused 177 deaths. Even if these methods of inducement could be precise enough to control the scale of movements in stressed rocks, a nuclear explosion or a vast reservoir hardly seem satisfactory alternatives to the earthquake hazards of San Francisco.

A more promising method of inducement was discovered accidentally at Denver, USA. Starting in 1962, waste fluids were pumped into fractured granite at the foot of a well 12,000 feet deep. In the eighty years up to 1962 there had been only three minor earth tremors in the area, but from 1962 to 1968 there were 610 small quakes. It was fortunate that Denver was an aseismic area and that the relationship of pumping to earth tremors was recognised, which led to the pumping being stopped. The correlation was in fact very good, and with a flow of over six million gallons of fluid per month there were over fifty minor quakes a month, mostly originating on a fault zone just below the bottom of the well – and the tremors started just seven weeks after the beginning of pumping. Clearly the stessed rocks were being luburicated at depth, and there appeared to be a precise method of controlling the movement. Water injection operations in oilfields – a standard practice to force out more oil than will emerge under its own pressure – have confirmed the results from Denver, and water pumping does seem capable of inducing many small tremors in place of one large one. It has been suggested that the locked zones of the San Andreas Fault should be triggered in this way before stresses accumulate to dangerous levels; but one wonders who would dare tempt providence by interfering with such a potential time-bomb as the San Andreas Fault.

Earthquake protection and zoning

Earthquake prediction does not look like being accurate enough to be a significant aid – all we can know is where a major quake must be expected some time in the future. Protection against earthquake damage is therefore vital, and basically comes down to two courses of action. First the most obvious danger areas must be avoided – and as the total evacuation of places such as the Californian coastal cities is not feasible, this demands zoning on a smaller scale to minimise the risk as far as possible. Secondly we must ensure that buildings in quake-prone areas are as safe as possible and are not adding to the hazards: while in practice the earthquake-proof building does not exist, the earthquake-protected one is within the scope of design.

To a large extent the dangerous features of buildings can be discovered from the experiences of past earthquakes. The mud, wattle and timber buildings with heavy stone roofs, which are so common in Asia and South America, are about the worst possible for an earthquake area. Top-heavy buildings of any sort, even upper floor parapets, should be avoided, and it was found in recent California earthquakes that a double ground-floor garage significantly weakened a house. Modern reinforced-concrete buildings generally survive well, though the theoretically applied design criterion may be open to question in the case of a horizontal acceleration equivalent to the Earth's gravity such as was recorded in the 1971 California quake.

Some modern 'daring' concrete architecture may be lacking in the conservatism which is necessary in earthquake regions, but worse is the danger of inferior concrete which may too easily exact its own payment. Damage in the Italian quake of 1930 was largely caused by heavy rounded stones used in the buildings, and there were many failures in the Skopje earthquake of 1963 due to a poor bind by concrete on unwashed aggregate. 'Pancaking' of buildings in Skopje also demonstrated the inadequacy of good reinforced-concrete floors supported on unreinforced masonry walls. Poor foundations are of course disastrous, whether they are just inadequately compacted fill or underconsolidated sediments, as was the case at Niigata in 1964. In contrast, an earthquake-protected building will be of reinforced concrete, with a steel frame, deep foundations, and a light roof and short chimneys. Apart from the fire hazard, wooden buildings – either log cabins or timber-frame houses – have repeatedly proved to be the safest in an earthquake. The Japanese have found corrugated iron or asphalt sheet far better roofing material than traditional tile, and the Imperial Hotel built in Tokyo just before the 1923 earthquake was, for its day, a classic in thoughtful design: it had deep foundations, tapered upwards to a light copper roof, and it even had an ornamental pond in the centre which saved it from the fire following the quake.

The main problem with earthquake protection is old buildings. New ones can, and should, be designed to adequate standards even at an increased cost, but the cost of demolishing old structures and rebuilding them just as a safety measure may seem excessive – until the consequences of a major quake in a crowed city are themselves priced. Even with good construction practice it is difficult to avoid the threat of resonance in high buildings when slow earthquake waves happen to coincide with their natural period of motion. The alternative of protection by prediction also has its limits. Seismographs have been incorporated into Japan's high-speed Tokkaido railway so that trains will automatically stop should earth tremors pass a certain level. Even vague predictions by engineers can be used to lower water levels in reservoirs and increase the safety margins, but such warnings are going to have little effect on people's individual activities. It may be different in a regimented society such as China, but a recent survey in California showed that, among the few people willing even to discuss the matter, half would do nothing if an earthquake warning were issued. And most of the others would just pray.

If accurate prediction is not possible and if people are going to ignore a warning anyway, the best line of earthquake defence seems to be land zoning, to minimise damage. In this the details of local geology are of prime importance. Although in most earthquakes the ground shaking is more destructive than any total displacement, the outcrops of active faults are obvious hazard zones. Precise tracing of all known faults is therefore a first step in a zoning exercise, but it is complicated by the fact that faults commonly disintegrate into wide bands of branch faults, and also that new faults are likely to develop or old 'stable' ones may move for the first time. The 1971 San Fernando earthquake originated on a fault thought to be inactive – so geological mapping must record all faults regardless of age, and they must then be avoided. There is now in California a ban on new building within 125 feet of a known fault (with the exception of small single-family homes which can approach to within 50 feet), and if the fault is not adequately located the building limits are much further out. Some structures have to cross active faults. The aqueducts feeding water to Los Angeles cross the San Andreas faults, and flexible joints are incorporated, but it is heartening to see that plans for a nuclear power plant almost astride the same fault, further north at Bodega Head, have recently been dropped, though only after heavy pressure from environmentalist groups.

Undoubtedly the most important aspect of earthquake zoning is the foundation strength of the ground. Bedrock is the best, and geologically young, unconsolidated, saturated muds are by far the worst. There is a direct relationship between rock strength and earthquake damage, which, though it barely lends itself to quantitative analysis, does provide the best guide to relative safety zoning. In unconsolidated sequences silts or sands with grains of a uniform size are most prone to liquefaction and must be a prime consideration in zone mapping, particularly when

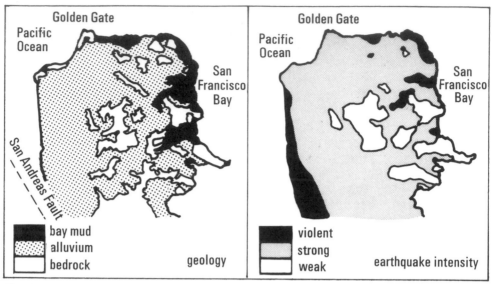

Earthquake damage in 1906 in San Francisco (right) shows a very close correlation with the areas of poor foundation rock (left).

they are both shallow and saturated. It has also been found that amplification of seismic waves is greatest where soft sediments directly overlie solid bedrock rather than other layers of progressively more consolidated sediment. The distribution of coastal sediment should therefore play a major part in the planning of cities such as Tokyo and San Francisco, but this raises the question of what alternatives there are in such crowded urban areas.

Other factors in earthquake zoning are the possibility of inundation by tsunamis and the hazard from landslides triggered by earth movements. The latter again tends to be qualitative, as in practice its assessment consists of recognising pre-existing landslips likely to move again and assessing the stability of any other unconfined slopes. On a broader scale, California's San Andreas Fault can be zoned into sections where slow creep is taking place and other sections which tend to lock and then break, thus causing earthquakes. But the conclusion from this – that both San Francisco and Los Angeles are sited in dangerous zones – is of no practical value. Identification of hazard zones is not precise enough to precipitate the relocation of existing buildings and towns: it can only aid in planning the new. The city of Valdez was resited on bedrock after its destruction in the 1964 Alaska earthquake, as its original site had been on soft delta sediments. But the bad ground which aided the destruction of Managua, Nicaragua, in the 1972 earthquake was almost unavoidable, and the city was rebuilt on the same site, the only concession being to leave open belts along the lines of the five faults which were active in 1972.

The future

If a repeat of the 1906 earthquake hit San Francisco today, at least 2000 people, and maybe more than 100,000, would die. The figure would largely depend on the time of day and on the number of dam failures. But another earthquake in San Francisco is a certainty. The city lies on one of the world's most active faults, and it *will* move again – sometime in the not too far distant future.

What is being done about this awful threat? The answer is depressingly little, partly because of the unmanageable scale of the problem, but partly also because of public indifference. The material damage from a major earthquake in modern San Francisco would run to billions of dollars, with an even greater additional cost in terms of lost productivity. Yet planning and design could reduce this figure substantially. A recent survey estimated that California could save $38 billion in future earthquake damage by spending $6 billion now on reconstruction and relocation. Is a one-to-six ratio reasonable as insurance against losses in an unknown event at some undated point in the future? It may seem doubtful – until of course the priceless value of human life is added in. There are too the enormous political problems involved for cities or state governments trying to spend this amount of money. But there are precautions which can be taken at virtually no cost.

Enough is known about the geology of San Francisco and the San Andreas fault system to be able to predict accurately the hazardous areas, along the fault lines and on areas of weak sediment prone to vibration. But nobody really accepts the responsibility of avoiding these hazard zones. There is an enormous communication gap, between individuals' knowledge of local ground conditions and public appreciation of hazards and planning policy. The actual line of the active faults obviously presents the most immediately dangerous sites in the case of any earthquake. Today, building along the fault lines is banned by Californian law; it is accepted that ideally these narrow belts of land are best left for parkland, golf courses or even highways as long as major bridges are not involved. But this has not always been the case, and the errors of the past remain unremedied. Why are so many buildings still in use when it is known that they are astride the active faults? Why is the San Andreas Fault straddled by two housing estates in the western suburbs of San Francisco?

Worse still is the situation in Oakland – on the inland side of San Francisco Bay. It lies on the Hayward Fault, a very active branch of the San Andreas system which moved in the big earthquake of 1868. If it is dangerous to have houses built across the fault it is even more so to have multiple-occupancy buildings in the same situation. Yet, in Oakland, there are fourteen schools, two hospitals, and the football stadium at the Berkeley campus of the University of California, all directly on the trace of the Hayward Fault. The hazard is known, and it is ignored. The analogy is at Anchorage in Alaska. There, the potential failure, under vibration, of the Bootlegger Cove Clay was described in the US Geological Survey report of 1959. But the houses were built on Turnagain Heights and the school was built on Government Hill – both underlain by the clay. And in the 1964 earthquake they all fell down. And everyone said what a tragedy it was.

So what will everyone say if – or is it just when? – the Hayward Fault moves again under Oakland, and hundreds of people die in the wreckage of the football ground, the two hospitals and the fourteen schools?

VOLCANOES

At four o'clock in the afternoon of 20 February 1943, Dionisio Pulido was ploughing a field near his village in western Mexico, when a narrow fissure 50 yards long opened in the ground. Half an hour later he saw smoke issuing from one point in this fissure, and within a few minutes the smoke was being blasted out, accompanied by a whistling noise and a shower of fine dust. Pulido ran to tell his fellow villagers, and when they returned they saw more dust and fine stones being blasted from the vent. The first explosion came at ten o'clock that night. Stones and incandescent rocks were thrown out, and a column of ash rose high into the air accompanied by a tremendous roaring sound. Paricutin volcano had been born.

Paricutin's appearance was not entirely unheralded. Earth tremors, which are not unusual in that part of Mexico anyway, had greatly increased in intensity for a couple of weeks previously and had been associated with various noises from beneath the ground around the village of Paricutin. But once the surface vent was formed, the volcano grew with impressive speed. The cone of volcanic ash centred on the vent was 50 feet high the next morning; within a week it had reached 400 feet, and after a month it stood 1000 feet above the fields and was nearly a mile wide at its base. Its growth was accompanied by numerous explosions, small and large earthquakes, volcanic bombs raining over the countryside and a column of ash and vapour climbing more than 5000 feet into the sky. After four months, the crater started to fill with lava, and flows of lava emerged from fissures in the flanks of the cinder cone. At rates of 100 feet per hour or more the lava flowed across the countryside, the furthest flows extending 3 miles from the vent. The ash explosions and lava flows continued. Then, after nine years, Paricutin volcano ceased to erupt. A mountain of ash 1350 feet high stood on Pulido's field, lava flows buried the village of Paricutin and half buried a second, and for miles around the countryside was covered in a thin layer of ash which effectively killed off all the vegetation.

An erupting volcano is probably nature's greatest spectacle. It is formed where molten rock, or magma, rises towards the earth's surface at some weakness in the crustal rocks. Magma is generated by enormous concentrations of heat in relatively local pockets rarely more than 75 miles below the surface, and is totally unrelated to the great mass of molten material which forms the core of the Earth. The hot magma tends to rise towards the surface: if it actually emerges as liquid molten rock it is known as lava, but frequently its upward progress is interrupted so that it partly cools, partly solidifies, and is then broken up by accumulating pressure. In this case it is blasted through the surface in the form of rock fragments, and these form the volcanic ash. Lava and ash are the two main components of any volcano, but beyond this the similarities between different volcanoes may be very few. Paricutin erupted for nine years and then completely ceased activity, whereas Stromboli, off the coast of Italy, has been exploding and erupting in a fairly mild way since before history. The volcanoes of Hawaii have for centuries been quietly producing enormous quantities of lava, while Krakatoa became famous with one single gigantic explosion.

At present there are about 500 volcanoes around the world which can be considered active, in that they have erupted during historic times. There are many more which can be described as dormant: they are not known to have erupted for thousands of years but could return to activity at any time. Mount Lamington in New Guinea erupted violently in 1951 when it had been thought to be inactive. Volcanoes are described as extinct when there is no chance of renewed eruption, and this is usually only when there has been a change in the geological environment which has effectively defused a once-active volcano. Over the millions of years of geological history volcanoes have existed in almost every part of the world, and have formed enormous volumes of rocks. The entire landmass of Iceland has been thrown up out of a continuous series of volcanoes. Today volcanoes are found only in restricted belts around the world which is perhaps fortunate because although a volcano may be a fantastic spectacle, to anyone in the wrong place at the wrong time it can also be a disastrous one. On average nearly a thousand deaths every year can be attributed to volcanoes. This figure includes those who die of starvation because their crops have been smothered by a layer of ash, but it also includes those suffocated by heavy ash falls, or even consumed in the fires of volcanic lava.

The nature of volcanic activity

Laki and Vesuvius are two very different types of volcano: different in the way they erupt, different in the landforms they have created, and different in their effect on people living in the region. The Laki fissure is a 15 mile long line of volcanic vents oriented northeast–southwest and located just west of the Vatnajokull, Iceland's largest icecap. Fissure volcanoes are normally notable for the enormous quantities of lava which they emit, and Laki was no exception – its 1783 eruption was the most effusive to have taken place anywhere in the world for well over a million years. Preceded by a series of earthquakes and gas emissions, Laki burst into activity on 8 June of that year, blasting ash and steam high into the air from a whole line of vents. Then, three days later, the south-west end of the fissure started to emit lava and the north-eastern end followed suit late in July.

The lava was a very fluid basalt, and vast quantities of it rapidly flowed away down the pre-existing valleys in the area. The Skaftar Valley was completely filled with lava even though in places it was over 600 feet deep, and a 100-foot-high flow front advanced over 35 miles down the valley. In places the lava overflowed the valley, and it spread across a 10-mile-wide front where it arrived on the coastal plain. An almost equally long flow filled the Hverfisfljot Valley, and at the end of its six months of activity the Laki fissure had poured out 2.9 cubic miles of basalt to cover 220 square miles of the Icelandic countryside.

Unfortunately the effect of Laki's eruption was not only felt in the lava-filled valleys. Thirteen farms were engulfed by the lava, although because a flow rarely moves fast enough to catch a man few lives were lost in this way. But the side-effects were on a horrifying scale. Rivers diverted by the lava flows inundated great areas of farmland, and glacier ice melted by lava added to the flooding. Ash rained down, burying and killing the vegetation, and great clouds of poisonous sulphurous gases swept across the country. The result was the death of over a quarter of a million sheep, cattle and horses – three-quarters of the country's total livestock. In the isolated farming community which Iceland was in the eighteenth century, this in turn brought on an appalling famine, which was aggravated by a very hard winter immediately afterwards, and nearly 10,000 people died. Laki cost Iceland just a fifth of her population.

Vesuvius, in southern Italy, is today probably one of the best-known volcanoes in the Western world. But in the year AD 79 it was just an attractive conical mountain, thought to be an extinct volcano, overlooking the Bay of Naples. The people who lived in the towns and villages nearby were basking in the prosperity of the Roman Empire at its height. On Vesuvius itself, intensive cultivation reached almost to the summit, reaping the benefits of the rich soils which typically develop on volcanic ash. All that was to change.

Nobody paid much attention to the earthquakes which had rocked the area around Vesuvius for the previous seventeen years – after all, earthquakes were common enough in southern Italy and the volcano was supposed to be extinct. Early on the morning of 24 August, few people were at first concerned by the cloud of ash and steam which rose above the volcanic cone, but their complacency rapidly disappeared as Vesuvius started to shoot ash thousands of feet up into the sky in a massive eruption which continued for two days and nights. Fine ash mixed with larger pebbles (known as lapilli) rained down on the surrounding villages and countryside. There was so much ash in the air that sunlight was completely blotted out, and the unceasing inky darkness added to the confusion. In some places rocks the size of a man's fist or even larger hurtled down from the sky, making it dangerous for people to walk in the open without pillows tied over their heads, and the presence of noxious volcanic gases made breathing difficult. Meanwhile the static electricity in the rising plume of volcanic ash caused violent lightning and local storms, and earthquakes continued to rock the area; tsunamis in the Bay of Naples caused the sea to retreat from the foreshore and pound back relentlessly.

When all this activity had continued for a whole day, the people must have thought that their world was coming to an end, and most had had enough. Thousands of them ran for the open country away from Vesuvius, or set sail in their boats, and over most of the region the rate of accumulation of the ash was slow enough to allow the majority of people to escape. In the town of Pompeii, however, conditions were rather different. Being immediately downwind of the volcano, it was rapidly covered by a thick layer of ash. By the time the terrified inhabitants realised the seriousness of their plight the ash already lay thickly in the streets and continued to rain heavily down – the whole scene in pitch darkness, as no sunlight could penetrate the hanging ash cloud. Eventually most people tried to escape, but many left it too late. The combination of soft ash on the ground, ash raining from above and the air full of sulphurous fumes was too much. They stumbled and fell to their deaths in the streets, their hands clutched to their faces, and were rapidly buried by more ash. Some chose to stay in their homes, protected from the ash – but the fumes were insidious and hundreds died indoors of asphyxiation, while others

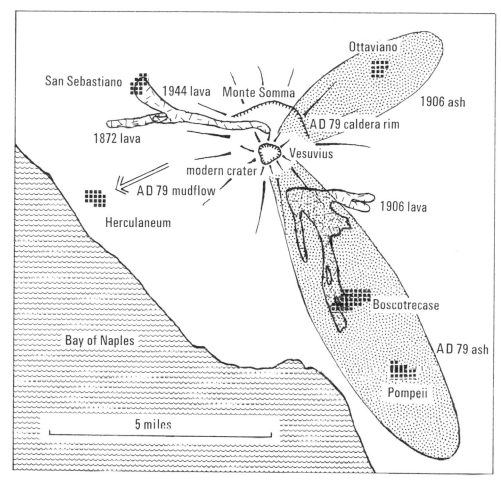

Lava flows and ash deposits from some of the major eruptions of Vesuvius which have taken place from AD 79 to the present century.

were killed when the roofs of their houses collapsed under the weight of the ash. At the end of the eruption, Pompeii lay buried beneath 10 feet of ash, and of the original population of 20,000, one in ten lay dead in the ruins of his town.

On the other side of Vesuvius the town of Herculaneum had not been buried by ash, but still it was doomed. High on the slopes of the volcano huge amounts of ash were balanced precariously on slopes, and were then inundated by really heavy rain from the local storms generated by the eruption. Fortunately, by then, most of the population of Herculaneum had been driven away by the terrifying activity of the volcano, and only about fifty people remained in the town when it met its own special fate handed out by Vesuvius. The saturated slopes of loose ash became unstable and started to slide, developing into semi-liquid mudflows which swept down and completely buried Herculaneum – some parts to depths of over 50 feet.

After two days of furious activity the eruption ceased, and the survivors could see that the top of Vesuvius had been replaced by a caldera – an enormous crater two miles across, formed by inward collapse due to the weakening of the underground

31

pressure which had powered the eruption. Part of that caldera wall is still visible as Monte Somma, for the present summit cone of Vesuvius has been built up just south-west of the original one by various periods of rather milder activity which still continue today. Meanwhile the mudflow of Herculaneum set solid, and both it and Pompeii, under its preserving layer of ash, lay forgotten – until their discovery turned yesterday's catastrophe into today's archaeological bonanza.

As Laki and Vesuvius show, volcanoes vary enormously, and almost always it is the composition of the magma which causes this variation. Magma consists essentially of a melt of silicates of various metals, and the total amount of silica (normally between 50 and 70 per cent) strongly influences its viscosity. This directly influences not only the rate at which lava will flow and spread out, but also the flow of gases within the magma. At the very high pressures found at the considerable depth below the surface where the magma is formed by local rock melting, many gases are soluble in the silicate melt. But as the liquid rock moves upwards, into levels of lower pressure, the gases form bubbles in the magma. They may then either escape quietly, or the bubbles may be held in the magma, containing their gases at explosive pressures. Silica-rich magmas are likely to have higher gas contents anyway, and their high viscosity tends to restrict any escape of the gas. The extrusion of such a gas-charged magma in a volcano therefore causes a more explosive type of eruption with larger proportions of ash.

Basaltic magmas are the commonest silica-deficient ones, and when extruded from volcanoes they form extremely mobile lavas. Laki was a typical fissure volcano in that its magma was basaltic and spread out in extensive lava flows. Eruption of basaltic lava from a single 'central' vent results in lava spreading out in all directions and progressively cooling down and solidifying so that it builds up a large conical heap. The extreme fluidity of basalt, however, ensures that this type of cone is relatively flat, with slopes of only 2–10°. Mauna Loa and the other volcanoes of Hawaii are the best examples of this type, which are known as shield volcanoes. These contrast with the well-known conical shape of volcanoes such as Japan's Mount Fuji, with slopes of around 30°. The steeper slopes are due to the fact that these volcanoes are composite, that is they are built up of alternating layers of lava and ash emitted from a central vent, with each layer thinning away from the vent. The ash content of the composite volcanoes indicates a greater degree of explosiveness which is due to the higher gas content of the lava. These are also most commonly basaltic in composition, and the low viscosity of the magma ensures a steady escape of the gases and a constant jetting out of the ash without any major explosions. The third type of volcano, the almost purely explosive form emitting ash but little lava, may range from quite small cinder cones rarely more than 200 feet high, to the violently explosive forms such as the famous Krakatoa. In the latter the very viscous nature of the silica-rich rhyolitic magma ensured the temporary blocking of the lava vent and the consequent build-up of gas pressures until they were released with devastating effect.

Clearly a volcano, whether it produces ash or lava, represents – unless it is of very modest proportions – a hazard way beyond the control of man. The Columbia Plateau occupies about half the state of Washington, besides large areas of Oregon and Idaho in the north-west of the United States. It is made of lavas which were poured out of fissure volcanoes twenty million years ago to cover an area of 50,000 square miles, and an eruption of the same scale today would be an incomparable disaster. On a smaller scale, the modern Italian volcanoes demonstrate well the dangers of lava. Etna, on the isle of Sicily, is Europe's largest volcano, a composite one which is today in a state of almost continuous activity. In 1971 an eruptive phase started with both ash and lava production from the main summit cone. The lava demolished a volcanological observatory and then swept down and ruined the best ski slopes along with the cable-way built to serve them. All this explosive activity effectively de-gassed the magma, so that it was followed by a peaceful phase of lava production. This lava emerged from a fissure lower down the slopes of Etna and flowed into vineyards and farmland, destroying houses, roads and bridges but fortunately avoiding the main villages. Although lava tends to flow downhill like any fluid, it can break out and behave unpredictably – as was once horribly demonstrated on Vesuvius. This Italian mainland volcano has had various short phases of lava production: in 1906 a fissure eruption on the south flank produced lava which partly destroyed the village of Boscotrecase. In 1872 a lava phase attracted tourists high on the mountain to watch the eruption; a group of twenty-two visitors were so engrossed in the volcanic display that they did not notice until too late that two lava flows had looped round them and rejoined, completely cutting off their escape route. As the flows increased their island of rock was slowly overrun, until they too disappeared.

Fragments blasted out of a volcano are often called volcanic ash, but the correct term is tephra. Tephra consists of material of all sizes: the sand size or finer is strictly the volcanic ash, fragments up to $2\frac{1}{2}$ inches are known as lapilli, and even larger are the bombs and blocks. Blocks are broken fragments of solid rock, and bombs are material ejected as clots of liquid lava, cooled and solidified in mid-air. The lapilli and ash may similarly be of either origin. A tephra fall does not have to be as thick as that which buried Pompeii to be utterly disastrous. Three feet of ash is enough to kill practically all vegetation with obvious consequences to an agricultural economy, and even smaller quantities can spell disaster to animals. Besides losing their food supply when it is buried by ash, animals can easily be killed off by eating small amounts of the indigestible ash on grass. Thousands of sheep died in Iceland in 1970 when an eruption of Hekla produced an unusually fluorine-rich ash, so that where the fluorine combined with the grass it produced a poisonous diet.

Enormous quantities of tephra heaped on the steep slopes of a classical conical volcano provide a dangerously unstable situation, especially if saturated with water from the heavy local storms often generated by an eruption. The finer tephra – the ash – can very easily start to move down the volcano, and although it may do so when it is dry and even still hot, it more usually moves as an almost liquid mudflow. Such a flow from Vesuvius buried Herculaneum, and mudflows are very common on some of the Indonesian volcanoes, where they are known as lahars. Although modern examples are limited in extent, prehistoric volcanic mudflows cover 4000 square miles in the Yellowstone Park area of the United States. The most fluid and mobile mudflows are caused by enormous amounts of water being added suddenly to the ash through the volcanic melting of snow or ice. The Electron mudflow on America's Mount Rainier took place only 500 years ago; started on Rainier's summit by lava melting snow and wet frozen ground, it extended right out to the plains to the west, to the sites of several modern towns near Tacoma. In 1877 an eruption melted the summit icefield on Cotopaxi, in Ecuador, and the resulting floodwater mixed with unconsolidated ash to form a really fluid mudflow which damaged a village 150 miles downstream. This flow was so mobile, with such a small proportion of ash in it, that had it occurred in Iceland it would probably have been called a *hlaup*. This is a volcanic hazard almost peculiar to Iceland – a flood produced by volcanic melting of glaciers. Iceland has at present two major volcanoes beneath its icecaps – Grimsvotn beneath the enormous Vatnajokull, and Katla beneath the smaller Myrdalsjokull near the south coast. Grimsvotn volcano has directly above it a lake covering an area of 14 square miles, surrounded by great ice cliffs. Due to ice melting beneath it the lake steadily rises in level, until the water escapes through a series of subglacial tunnels and spreads out across the barren wasteland of the coastal plain in immense floods. Within a few days the level of the lake may drop by over 600 feet, and the release of pressure triggers further activity in the volcano below. The Grimsvotn floods are predictably regular – every ten years up to a massive flood in 1934 and since then every five years. More unpredictable, irregular, violent and dangerous are the floods from the Katla volcano. There is no surface lake above Katla but enormous quantities of meltwater are generated beneath the ice-cap. The great flood in 1918 maintained for two days a flow of around half a million cubic yards per second – double that of the mighty River Amazon. Fortunately the Katla *hlaup* only affected an almot unpopulated outwash plain leading down to the coast of Iceland.

The last two components of volcanic eruptions – water and gas – are usually only minor features which do not represent great hazards. Indeed many of the geysers of the world, the volcanically powered hot-water fountains, are popular tourist attractions – the Old Faithful at Yellowstone in the USA or the original Geysir in Iceland for example. Seeping gas has been known to kill sheep on the flanks of Iceland's Hekla, and may also have killed many of the people of Pompeii. But gas and water, in the form of steam, when at enormous pressure provide the explosive mechanism behind the most violent and catastrophic volcanic eruptions.

Volcanic violence

An active volcano can never safely be described as peaceful, but there are certainly degrees of violence to which any eruption may rise. Santorini and Pelée were both extremely violent in their own ways, but perhaps the best known of all the world's violent volcanoes was Krakatoa. Lying in the Sunda Straits between Sumatra and Java, the island of Krakatoa was just part of a massive complex volcano which rose barely above sea level, and on the island were three distinct vents built of andesitic lava and ash. As first recorded by Europeans, Krakatoa had been dormant for two centuries before bursting into activity on 20 May 1883. For three months it variously exploded and produced ash clouds. Nobody lived on the island and the people of nearby Sumatra and Java had almost become used to it, when on 27 August of that year it blew up in four enormous explosions. The third was the greatest and it was heard over 3000 miles away, and ash was blasted so high into the air that it encircled the world. Tsunamis generated by the explosion swept the surrounding shores, and a town called Merak at the head of a tapering bay was annihilated by a wave 130 feet high. Over 36,000 people died in these mammoth tsunamis. Most of the island of Krakatoa just disappeared. The ash which landed nearby was shown to be 95 per cent original material and only 5 per cent broken

34

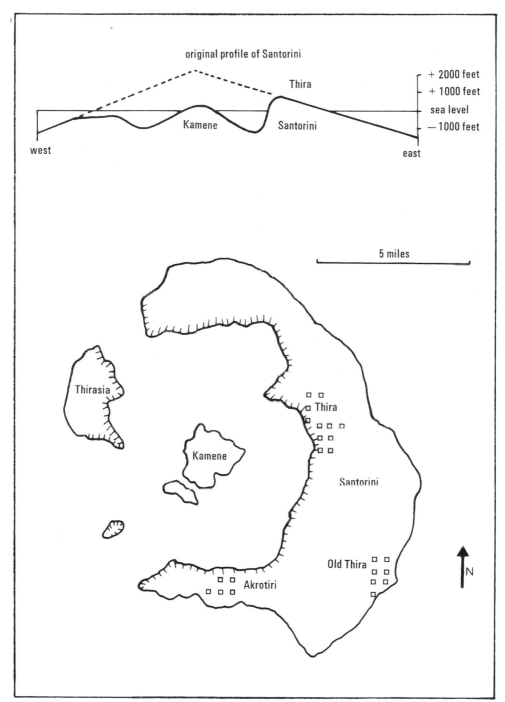

The arc of islands which is all that is now left of Santorini after its cataclysmic eruption over 3000 years ago.

rock, so much of Krakatoa must have fallen back into a caldera collapse. The power of the explosion may have owed much to its location at sea level. It is probable that the early phase of activity, violent enough in its own right, opened up ground fissures which let the sea into the magma chambers below, there to generate enormous quantities of steam. The combination of this steam and the volcanic gas in the viscous magma was enough to blow up Krakatoa, and seawater may also have played a part in the comparable explosion of Santorini.

Santorini is the most southerly of the Cyclades Islands in the Aegean Sea. In the year 1500 BC the island was an imposing site, about 10 miles in diameter, rising in its centre to a high volcanic cone. The island was well populated; the city of Akrotiri, on the southern side, housed some 30,000 people and was one of the main cities of the Minoan civilisation centred on Crete 70 miles to the south. The geology of the island was that of a composite volcano where tephra and lava had emerged from a number of centres, and continued small-scale activity clearly labelled Santorini as dormant, not extinct. But all this changed in, or close to, the year 1470 BC. Then, the volcano entered a far more dramatic phase of eruption. Earthquakes shook the island and ash was blasted high into the air. At first the people repaired their damaged homes and tried to live with the rain of volcanic ash, but later it seems they gave up the fight and there was a mass exodus from the island – so far not a single body has been found in the buried city of Akrotiri.

The people's departure was timely for, shortly after they left, Santorini exploded in one incredible cataclysm. Pent-up gas pressures overcame the strength of the rock, and blasted enormous quantities of ash, pumice and rock into the air. The tephra built up to a thickness of 200 feet on parts of the island, was 4 inches thick as far away as Crete, and still lies as a recognisable layer over the whole seabed of the Aegean. With this gigantic escape of rock and debris, the volcano of Santorini collapsed in on itself. The central cone fell into a huge caldera, with the island rim broken by cliffs dropping a thousand feet into the sea which is itself another thousand feet deep in parts of the drowned crater. This is how Santorini appears today except for the addition of Kamene Island, built up in the centre of the caldera by a small volcano which is still periodically active on a small scale.

Unfortunately the collapse of the caldera and the burial of Akrotiri beneath the ash were not the only effects of Santorini's massive explosion. Great sea waves, volcanic tsunamis, radiated from the island, and it is likely that when they hit the north coast of Crete they washed up to heights of 160 feet above normal sea level, causing terrible destruction. Santorini may therefore claim to be one of the most catastrophic volcanoes ever known to man, in that it saw the end of an era. The great Minoan civilisation ended at around 1450 BC. The destruction of the Minoan cities on Crete's north coast, the damage to agriculture by the ash fall, even the complete loss of Akrotiri, seem to have triggered the final collapse of a civilisation already groaning under the weight of excessive affluence, administration and internal strife. The stories of the destruction and disappearance of an important island and city must have spread with awe around the Mediterranean peoples of the day, and so Santorini gained its place in mythology as the lost land of Atlantis.

In 1902 the city of St Pierre had a population of around 30,000 and was one of the main commercial centres of the Caribbean. It lay near the northern end of the then French island of Martinique, just 4 miles from, and 4000 feet below, the summit of Mount Pelée. Pelée was a dormant composite volcano, a classical cone rising to a small double crater. Eruptions had first been recorded in 1635, and there was further minor activity in 1792 and again in 1851 when St Pierre was covered in a ghostly layer of fine white ash. The lavas and ashes of Pelée were andesites and dacites – a fact that today would give some cause for concern, because magmas of these compositions are very viscous and therefore prone to accumulate gases to dangerously high pressures.

When the volcano started a new eruption at the beginning of May 1902, the potential scale of the danger was not appreciated – even though earthquakes shook the area, fissures opened in the ground, boiling springs burst from the slopes of the mountain, and on 5 May a mudflow of hot ash swept down the west slope of Pelée, overran a sugar factory and caused over 150 deaths. At night the flames and ash plume of the volcano struck terror into the people who lived nearby, and the next day red-hot ash rained down on St Pierre until it was a foot deep and had started numerous fires. But local government elections were due on 10 May, and the authorities, with the aid of the politically influenced local newspaper, did all they could to say the volcano was safe and exhort the people to stay in their homes – which they had to do to be eligible to vote. The next day, 7 May, was chaos. The ash and fumes made life almost unbearable in the town, and many visiting ships in the harbour weighed anchor and left. Still the governor urged the people not to panic, and he even moved into the town from his capital at Fort de France. A few people left their homes, but even more arrived from outlying farms to seek shelter in the town. St Pierre should have been evacuated but it wasn't – politics won over scientific (and common) sense.

At 7:50 on the morning of 8 May a series of violent bangs shook Mount Pelée. Then at 7:59 two great clouds of incandescent gas and red-hot ash exploded from the summit. One cloud was blasted high into the air, but the other came out of the side of the volcano. With its suspended load of ash just heavy enough to keep it to the ground, it roared down the side of the mountain in a dead straight line, over some low ridges, and in three minutes covered the 4 miles to St Pierre. 'The city was blotted out by one great flash of fire', were the words of Assistant Purser Thompson on a ship in the harbour. The blast of this glowing cloud was enough to smash the strongest buildings, uproot great trees, and wreck seventeen ships in the harbour (Thompson's ship was one of only two to survive). But worse was the heat; when the cloud hit the town its temperature was nearly 700°C – enough to boil the water in the harbour. And enough to kill 30,000 people, including the governor, in less than a minute. The hot gases and lack of air meant that fires were not easily started until the air returned later to the charred town. Most people died when their lungs were burned out, though many corpses were found shrivelled or blown due to their body fluids having turned to steam and then evaporated. Incredibly, there were two survivors in the town. One was in the almost sealed condemned cell of the town jail, and though horribly burned he survived three days without food or water before he was rescued. The other was a shoemaker, Leon Compère-Leandre, who, by a freak of air movement, survived in his own home when everyone around him died, and lived to tell his story: 'I felt a terrible wind . . . arms and legs burning . . . four others crying and writhing in pain . . . after ten seconds the girl fell dead . . . the father was dead, purple and inflated . . . crazed I awaited death . . . after an hour the roof was burning . . . my senses returned . . . I ran.'

After the eruption of the glowing cloud, a great tower of nearly solidified lava rose vertically out of the summit of Mount Pelée until it stood 840 feet high and some 400 feet in diameter. Three months later another glowing cloud swept the east slopes of the volcano and killed another 3000 people. After a year the lava tower had crumbled into a heap of debris, and the eruption was over.

The East Indies have more than their share of violent volcanoes. Tambora on the island of Sumbawa, east of Java, exploded in 1815, and here the main damage was caused by the widespread carpet of ash which killed off vegetation on Lombok and other islands, resulting in a famine in which between 50,000 and 100,000 people died. Papua's Mount Lamington was thought to be an extinct volcano until it started to erupt on 15 January 1951, with frequent explosions. After five days, an enormous explosion blasted an ash cloud to an altitude of 43,000 feet in two minutes, and at the same time a tremendous base surge developed. This is the explosive cloud that is formed in any large explosion and sweeps the ground at low level. This base surge is very similar to a glowing cloud, like that of Mount Pelée, except that it is not directional. Lamington's base surge covered 90 square miles, completely flattening mature forests and totally destroying the town of Higatura and its 2900 inhabitants.

One feature that links all these violent eruptions is that they occur on volcanoes containing the more viscous types of magma — either rhyolitic, dacitic, or sometimes andesitic. Lavas of these types are found throughout the geological record and prove that volcanic violence is not a new development on Earth. But the world's fossil volcanoes also contain a type of rock called ignimbrite which is best described as a welded ash, because when the ash fragments landed on the ground they were still so hot that they instantly welded into a solid rock. The Mount Pelée type of glowing cloud was once thought to form ignimbrites, but though it is certainly of high enough temperature it deposits very little ash – there was only a thin layer on the ruins of St Pierre. Man has not yet observed an ignimbrite eruption – which is perhaps fortunate because the known fossil ones cover enormous areas, must have formed very rapidly, and seem to represent the ultimate in volcanic destruction, the effects of which in a populated area defy speculation.

Minimising volcanic damage

Icelanders have long been used to volcanoes erupting in various parts of their island country, but never, before 1973, had they been threatened by a volcano so close to one of their major cities. Vestmannaeyjar is the nation's major fishing port and lies on Heimay, the largest of the Vestmann Islands which are a group of volcanic islands just off Iceland's south coast. The town is overlooked by the mountain of Helgafell, a volcano which had been extinct for 5400 years – until 1973. Then, preceded by only twenty-four hours of minor earth tremors, a 1300-foot-long fissure opened up on the flank of Helgafell immediately above the town and started to pour out lava. This was in the early hours of the morning of 23 January 1973, and later in the day the fissure extended to nearly a mile, fountaining lava 300 feet into the air. Fortunately the fishing fleet was in harbour, and within the day practically the whole population of the island, over 5000 people, was evacuated to the mainland, a few volunteers staying behind to lead the defence of their town.

Lava poured down into the sea east of the harbour, and within a couple of weeks

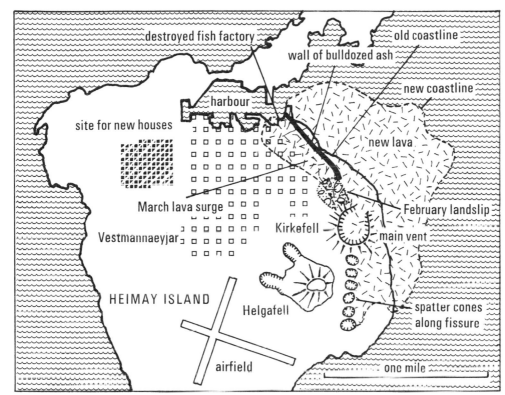

The island of Heimay, showing the town of Vestmannaeyjar threatened and encroached upon by the 1973 eruption of the Kirkefell volcano.

the land area of the island had been increased by nearly a square mile. The lava flowed down at a rate of up to 3000 cubic feet per second, and as it was a fairly viscous alkaline-rich magma there was also considerable production of ash. Much of the fissure was soon blocked, and the majority of ash then came from a single point, building up a cone over 650 feet high – which was christened Kirkefell. During the first two weeks ash rained down on the town, and although it was enough to bury some houses, the men who stayed behind used their time mainly clearing ash off the house roofs to prevent collapse under its sheer weight. On 4 February there was renewed production of a very fluid, more basaltic, lava which flowed at a speed of two miles an hour into the sea just outside the harbour mouth, threatening to block it. The thick fall of ash was put to good use by being bulldozed up to form a wall which deflected the lava away from the town. On 15 February gas was found to have accumulated in some of the houses; one man died in a dense pocket of it, and so the rest of the rescuers retreated to the higher parts of the town. The next day the library roof collapsed under the weight of uncleared ash.

On 20 February there was a huge landslip on the side of the Kirkefell cone. A thick mass of ash slipped where it lay on still-molten lava, and this marked a slight change in events as more lava poured down towards both the town and the vital harbour entrance. A few days before, an experiment had been started of spraying cold water on to the lava, in an effort to cool it down and slow its advance. This was so successful that by the end of the month a ship was standing in the harbour mouth pumping 750 gallons per second of seawater on to the lava – and due to both these efforts and a share of good luck the harbour mouth actually ended up better protected than it had been before. In March there were two lava surges down towards the town. The wall of bulldozed ash was topped as the lava advanced at walking pace; seventy houses and one of the three fish factories were overrun. More pumps were brought in and a total of 13,000 gallons per second of water was sprayed from forty pumps on to the western edge of the lava. A single pump took two weeks to cool the lava within its reach before it was moved to a new site, and ash roads were bulldozed on to the hot lava so that pumps could be placed to cool the lava further in and prevent it overriding the chilled margin.

By the end of April, after three months of activity, the Kirkefell eruption ceased, but a quarter of the 1200 houses of Vestmannaeyjar lay buried by lava or ash. In July the people moved back into the town. Their harbour – and livelihood – was still there, and many of the buried houses were able to be dug out. The ground was still hot, mainly due to the hot water in it and to steam feeding through from the lava, but the ash was easily moved and even the blocky lava flows could be scraped cleanly off the roads – they had not welded to the road surface because of the continual layer of chilled lava which tumbled from the flow fronts and formed carpets for the molten lava. The vast supplies of ash were used to level a lava field west of the town, where construction started to replace the few houses irretrievably buried, and life on Heimay continued almost as before. However, the cost of the eruption was estimated at around £20 million. Nearly half of this was raised by the government through a special tax levied on the whole country; this lasted only for a year but in that time took about 10 per cent of the Icelanders' personal income.

Kirkefell's eruption in 1973 and the very successful efforts at minimising the damage to the town of Vestmannaeyjar admirably demonstrated that volcanic activity should not be regarded as a totally immutable catastrophe. Ash falls do not present a major hazard, unless they are exceptionally heavy or of the hot weldable type, or unless they are not treated with due respect and precaution. Grazing animals may suffer from very slight ash cover and their evacuation to uncontaminated pastures is an immediate necessity. In urban areas the most urgent task is to prevent excessive ash accumulating on roofs, which can lead to their collapse under the weight – especially when the ash is wetted by the rain storms commonly generated around erupting volcanoes. Loose cold ash is easily swept off house roofs, as it was at Vestmannaeyjar. What not to do was shown by the villagers of Ottaviano in southern Italy when Vesuvius erupted in 1906: they all rushed to the church to pray, where most of them were killed when the church roof collapsed under the weight of ash.

The threat of lava flows can be reduced in any of three ways – by deflecting, disrupting, or stopping them. In 1951 Mihara volcano erupted on the Japanese island of Oshima, not far south of Tokyo, and a building known as Kako Jaya (the Crater Teahouse) was swamped by lava. The very low destructive strength of lava was demonstrated when the molten material merely flowed into the building through the windows on one side and then out through the doorway and windows on the other. The survival of the relatively frail walls of the building awakened the local people to the possibility of constraining the lava when it continued to fill up the summit caldera and threatened to flow out through a notch in the rim on to the village of Nomashi. The villagers built a wall in the notch and cut a trench in

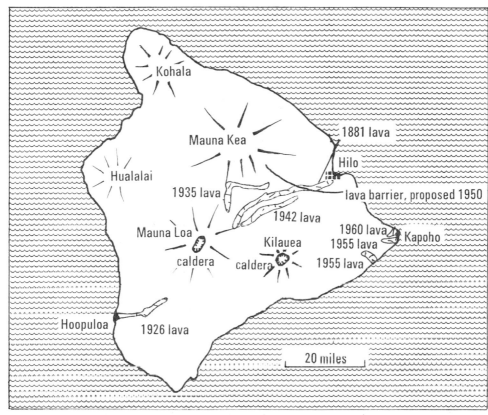

Hawaii, with some of the lava flows from Mauna Loa and Kilauea which have threatened the coastal towns and villages.

another one to allow the lava to flow harmlessly away down an unpopulated slope. As it turned out, the lava never quite reached the wall, but the villagers' action was a model of clear thinking. Earth walls can be just as effective as masonry in diverting lava. Hawaii's Kilauea erupted in 1955 and threatened the village of Kapoho, but a major flow was diverted by an old railroad embankment. Specially bulldozed walls have been shown to be perfectly adequate in diverting flows. They should ideally be oblique to the line of the flow, and can only work where the topography allows a lateral diversion of the lava into a line where it can cause no damage. Walls need only be about 10 feet high, as long as they avoid steep slopes where the lava flows may gather more momentum. Experience in Hawaii has shown that the walls should best be of large and heavy rocks, as ash may float away on the lava, although the ash wall bulldozed on Kirkefell in 1973 was successful until it was completely overridden by lava.

In 1669 Etna erupted on Sicily, and a lava flow threatened the town of Catania. As is usual the lava stream was flowing between self-made banks, or levees, of chilled lava blocks, and the people of Catania realised that if they could breach one of these banks they could let the lava flow away laterally and remove the impetus at the front of the flow as it advanced towards their town. Armed with iron bars and clothed in wet cowhides the Catanians successfully breached the bank and diverted some of the lava – unfortunately though towards the town of Paterno. A spectacular confrontation between the citizens of the two towns then ensued, and as a result the lava was allowed to return towards, and destroy part of, the town of Catania. The modern equivalent of this disruption and diversion of lava was carried out in 1935 in Hawaii, when a flow from Mauna Loa threatened the town of Hilo. The flow was successfully bombed, from airplanes, and as the lava spread out through the breaches on to the mountainside it lost its impetus and cooled down. The small amount of lava left in the original channel then cooled and solidified, and the flow of lava towards Hilo was completely stopped within two days. Hilo is very dangerously sited in the direct natural line of any flows from Mauna Loa, and in 1942 bombing was again used to divert lava threatening the town. It has been proposed that long diversionary walls up the hillside above Hilo could insure against further damage, but so far the money for such plans has not been found. Bombing might also be used to breach a crater wall and release a lava lake in a harmless direction. This was considered in the case of Kirkefell's 1973 eruption, but was not attempted because of the threat of disastrous explosive activity if the sea broke into the underground lava reservoir.

Amid totally unwarranted derision from local officials, the fire chief at Kapoho village, threatened by the 1960 eruption of Kilauea, sprayed water on the advancing lava. His aim was to cool the lava and solidify it, and he successfully showed that even a small amount of water did have a significant effect. Thirteen years later his bold lead was followed by the Icelanders at Kirkefell with the success already described. Man it seems can stop a lava flow, even one of impressive size.

Lavas normally move relatively slowly, but very different defences must be mobilised against the threat of mudflows generated by masses of loose ash sliding off volcanoes. A small earth dam would be easily overtopped by a fast-moving, fluid mudflow, and perhaps the only chance of stopping a major mudflow is by catching it in pre-existing reservoirs whose water levels have been lowered following accurate predictions. Even this depends on dams being available, though it could be a defence for example in the case of renewed activity in the volcanoes of the Cascade Range in the US northwest. Some of the worst volcanic mudflows have been in Indonesia, where several villages now have artificial hills close to them to which the people can run for refuge from an advancing mudflow. The Indonesian volcano of Kelut has produced disastrous mudflows because of its large crater lake. A flow in 1919 topped an inadequate protective dam and killed over 5000 people. Dutch engineers subsequently attempted to remove the threat at source by driving drainage tunnels through the crater wall to lower the lake level, and the value of the scheme was proved in 1951 when a similar eruption cost only seven lives because no large mudflows were formed. Unfortunately the 1951 eruption damaged the drainage tunnels and also deepened the lake. Another lower tunnel was then driven towards the lake and the water was left to seep into it. But the rock was not permeable enough, the seepage was insufficient to lower the lake level, and an eruption in 1966 caused more massive mudflows and killed hundreds of people. Yet another tunnel was cut in 1967 and the lake was almost completely drained, finally removing any further threat.

Ash falls, mudflows and even some lava flows may be controlled, but it must be admitted that volcanoes can muster far more strength than man. Really massive

42

14 *The volcano of Taal blasts into a new phase of activity, showering ash on to the country surrounding the lake side.*

15 (above) *Smoke rising from the distant Kirkefell volcano forms a background to the houses of Vestmannaeyjar, already partially buried in ash.* 16 (below) *Apart from the burying of houses as above, the main damage to the town was caused by the lava flow which encroached upon its eastern edge, threatening to block the harbour.*

17 (above) *Vesuvius produced a spectacular cloud of ash during its eruption in 1944, but it had little effect on the city of Naples lying nearby.* 18 (below) *Lava fountains shadowing a tree foretell the imminent destruction of these houses near the Hawaiian village of Kapoho.*

19 (above) *The shattered ruins of St Pierre lie beneath the volcanic stump of Mt Pelée following its violent explosion in 1902.* 20 (below) *The railway station at the Italian village of Mascali is slowly overwhelmed by the lava spreading down from Mt Etna in 1928.*

21 (above) *An embarrassing 2-foot-high step in the road up the side of Mam Tor was a feature of the 1977 movements on this perpetually unstable landslide.* 22 (below) *Clifftop holiday houses at Skipsea, Humberside, are undermined by the successive failures of the crumbling cliffs facing erosion by the North Sea.*

23 (above) *Another segment of the chalk cliffs at Beachy Head, Sussex, threatens to crash to the seashore, following a series of similar landslides.* 24 (below) *This house on the cliffs on the south coast of the Isle of Wight was destroyed early in 1978, and joined a long list of homes lost from landslides in this area.*

25 (above) *The slipped face of Tip 7 looms behind the mass of black debris which descended on Aberfan in 1966, killing 109 children in the school.* 26 (below) *After the slide, the broken face of the tip revealed that this powerful spring was the real culprit of the disaster at Aberfan.*

27 (above) *Shattered buildings and a heap of debris bear witness to the flow slide which undermined the town of Nicolet, Canada, in 1955.* 28 (below) *A scar right across the valley marks the source and destination of the great rockfall at Frank, in the Canadian Rocky Mountains.*

lava flows may be insuperable, and the glowing cloud type of eruption, with or without ignimbrite formation, offer man no choice of defence. In these cases the only escape is to get out – and fast. The entire population of the tiny Atlantic island of Tristan da Cunha had to leave their homes on 10 October 1961, when a volcano opened up close to the only settlement on the island. It was not a major eruption by worldwide standards but it was too much in the cramped space on the island, and it was nearly two years before the islanders could safely return to their homes. More recently there was a much larger evacuation on the Caribbean island of Guadeloupe. The volcano of Soufrière erupted in August 1976, a great fissure opening on the flank of the summit cone and emitting powerful jets of ash. The particular fear was that Soufrière, which has a silica-rich magma similar to that of the nearby Mount Pelée, could produce a glowing cloud of the type that destroyed St Pierre in 1902. And beneath the fissure on Soufrière stood the old-established city of Basse Terra. While the volcano continued to rumble and splutter, 72,000 people were evacuated to the far side of the island away from the threat of a glowing cloud and instant annihilation. In the end the eruption just died away, and the people returned to their unharmed homes, but there is little doubt that evacuation was the only course open in view of the activity of Soufrière. The real problem in this case, and in so many others, is not just appreciating the dangers, but also predicting them – a difficult task indeed.

Prediction of volcanic disasters

Volcanoes are not distributed randomly around the world, but occur in quite distinct zones. This is fortunate for the countries that are, and always will be, completely safe from any possibility of volcanic eruption, though less so for the few countries which have more than their fair share of volcanic activity. A map of the world's five hundred or so volcanoes that have erupted in historic times shows clearly defined volcanic belts, with the Circum-Pacific belt containing the lion's share. The other obvious belt is in a line down the middle of the Atlantic Ocean, and these volcanic zones immediately bring to mind two other worldwide patterns – the distribution of earthquakes and the plate boundaries of the Earth's crust. Like earthquakes, volcanoes are essentially plate-boundary phenomena which indicate the enormous geological forces involved where the plates of the Earth's crust move against each other. The Pacific 'Ring of Fire' and the mid-Atlantic line are well-known plate boundaries, and the Mediterranean and East and West Indies boundaries also have their share of volcanoes. But there are other volcano areas, and the concentration in East Africa is particularly obvious. The volcanoes there are associated with the Rift Valley system, which is probably a very young plate boundary where Africa would be splitting apart if it were not for the far more powerful mid-Atlantic plate boundary compressing Africa. But even if we call the African Rift Valley a plate boundary, there are other volcanoes which are exceptions to the rule. The temporarily inactive volcanoes of the Saharan Tibesti mountains, as well as the better known and more active ones of Hawaii, are situated plumb in the centre of plates. Totally unrelated to plate boundaries, they owe their origins to hot spots in the Earth's internal structure, which have burned holes through the overlying plates.

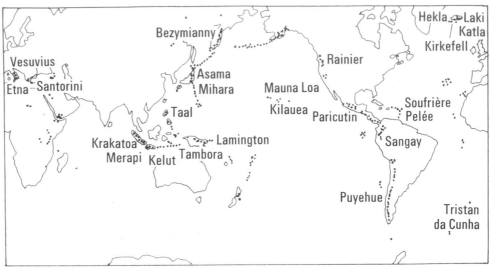

World distribution of volcanoes. Compare the map on page 6 for the connection between volcanoes and plate boundaries.

With most of the world's volcanoes lying on plate boundaries, the nature of the boundary can give at least some indication of the type of volcano to be found there. The Mid-Atlantic Ridge is a divergent plate boundary where the two halves of the Atlantic are pulling apart and volcanoes are forming the new crust in the spreading zone. In this case the magmas originate from the depths of the mantle and are therefore almost exclusively composed of basalt – the silica-deficient, highly fluid material which forms very mobile lava flows with relatively little explosive activity, typical of the Icelandic volcanoes. In complete contrast, convergent plate boundaries, which account for most of the Pacific Ocean rim, involve one plate being overrun, and destroyed, by another, with vast amounts of surface rocks being dragged down to great depths. At these depths the temperatures are high enough to cause melting and the generation of magma – which can on the convergent plate boundaries be of almost any composition. Most significant is the fact that these volcanoes can produce the viscous, gas-charged, silica-rich magmas which generate the more violently explosive types of eruptions. The island arc volcanoes situated very close to plate boundaries, such as in the East and West Indies, are characteristically silica-rich rhyolites, and with magmas of this nature the violence of Pelée or Krakatoa is only to be expected.

These very generalised geological considerations have absolutely no value in specific prediction of individual eruptions, but they do form a basis for evaluating risk in volcanic regions. Paradoxically, although volcanoes are such powerful destroyers they are also beneficial to man, for the soils which develop on recent volcanic ashes are extremely rich and conducive to intensive agriculture. The lands around and on the slopes of Vesuvius and Etna have always been well farmed, and the rich volcanic soils of Java support a very high population even on the flanks of Merapi, one of the most active and dangerous volcanoes in the world. The Philippines volcano of Taal is situated on an island in its own lake; it erupted violently in 1965, and the many island residents were evacuated just in time, but

44

they moved back on to the island only two days later. In situations like these, risk evaluation and the mapping of danger zones are of great value, even if only in minimising the extent of wholesale evacuation when an eruption is imminent. The basis of risk evaluation lies in geological and historical studies of the exact nature of previous eruptions, and inferring the likelihood of mudflows or the extent of lava flows as deduced from anticipated composition and viscosity, combined with consideration of the volcano's topography. The slopes of Kelut, in Indonesia, have been zoned according to the hazards from mudflows, and the Hawaiian volcanoes on the chances of lava inundation. The worst, or most hazardous, areas on Hawaii are along the active rift zone of Kilauea where any house has a one in forty chance of being destroyed by lava within twenty-five years – a figure which planners and engineers can use as a basis when development is proposed. The Cascades volcanoes of the north-western United States have been studied for risk zoning, because the area contains some major towns and cities, and past evidence is that one or other of the volcanoes is likely to erupt about once a century. The main hazard zones reflect the possibility of lava flows extending down valleys up to 10 miles from source, mudflows up to 12 miles, and ash up to double that distance downwind – though it is a lesser danger than the lava or mudflows. In addition these volcanoes are rich enough in silica to develop violent activity, but the chance of a really explosive eruption is so remote as to be economically not worth considering.

Beyond these broad geological implications, volcanic activity is both difficult and expensive to predict – though the costs of prediction can prove a long-term bargain compared to the cost of wholesale volcanic destruction. Even on a small scale prediction is not easy: in 1976 two Englishmen climbing the Ecuadorian volcano of Sangay died when the gentle rain of volcanic ash was replaced for an instant by a shower of blocks of red hot lava, and during both the 1971 and 1974 eruptions of Etna the Italian police had violent clashes with crowds of sightseers intent on getting too close to the lava. On this scale, the immediate danger should make any prediction acceptable and valuable to people at risk, but on a larger scale volcanologists are faced with the problem of a lack of alarm at events which are too distant until it is too late. Most predictions just cannot be precise enough, and false alarms and mass evacuations lead to disrespect for any warning. It is all too easy to placate a town's population if a volcano is anything less than perpetually active – as the successful 'don't panic' propaganda before the 1902 destruction of St Pierre demonstrated so well. In the face of all these difficulties it is encouraging that the science of volcanic prediction is beginning to show such creditable results.

The first and most obvious way to predict volcanic eruptions is on the basis of recognisable cycles or patterns of events, but unfortunately these are rarely accurate enough. Not one volcano has yet revealed a recognisable cycle of activity which can be used to foretell the time of an eruption more accurately than within a decade or so. In addition, the violent and destructive eruptions of Mount Lamington in Papua in 1951 and of Bezymianny on Russia's Kamchatka peninsula in 1956, both previously thought to be extinct, effectively minimise the value of predictions based on previous events. More useful are patterns of activity within the period of eruption. Lava always started to pour out of Mexico's Paricutin volcano a short time after ash explosions had built up to a maximum and had then suddenly stopped. The danger of a sudden break in activity in the potentially explosive silica-rich volcanoes is now recognised. In 1902 Mount Pelée built up to a crescendo of activity before suddenly stopping; for four hours the gas pressure built up inside the volcano before it exploded in its now famous and catastrophic fashion. A similar sequence of events today would be taken as a sign for immediate evacuation of the area – as happened at the nearby Mount Soufrière in 1976. Some volcanoes appear to erupt more commonly at times dictated by external processes, such as climatic changes or earth-tide effects, and Chile's Puyehue erupted in 1960 just forty-eight hours after a major earthquake centred 180 miles away. Unfortunately such trigger mechanisms are so little understood as yet that they can only be useful in alerting volcanologists to intensify their monitoring of more precise methods of prediction.

As magma starts to rise towards the vent inside a volcano, some of its heating effects may be detectable before the actual eruption. Thermally sensitive infra-red air photographs have been used to detect surface heating of this nature, but any recognisable increases in temperature give too little notice of any impending eruption to be of much use. This same heating may cause the waters of perennial springs and fumaroles to rise in temperature, and this effect is noticeable rather earlier than the rock heating. The 1965 eruption of Taal, in the Philippines, was predicted because of a temperature rise in the crater lake water; consequently there was a rapid evacuation of the area and only 190 people died in what proved to be a very violent eruption. Heating also has the effect of demagnetising rock, as the various magnetic mineral grains are warmed beyond their curie points, and this effect can be monitored by surface magnetic surveys. A marked magnetic loss has been recorded on the Japanese volcano of Oshima prior to an eruption from a pool of relatively shallow magma, but magnetic effects have not been found significant on the Hawaiian volcanoes which are seemingly fed from deeper magma accumulations. But it is the gases from fumeroles that may yet provide one of the most useful means of prediction. On some Japanese volcanoes fumarole gases have been found to contain much higher contents of chlorine and sulphur dioxide just before eruptions – though this has not been confirmed on other similar volcanoes. As the gases of a volcano are so clearly related to the details of the mechanism of any eruption, their study may yet reveal very useful methods of prediction.

When it is appreciated that a volcanic eruption involves the upward displacement of millions of tons of molten rock, it would seem simple enough to detect the movement before an eruption actually took place. This can in fact be done in two ways: by measuring small surface displacements, and also by seismic recording of shocks and tremors from underground movements. Magma is generated at considerable depths within the Earth's crust and then moves upwards due to its low density compared with surrounding, cooler, solid rocks. Just before its eruption on the surface, its movement into the the heart of the volcano causes a regional tumescence – a doming and uplift of the volcano itself. Accurate surveying of the surface can detect and measure this by measuring either elevation, distances between points across the tumescence, or tilting. The latter is usually measured because tiltmeters consisting of fluid-filled pipes connecting two reservoir containers are relatively simple and inexpensive to make, with a sensitivity to detect a change in slope of one in a million. Eruptions of the Hawaiian volcano of Kilauea have been intensively monitored by the US Geological Survey, and even though the total uplift of the volcano summit there may be as much as 3 feet, tiltmeters are the most frequently used instruments. Through 1958 and 1959 the volcano steadily swelled, and then in November 1959 the tumescence rapidly increased until minor eruptions took place in the last months of the year. But the tiltmeters recorded continued swelling and further eruptions were predicted; in January 1960 a major eruption produced large amounts of lava, and the tumescence ceased before the eruptive phase died away. The other effect of magma's upward movement in a volcano is the generation of small earthquakes, and these can be detected on standard seismographs. Many small tremors shook the area around Vesuvius for sixteen years before its eruption of AD 79. The significance was not then recognised, but today an increase in the frequency of tremors is one of the most reliable methods of volcanic prediction. A network of seismographs can not only detect tremors but also determine the position and depth of their origin – which is important when tracing the movement of magma up through the core of a volcano. Eruptions of Japan's Asama volcano are predicted on the frequency build-up of tremors within 1000 yards laterally or vertically of the vent. On Kilauea earth tremors average six a day, but in early 1955 there was a marked increase in frequency with an increasingly rapid build-up to 600 a day on 26 February. An eruption was predicted as imminent, and did in fact occur two days later. But there were more tremors centred underneath the nearby village of Kapoho, which was evacuated just in time before a second eruption. This locating of tremors was useful to the people of Tristan da Cunha during the disturbance of 1961, even though they had no instruments. By sending men to the other side of the island they recognised that the shocks were strongest on their side, and they therefore evacuated their homes just before the volcano erupted right next to them.

A combination of tilt and seismic monitoring can provide a very valuable guide to predicting a volcano's behaviour, but there is unfortunately little alternative to expensive networks of instruments because, except in a few special cases, other methods of prediction are so far too vague. Even just an automated package of instruments connected to a radio transmitter on each of the world's potentially eruptive volcanoes is both practically and economically a luxury, and single instruments are barely adequate for prediction. The US Geological Survey's network of monitors on Kilauea and the other Hawaiian volcanoes do show that, with experience and a genuine familiarity with a volcano, prediction is no longer a dream. One evening in 1973 hundreds of tourists were watching the activity of Mauna Ulu, a small vent on the flank of Kilauea. The Volcano Observatory then detected a strong tremor and noted that the Mauna Ulu lava lake had started to drain out; the tiltmeters recorded a sinking of the Kilauea summit. Everyone was evacuated from the area, and four hours later an eruption cut all the access roads.

The future

In many ways, volcanoes are now the best understood of the major geological hazards, and therefore the least threatening. This is not to say that volcanoes can be controlled – indeed it is inconceivable that man should ever be able to control or even influence a full-scale eruption. But volcanoes are sufficiently understood now for their activity to be adequately predicted – given that most eruptions are relatively slow events. Timely evacuation can eliminate the hazard to human life, even though destruction of buildings may still have to be accepted as inevitable.

The 1955 eruption of Kilauea, on Hawaii, caused damage to the tune of over $2 million damages – but not one life was lost. Only a few miles away lies the town of Hilo, partly built on the 1881 lava flow from the volcano of Mauno Loa. In July 1975 a summit eruption of Mauno Loa put the civil authorities of Hilo on permanent alert for six days, after which micro-earthquake activity and contraction of the volcano suggested that the threat had passed. But past events on Mauno Loa indicate that this could be followed within the next few years by a more dangerous flank eruption capable of pouring lava into the town of Hilo. However, while monitoring of movement and earthquakes continues, no other precautions are needed. Any threat to the town will build up so slowly that lava diversion walls could be built as and where needed. Experience on Hawaii, and of course at Iceland's Kirkefell eruption in 1973, demonstrates how minimal is the threat offered by volcanoes of this type. But that is only half the picture.

The real danger is from the more violent types of volcano in the less well developed parts of the world where monitoring cannot be so comprehensive. New Guinea's Mount Lamington killed 3000 people in its 1951 eruption – mainly because the villagers of Higatura received no warning. In this situation danger zoning is probably the only available defence – and even this is lamentably inadequate in many parts of the world. Crash programmes of hazard zoning on many volcanoes in populated areas could be a worthwhile planning aid to be carried out well before the first rumblings on an impending eruption. But even then contingency plans may require further action to avoid disaster. It can be reliably predicted that in the next eruption (whenever that is) of the El Teide volcano on Tenerife Island, villages on its east side have a one in three chance of receiving more than 3 feet of ash. While offering only a minor threat in itself this could disastrously hinder any evacuation in the event of much more dangerous subsequent ash flows.

Volcanoes always have the advantage of surprise, and in this respect the final word should rest with Alaska's Mount Katmai. On 6 June 1912 this volcano erupted violently, and in a single day deposited ash averaging 100 feet deep over more than 100 square miles of countryside. It was fortunate that the area was only unpopulated forest and tundra. Yet Katmai is only one of the volcanoes in the great 'Ring of Fire' that borders the Pacific Ocean, and of the whole volcanic belt only the northern section through Alaska and Kamchatka is so thinly populated. The same type of potentially violent volcano exists in many other places, ready to erupt on the same or an even bigger scale. And what could man do if Katmai was repeated in Oregon, Mexico, Chile, New Zealand or the East Indies, all of which contain the same type of volcano – waiting to erupt?

LANDSLIDES

The road between Hope and Princeton crosses the Cascade Mountains in southern British Columbia, Canada, almost due east of Vancouver, and nearly twelve miles from Hope it passes along the foot of the steep western slopes of Johnson Peak. Just before dawn on 9 January 1965, three vehicles were on the road when 130 million tons of rock slid down off Johnson Peak. The landslide buried two miles of the road, and all four people in the vehicles died.

The Hope landslide was one of those isolated but completely natural events in which hillside erosion takes place not as a slow steady process but in a sudden violent movement. There were no surviving witnesses at Hope, but the slide must have been almost instantaneous. The bulk of the slide moved around 8000 feet over a vertical descent of 2400 feet, and debris carried 500 feet up the opposite side of the valley indicated a speed well over 100 mph. Like almost any other slope in a comparable climatic regime, the western face of Johnson Peak had been undergoing continuous erosion for thousands of years. Rainwash, soil creep, scree development and gulley erosion had caused the surface material to move downwards, and rivers had then removed the debris from the foot of the slope. On most slopes this sort of slow erosion can continue unchecked, but on Johnson Peak a particular set of geological circumstances had combined to interrupt the process. Easily sheared greenschists and metamorphosed volcanic rocks, with sills of felsite included, all dipped roughly parallel to the hillside, so that relatively thin sheets were prone to move down and break away to form significantly large landslides. On that January night in 1965 two minor local earthquakes provided the trigger mechanism to set the slide in motion. It is geological details such as these which may combine on certain hillsides to transform the normal slow progress of erosion into landslide activity on a scale which can range from the minor inconvenience to the major catastrophe.

Landslides occur when either natural or man-induced processes leave masses of rocks with inadequate support where they underly hillsides. A theoretical consideration of the forces involved on any sloping mass of rock should be able to reveal the likelihood of slope failure – or the development of a landslide; but unfortunately, in practice, the science of rock mechanics cannot really cope with the almost infinite variation in styles of rock fracture, and if fracture patterns, or internal frictional resistances, or the degree of sediment cohesion deep down cannot be accurately assessed, neither can slope failure be accurately predicted. This may appear unduly pessimistic, for even qualitative considerations of the geology of slopes can reveal many potential failures, but the continued occurrence of landslides, involving considerable damage and even loss of life, proves the difficulty of assessing the various factors involved.

49

Enormous vertical, or even overhanging, cliffs in places like Yosemite in California or the Dolomites of Italy demonstrate just how stable rock may be when it is both strong and relatively little fractured. As a rule of thumb, engineers use an angle of 70° for a safe, permanent slope in hard massive rock with randomly oriented joints, although slopes of less than 7° have been known to fail in some poorly consolidated clays. In any case of slope failure there are usually two features to be considered – the root cause, and the actual trigger to the individual event. The most common causes are either lack of internal cohesion in unconsolidated materials, or unsuitably placed planar weaknesses, such as joints or bedding planes, in solid rocks. In both cases these are static geological conditions which should be recognisable and predictable. Perhaps more difficult to understand are the various trigger mechanisms. Disturbance of potential slide masses is an obvious trigger, whether it is by overloading due for example to building, or by vibration from either constructional activity or earthquakes. Removal of the toe of a mass of rock, leaving it perched on an excessively steep slope, has been responsible in some way for most of the world's largest landslides. The toe removal may be as obvious as coastal or river undercutting, as remote as ancient glacial oversteepening, or as potentially suicidal as the excavation of road cuttings. The other widespread trigger mechanism is water: most often it is a hazard when added to unstable material which is then softened and weakened, but its removal and the subsequent desiccation of clays may also promote slides. The weathering of rocks, changes in vegetation, alternate freezing and thawing, and long-term soil creep are just some of the other natural triggers to landslide development, but many large landslides are set off by the combination of a number of these factors, as a few examples will show.

Attempts have been made to classify landslides, but without much success. This is essentially because there are no one or two parameters which can be used to establish a classification and yet also have some relevance to the causes and mechanisms involved. Landslides vary enormously in size, and can travel at a vast range of speeds. They may consist of large, relatively unbroken slabs of rock, totally fluid clay or piles of broken rock debris. The geological structure and the site of the slip material are obviously very varied, and this will have the greatest bearing on the cause of the movement. In the following descriptions only a very loose sub-division of landslide types is used, and geological factors are emphasised to try to understand how the more catastrophic landslides can develop.

Rockfalls

Many of the largest, most spectacular and most destructive of the world's landslides have involved a certain amount of free fall in the moving material, and can therefore be called rockfalls. Most of the larger examples were in fact complex landslides, in that they also involved shearing and sliding on discreet planes. Rockfalls characteristically consist of broken rock debris and, once set in motion, travel with terrifying speed over surprisingly great distances.

It is almost impossible to appreciate the vast scale of the larger rockfalls, but some bare statistics on the prehistoric Saidmarreh landslide in Iran make sobering reading. An inclined slab of limestone 1000 feet thick slipped off the ridge of Kabir Kuh, into the Saidmarreh Valley. The slipped block was 9 miles in its horizontal

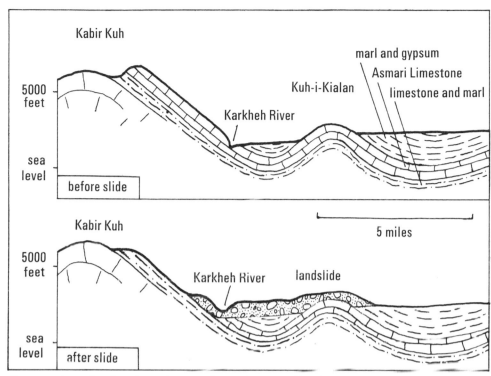

Cross-sections showing the rock formation before and after the enormous prehistoric landslide at Saidmarreh in southern Iran.

length and 3 miles across. As it slipped down Kabir Kuh it lost over 3000 feet in altitude and gained an enormous momentum, so that it then hurtled as a mass of broken debris right across the 5-mile-wide Saidmarreh Valley. At the far side, it still had enough speed to climb over the 1500 foot high ridge of Kuh-i-Kialan and continue until the furthest part came to rest 11 miles from its source. The volume of the slipped material was about 5 cubic miles and it weighed around 50 billion tons. The debris formed a massive dam in the valley and impounded a lake 40 miles long and 600 feet deep, now drained out through a gorge incised in the landslip material. The figures are staggering, although admittedly Saidmarreh is the largest landslide known in the world. As it pre-dated man's inhabitation of the area it did no measurable damage, but the prospect of a Saidmarreh-sized landslide in a populated area is truly horrifying.

The Saidmarreh slide lies some 60 miles north-west of Dezful on the western side of the Zagros Mountains in southern Iran. Its geology typifies that of many major landslides. Kabir Kuh is a hill whose surface follows the shape of the upfolded limestone of which it is formed – in other words, is an anticlinal stratimorphic mountain of the type for which the Zagros is justifiably famous. Its outer sheath consists of the massive Asmari Limestone, and it was this that formed the landslide. It dips at an angle of 20° towards the valley and is underlain by thin bedded limestones and marls. The Asmari Limestone is cut through at the top of the hill, where the crest of the anticline is breached, and on the site of the slide it had been

51

largely removed at the foot of the slope where the Karkheh River had swung to the south and cut into the flank of Kabir Kuh. This great slab of limestone therefore rested on the inclined surface of weak marl, with its toe support eroded away and probably broken through on both sides by steep ravines draining off the hill. It was classic landslide potential. The Zagros Mountains are seismically active, and almost certainly an earthquake triggered the movement. Once started, it must have spread with terrifying speed and ease across the marl and gypsum surfaces of the valley floor. As it moved the massive limestone broke up: much of it is now fine rubble, though there are still blocks weighing up to 2000 tons visible on the surface over five miles from their source. The original structure of the dipping limestone overlying the shale would have easily allowed water to reach the limestone – shale boundary, where it would have provided uplift pressure by its own hydrostatic head. (Hydrostatic head is the pressure exerted by the water which is due solely to its depth and does not involve any movement.) This would have greatly reduced the stability of the rock mass, as would the forming of basal limestone solution cavities. The water would then have aided the actual movement, and in addition the gypsum and marl valley floor would have provided a surface of relatively low frictional resistance. But beyond that, there is considerable debate as to just how such a volume of rock managed to slide so far.

The essence of the dispute on how rockfalls actually move concerns whether the debris flows or slides as a mass over a single plane of movement. Problems concerning friction at the base of a landslide made the idea of flowing debris more attractive until evidence from America's Blackhawk landslide suggested an alternative. The Blackhawk slide fell about 4000 feet from the mountain of the same name in southern California in some prehistoric period: it consists mainly of marble. It has been suggested that the slide moved almost as a single unit, gaining a nearly frictionless ride on a cushion of compressed air. The slide could have gained its air cushion by 'taking off' as it crossed over a low-resistant ridge. This theory is supported by the marginal ridges of debris formed where material was dropped as air leaked from the edges of the slide-mass, and by debris cones on the landslip formed by air leakages blasting up through holes in the main mass. Although the morphology of the Blackhawk slide debris does lend itself to the air cushion theory, there were no witnesses to the event, so it is perhaps more helpful to look at some more modern rockfalls.

In 1881 a large chunk of a mountain called the Plattenberg fell over 1500 feet and landed very close to the village of Elm, near Glarus in eastern Switzerland. Astonishingly, the fall was almost entirely the work of man: a large quarry had been cut into the slate of the mountain, forming a gash 600 feet long and some 200 feet deep. The overhanging upper wall of the quarry was not supported, and by 1876 its movement was made apparent by the opening of great curved fissures higher up the mountain. Five years later the fissures were still larger and at one place absorbed a small stream. By 8 September 1881, the main fissure was over 10 feet wide, and creep rate and creaking noise from the rock were such that quarry work was suspended. At 5:15 pm on 11 September there was a small landslide above the quarry. People in the village below watched in awe and amazement, and seventeen minutes later there was another small slide. Then for four minutes the mountain was still – until the whole mass of slate above the quarry broke away. It crashed on to the quarry floor and then almost took off out into the valley like a great water spout.

Over 400 million cubic feet of rubble crashed to the valley floor, bounced 340 feet up the opposite wall, turned and in less than a minute careered down the valley nearly a mile before coming to a sudden stop. Fortunately it missed the centre of Elm, but 115 people lay dead under the debris.

With its spectacular take-off from the perched quarry floor it is quite feasible that the Elm rockfall could have ridden down the valley on a cushion of trapped air. That it managed to override some patches of vegetation almost without disturbing them seems to confirm this theory, but there is also strong evidence that the debris flowed as it was fluidised by air and dust inside it. A survivor who just managed to run away from the slide's path in time described the surface of the moving debris as a rolling and heaving mass reminiscent of a 'boiling cornstew'. Another old man was buried up to his shoulders in the kitchen of his own home by debris which flowed around him without injuring him. With other houses unharmed but filled with debris in similar fashion the concept of flow as opposed to a single sliding mass does seem more tenable, and model experiments also support the flow theory. Either theory explains how rock falls can move so far and so fast out over almost level ground once they have gained momentum. Unfortunately at present nobody who champions one theory will accept the other. Only when a clearer understanding is reached will it be feasible to make reliable predictions on just what areas are in danger from potential rockfalls.

Rockfalls are all too common in young mountain regions such as the Swiss Alps, and are an almost indefensible hazard for some villages in the deepest valleys. In 1618, 2430 people died when the southern Swiss town of Pleurs was buried by a massive rockfall from the slopes of Monte Conto, but it seems that, as at Elm, this fall was triggered by indiscriminate quarrying into the mountain slopes. Also in Switzerland, an interglacial landslide at the site where the village of Flims now stands, just west of Chur, blocked the Rhine valley so that a lake was formed, at first 650 feet deep. The lake no longer exists, as the Rhine has easily cut a new channel through the massive debris bank of the rockfall, which is itself now stable and presents no threat to Flims, built upon it.

A debris-dammed lake still survives from the largest rockfall of modern times: in 1911 some 5000 million cubic yards of rock crashed into the Murgab River valley in the Russian Pamirs. One village was buried, and another drowned as the lake, Sarezskoya, formed. The debris dam is now 1000 feet high and the lake is 45 miles long. Eighteen years previously a massive fall occurred in the heart of the Indian Himalayas. A mountainside of dolomite fell into the Birehiganga River valley near the village of Gohna, north-east of Delhi. The debris formed a dam 980 feet high and two miles long behind which a lake rapidly built up. The lake level was carefully monitored so that a year later it was accurately predicted when it would overflow its dam. A mass evacuation of the valley below ensured that no lives were lost, even though whole towns and villages were swept away when the overflow water cut a notch through the fallen debris and rapidly lowered the lake level by 390 feet, with a proportionately massive flood.

The Pamir landslide of 1911 provoked considerable interest at the time because it occurred simultaneously with a minor earthquake. At first it was thought that the massive rockfall had caused the quake, but subsequent calculations of the energies involved disproved this. The earthquake was found to have triggered the fall – as is now known to be a common occurrence. Just before midnight on 17 August 1959,

53

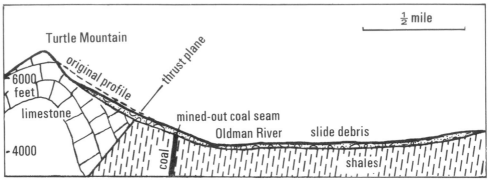

A cross-section through the central part of the Frank landslide, where the limestone was so dangerously inclined above the critical coalmine workings.

twenty-seven people died when a landslide hit their campground beside the Madison River in Montana, USA. The slide, best described as a rockfall, came from the steep canyon walls and was the direct result, and indeed the worst consequence, of an earthquake of magnitude 7.6 centred beneath Hebgen Lake. The fallen material was a mixture of dolomite and schist. Originally the nearly vertically bedded dolomite formed the lower part of the canyon wall, virtually supporting the schist behind and above it, which was in itself unstable because it dipped at 50° towards the canyon. The wall was able to hold until the earthquake vibrations weakened the dolomite buttress just too much. Peru's disastrous earthquake of 1970 had only a slightly greater magnitude (7.7) but it released a massive fall of rock and ice high on the mountain of Huascaran which hurtled down a valley on to the town of Yugay – killing over 10,000 people.

Landslides are typical features of earthquakes in mountain regions, but perhaps more disturbing are the landslides or rockfalls which do not need such a jolt to set them in motion. A prime example of this was the rockfall at Frank, Canada, in 1903.

Just east of the Crowsnest Pass in the Rocky Mountains of the southern corner of Alberta, lies the small mining town of Frank, nestling in the floor of a deep glaciated valley. Looming 3000 feet above it, on its south side, is the precipitous slope of Turtle Mountain. All the higher part of the mountain is formed of Upper Paleozoic limestones, most of which are massive and strong, though they do include many weak, flaggy and shaley, beds in its lower part. The limestones form a steep anticline with the lowest section of the eastern limb overturned. The main feature of this structure is that the bedding is parallel to a large section of the slope overlooking Frank. The limestone is underlain by a major fault plane, for the whole mass now lies on top of a series of notably weak Cretaceous sedimentary rocks, which underlie both the scree slopes at the foot of the mountain and the alluvium and boulder clay covered floor of the valley. These Cretaceous rocks are nearly vertical in the vicinity of Frank, and they consist mainly of shale, with some interbedded sandstones and a coal seam 14 feet thick.

In 1901, a drift mine was started just south of Frank to work the coal beneath the eastern slopes of Turtle Mountain. The mining left nearly vertical open rooms, or stopes, 130 feet long, separated by pillars 40 feet long which contained manways and coal chutes. By October 1902 the stopes extended 2300 feet along the strike of the coal, and a certain amount of movement and squeezing of the pillars became a regular occurrence, particularly in the early hours of the morning. By April of the next year the coal was almost 'self-mining': blocks of coal, together with chunks of shale off the hanging wall on the western side, were continually falling to the stope floors where they were simply shovelled up by the miners. This was going on over a length of 1500 feet, and in places the stopes reached heights of 400 feet. Then, at 4:00 on 29 April 1903, the movement in the mine suddenly increased. The rocks creaked and groaned, the coal broke and fell from the roofs in vast quantities, and the manways began to visibly close up. The night shift miners made a very rapid escape from the mine; ten minutes later a loud crack was heard outside the mine, and the summit of Turtle Mountain fell into the valley.

Following the initial crack, there was a noise like a dull explosion, as over a thousand million cubic feet of limestone crashed down the mountain. There was a muffled thud as it hit the scree at the foot of the slope, and then shot out across the valley floor at more than 100 mph, almost taking off as it ran over a low ridge of sandstone. Roaring like a high-pressure steam vent and with a wind blast that blew people from houses nearby, it scoured out the bed of the Oldman River, and the front of the debris mass extended another mile, rising 400 feet up the opposite hill before it quite suddenly stopped. Less than two minutes after that first loud crack the jumbled mass of limestone blocks covered the mine entrance, over a mile of the Canadian Pacific Railway, a number of houses on the edge of Frank, and the bodies of at least seventy-six people who had died beneath it.

While the mining activity obviously played a part in triggering the movement, the Frank landslide is classic for the number of different factors which contributed to its origin. Of prime significance was the structure of the limestone, especially its angle of dip. Had the dip been a little flatter, the bedding would not have permitted movement so easily. Conversely, had the dip and the hillside been any steeper, this would have encouraged frequent small-scale rockfalls without a large build-up of unstable material. As it was, the bedding was at the critical angle and over a large area offered little support to the limestone of the summit slopes. In addition, the valley in which Frank stood had been excavated during Pleistocene times by a glacier, and the eastern flank of Turtle Mountain had been oversteepened by the ice so that the rock slope was left just steeper than the inclination of the joints over the middle section of the face. The resulting relationship between the joints and hillside made the rockfall inevitable – indeed it was remarkable that Turtle Mountain had survived so long after the Pleistocene retreat of the ice. The fractured limestone must have absorbed large amounts of water and suffered a considerable build-up of water pressure in its joints, and regular freezing would also have contributed to the rock 'heaving', though largely in the surface layers. Minor contributory factors to the rockfall were the warmth of the day before, when melted snow in the fissures must have been considerable, and the heavy night frost which followed, inducing expansion of that same water. Critically oriented joints parallel to the hillside could have originated from unloading of the limestone following the retreat of the Pleistocene glacier in the valley – these are always a problem in deep glaciated valleys but their extent at Frank is difficult to estimate in the heavily fractured limestone.

That the mining did not cause the rockfall by its vibrations was virtually proved by the stability of the mountain during a minor earthquake in the area in 1901. But the mining did remove the support from the foot of the mountain – except for the inadequate coal pillars – and the result was that the whole rock mass was placed in tension, almost hanging from the summit. Any movement or flexing of the limestone must have resulted in heaving and loosening on the critically inclined bedding planes. The orientation of some localised thrust breccia zones within the limestone eliminated any significance in their low shear strength, but their potential compressibility may have contributed to the buckling of the limestone. This buckling was all that was needed to trigger the rockfall, which natural processes had made a certainty long before the coal miners arrived at Frank.

After the disaster of 1903 there was considerable concern about whether the northern shoulder of Turtle Mountain could move in the same way and land square on the town of Frank. The geological structure there was the same, and large open fissures did exist along the ridge – though their significance was not known since it was uncertain whether they pre-dated the 1903 failure or even the 1901 earthquake. It was clear that a slide could develop in this position, in which case should the town be relocated? On the other hand if there was no mining directly beneath the town, and if mining was critical as a trigger, then Frank could be deemed reasonably safe. Even though mining did continue for a few years, the town remained, and a new fall has not occurred – which strongly indicates that the mining up until 1903 was a badly planned and self-destructive operation in the light of the very easily interpreted geology of Turtle Mountain. The grand-sounding Canadian American Coal Company really thought of very little beyond actually digging the coal out and making money.

Rockslides

The massive failure at Frank in 1903 involved blocks of limestone sliding along joint planes, but this was only the start of the movement, and it ended up as a jumbled pile of limestone debris. It can therefore be called a rockfall. In contrast, a rockslide describes a block of rock sliding on a single pre-existing plane surface, and moving virtually as a single unit. This is the type of landslide with the simplest geology, making it the easiest to recognise; unfortunately the simplicity does not extend to its prediction, as the impossibility of reliably estimating frictional support at depth makes the time factor very wide-ranging.

In most cases the planes of weakness responsible for these rockslides are bedding planes in sedimentary rocks, though schistosity planes can have a similar effect in metamorphic rocks. Low shear strengths in either structure are commonly the result of included beds or zones of platey minerals – either clays or micas. Slides then occur where the planes of weakness are inclined steeper than their angles of friction and meet a ground surface which slopes even more steeply than the dip. A classically simple example took place in 1806 with the failure of the slopes of the Rossberg, a small mountain not far east of Lucerne in Switzerland. A slab of Tertiary conglomerate 200–300 feet thick dipped at angles of 19–21° and formed the southern slope of the mountain, where it sat on a similarly dipping bed of bituminous marl. At the foot of the slope, erosion had cut through to the marl, leaving the conglomerate unsupported except by friction on its sloping base. Then, in 1806, a large chunk of the conglomerate slid down into the valley, landing on the village of Goldau and killing 457 people.

It is amazing that so many of this type of rockslide, which involve such simple geometry, should have been caused by man removing the foot support of potentially unstable rock slopes. A hillside near Tyn nad Vltavou in south-western Czechoslovakia had a slope of about 30° and was cut in biotite gneisses dipping in the downslope direction at 40°. This was therefore perfectly stable until, regardless of the geology, a road was cut into the slope. The road had a cutting wall at an overall angle of 55° – and the perfectly predictable consequence was that the cutting failed as the gneiss slid down on to the road. At Matlock, in Derbyshire, two houses were built beneath an old quarry face in the steep-sided Derwent valley, even though the limestone in the face dipped steeply down towards them. On 10 January 1966 a large slab of the unsupported limestone, bounded at the back by a mineral vein and sitting on a thin clay layer, slipped slowly downwards, and ten hours after it had first creaked and groaned it had caused the complete collapse of the houses.

Less geometrically simple than the rockslides on inclined weaknesses just described, are slides developed where a strong and resistant bed sits – even horizontally – on a thick bed of weaker rock such as clay. Then large blocks of the upper bed are displaced en masse due to the plastic deformation of the underlying clay – a displacement which may be in any of three styles. The blocks may just settle and move outwards, as has happened many times on the edge of the St Raphael plateau in the city of Algiers. The most recent seriously damaging movement was in December 1943 when a limestone block of 5,000 square yards settled 23 feet into the underlying marl being squeezed out from beneath the plateau, fortunately without any tilting, which would have destroyed the houses on it. If more clay is squeezed out from under the extreme edge of such a plateau, the movement of the overlying stronger rock may involve some rotation as it dips down away from the high ground. The overall cross-section of such a disturbed structure earns it the apt title of a camber fold, and the overlying rock may then slide as well as settle on its inclined seat of plastic clay. The outcrop of the Magnesian Limestone, overlying a thick marl, between Nottingham and Doncaster in England forms a cambered escarpment which frequently moves, causing small-scale damage. Alternatively, if the underlying clay does not deform plastically but instead shears along a cylindrical surface, the blocks of the upper resistant bed move with a backward rotation so that they end up dipping in towards the hill. Slides of this type are well developed in the basalts overlying weak clays, along both the Antrim coast of Northern Ireland and the east coast of Scotland's Isle of Skye. The Skye landslips are less well known because they lack the spectacular but easily damaged coast road of Antrim, but the largest prehistoric slides on Skye involved movements of nearly a mile and rotation from an original horizontal to the vertical. The one feature common to all these rockslides is the existence of clay beds overlain by stronger rock – the classically unstable situation which should be so easily recognised.

The valley of the Gros Ventre River, just south of America's famous Yellowstone Park, is prone to landslides because of its distinctive geology. The south side of the valley is formed in Carboniferous sandstones, shales and limestones which dip north at between 18° and 21°, almost parallel to the valley slope, and this dip is maintained in the younger beds forming the northern side of the valley. About midway along

57

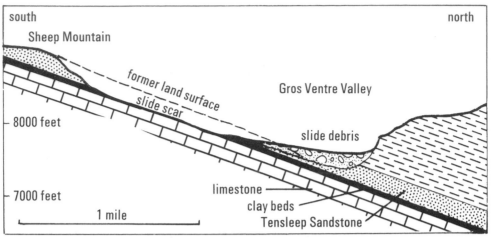

This cross-section through the Gros Ventre landslide is a classically simple example of a mass of sandstone slipping after being undercut by a river.

the south side, a spur of Sheep Mountain was formed in the dipping Tensleep Sandstone, which rested on thin shale beds separating it from a massive limestone beneath. Furthermore the river had cut down through much of the thickness of the Tensleep Sandstone, thus creating a potentially unstable situation with the mass of sandstone almost unsupported except by friction on the sloping shale beds. That at least, was the situation up until 1925. For, on 23 June of that year, after a period of heavy rain and snowmelt, a massive landslide carried the spur of Sheep Mountain down into the Gros Ventre valley.

Within a few minutes a vast sheet of the Tensleep Sandstone, 5000 feet long, 2000 feet wide and up to 200 feet thick, slid down into the valley floor. The front of the slide rose over 320 feet up the north slope before it came to a stop, forming a barrier 225 feet high across the river. Only a crest of sandstone was left on the scarred face of Sheep Mountain, most of which had been stripped to the limestone. The forest which used to be there largely survived, but it now stood on the barrier in the valley bottom. Many trees still stood upright, some had been killed, and many others had been knocked over but had survived – and can be seen today, weirdly shaped, with their later growth rising vertically from the older fallen trunks. The sandstone had been rather crumbled, but the lack of churning about during the slide movement is demonstrated by the survival of the forest and the scarcity of trees buried in the debris. Fortunately the slide caused no damage and took no lives, but it did dam the river which therefore built up into a lake and flooded a few ranches up-valley. Some of the water drained out through the slide debris, but on 18 May 1927 the spring melt overflowed the dam and scoured a deep channel through it. The event had been anticipated by the local forest ranger who, with only an hour to spare, warned people living downstream to move out quickly. As the lake partly emptied through the new channel a massive flood lasting five hours swept downstream and demolished the village of Kelly, where six people too slow off the mark were drowned. Today the lake is almost totally drained and the river cascades peacefully through its ravine cut in the slide debris.

58

The geology of the Gros Ventre slide was classically simple, and a slide on some scale was reasonably predictable. But the geology gave no clue as to the timing of the event. The trigger that was needed to set it off was provided, as it is in so many landslides, by water – the rainfall and snowmelt of the 1925 spring.

Water in landslides

Water, in the form of both snowmelt and rainfall, is known to be an important factor in landslide activity all over the world. One of Nepal's two main roads south towards India, that from Pokhara, is blocked nearly every year by small-scale landslides which occur during the summer monsoon. Each year the debris is shovelled away, and the roads and hillsides remain stable and safe – until the next monsoon. Not far away, the monsoon in 1976 triggered a landslide which killed 150 people as it destroyed the village of Pahirikhet. In the Brazilian city of Santos 100 people died under landslides following a period of heavy rain during March 1956. Water, normally from rainfall, can trigger landslides in almost any unstable geological situation. Heavy rain frequently causes landslides in the hilly parts of Hong Kong when the surface cover of soil and weathered rock slips on the underlying granite; a single slide on 18 June 1972 was 600 feet wide and killed over 100 people when it destroyed shanty-town housing in the Kwun Tong district of Kowloon. In July of the same year, a day's rainfall of 16 inches triggered a landslide in consolidated Mesozoic shales and sandstones which destroyed 350 houses and killed 112 people on the Japanese island of Kamijima. In similar style, heavy rainfall in Norway on 13 September 1936 prompted a slide in poorly jointed granitic gneiss; the slide itself, from a very steep mountainside, caused no damage but it landed in Lake Loen and the wave set up by it destroyed a village on the far side with considerable loss of life.

It is popularly thought that the water triggers a landslide by its lubricating effect, but this is patently not so. Besides the fact that some minerals, including quartz, have a coefficient of friction lower when dry than when wet, most rocks and soils are permanently wet enough to contain thin films of water which are all that are needed for efficient lubrication. Instead, water prompts landslide movements in a number of other ways when it gets into the pore spaces or joint openings of potentially unstable material. Firstly there is its additional weight, though this is rarely a major factor. A long-term effect is the internal weathering of the material in the presence of water, which can include both the solution of cementing minerals and also the development of clay minerals by the hydration of other silicates; the latter is the nearest that water comes to 'lubricating' a landslide, when easily sheared clays are formed at the expense of stronger original minerals. But the weathering process is slow, and while it may explain the failure of a slope in one wet season and not in hundreds of previous ones, it is not the instant result of a single heavy rainfall. The heavy fall and sudden wetting has a different effect: it increases the amount of water in the ground and raises the pressure of the pore water by the raising of its own head. This is the major factor responsible for causing landslides. Increased pore-water pressure literally holds the grains of mineral, or blocks of rock, apart, reducing cohesion, surface tension and frictional resistance; if high enough it can even liquefy an unconsolidated sediment. And a day's heavy rain can raise the water table and

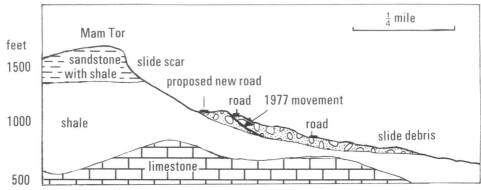

The Mam Tor landslide, showing the renewed movements of winter 1977 which resulted in serious damage to the road across it.

increase the pore pressures enough to cause a slide in material perfectly stable under any drier conditions. This was the cause of the earthslides of Hong Kong and Santos, and the rockslides of Goldau, Gros Ventre and Kamijima.

Such water pressure also caused the landslide on Mam Tor – a hill in the heart of England's Peak District, almost surrounded by landslides of varying antiquity and size. Locally it is known as Shivering Mountain – a name earned by the almost constantly moving slide on its eastern slope down into the head of Hopedale. Over thousands of years the movement of this slide mass has totalled around 1600 feet, and at present it slowly creeps a few inches or feet a year. Unfortunately the slide is crossed, twice, by a main road – which was built in 1802 and is an almost perfect example of where not to build a main road. However, the engineers responsible for it had, and have, an ideal excuse in that there is no reasonable alternative route for the road, so it is accepted that the road is constantly distorted by the steady creep of its foundations, and repair work is just a regular routine. But the winter of 1977 saw thick snow on Mam Tor until late February, when it rapidly melted during a spell of prolonged heavy rain. The water loosened the whole slide mass, and, almost as expected, it started to move on a scale which was well beyond that of slow creep. Tears and cracks opened up in the road, and sections of the road dropped to leave steps eighteen inches high in the surface. After a few weeks the movement ceased, but the road was so badly damaged that it was closed for nearly a year.

The water pressure which caused the landslide was initiated in the glacially oversteepened head of Hopedale where the Carboniferous sandstones and shales of the Mam Tor Series rest almost horizontally on the Edale Shales, so that water moving down through the sandstones was held up by the underlying shales. The 1977 movements only affected the already slipped mass, which consists of a mix of sandstone and shale. In this, substantial heads of water are easily transmitted down through the sandstone, sealed in by the shales, so that pore pressures can rise spectacularly. Pools of water rest on the slide debris, and boreholes drilled after the 1977 slip found artesian water at depths of over 65 feet. Earth and rock saturated on this scale is only too ripe for renewed failure. Although the Mam Tor road may be realigned to avoid the outcrops of the main shear planes developed within the slide mass, the only permanent means of stabilising the slope is a network of deep drains to prohibit any further build-up of the pore water pressures.

60

In the same way that artificial drainage can stabilise a landslide, as at Mam Tor, artificial flooding can cause a landslide, as was the catastrophic case at Vaiont. Lying in the Italian Alps north of Venice, the Vaiont River runs through a deep gorge cut in the floor of a broad glacial valley just upstream of its confluence with the much larger valley of the Piave River. The lower end of the gorge is cut in massive Jurassic limestones, and although the walls required some strengthening with anchor-bolts it was an ideal site for the Vaiont Dam completed there in 1960 for the Società Adriatica de Elettricito. Only 525 feet across its crest, the thinly arched dam was the world's second highest, at an impressive 875 feet. Unfortunately the excellence of the dam site was not matched by the rather difficult geology of the reservoir area.

The valley lies along a syncline in the Mesozoic limestones. The situation on the south side of the reservoir is worse, where the thick limestones of the slopes of Mount Toc dip steeply towards the syncline axis but then level out so that the Vaiont gorge cuts down through their toe. Many of the limestones are thin bedded and include partings of marl, and this mass of rock was essentially held in place on the side of Mount Toc by its frictional hold on the sloping beds beneath. Two sets of unloading joints, parallel to both the broad glacial valley and the incised post-glacial gorge, intersected just beneath the convex break of slope along the south shore of the reservoir, further reducing the slope's cohesion and stability. In addition two prehistoric landslides were recognised, close to Pineda and Casso. The geology therefore gave some cause for concern and, both before and while the dam was built, a number of geological studies were made in order to assess the potential of landslides from Mount Toc into the reservoir.

Inspections of the Mount Toc slope in 1957 and 1958 suggested that only small debris slides or rock falls not exceeding a million cubic yards could occur, and these provided no serious threat. The next year a seismic survey revealed solid rock at a depth of 65 feet below a veneer of loose debris. In 1960 a repeat survey didn't find solid rock until at depths of 160–240 feet, but the inference that this could be due to progressive break-up of the rock was not taken at the time. Boreholes drilled

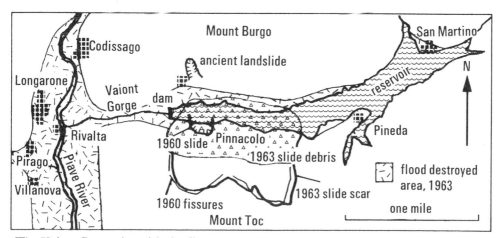

The Vaiont Reservoir, with the disastrous landslide from Mount Toc and the extent of the flood wave damage in the town and villages below.

in 1959 found no slide planes within the limestone – though events later revealed that the bores had merely not been deep enough. When filling of the reservoir started in 1960, the engineers set control marks in the ground so that any movement could be monitored. A slow lateral creep was noticed, but gave no concern. At the same time the rock spur of Pinnacolo, at the foot of the Mount Toc slope and projecting into the Vaiont gorge, was observed to tilt slowly, the rotational movement of the limestone blocks indicating that it was being pushed from the south. The movement of the whole slope accelerated in October 1960, and a long headcrack developed in the limestone, but when the reservoir level was dropped the movement ceased. On 4 November a small rockslide of 900,000 cubic yards of limestone descended into the reservoir in ten minutes – but this was almost as expected and again caused no concern. A report on the much larger movement in October laid the blame on the jointed nature and dip of the rock, the heavy rainfall at the time, and the buoyancy effect of the rising reservior level.

The movement of the whole hillside in October and November 1960 had averaged 1.5 inches per day for ten days on end, and it was recognised that the movement distinctly accelerated when the reservoir was filled to unprecedented levels. Consequently the filling was continued in stages, with continuous monitoring – which over the next two years bore out this relationship. By September 1963 the total movement of the Mount Toc slope, although it varied from place to place, was as much as 12 feet – most of which had taken place in the three periods when the reservoir level had reached new heights. To quote the engineer's report: ' . . . the movements generally had a higher velocity only if a new portion was wetted for the first time. . . . it was assumed that the mass would eventually reach a certain equilibrium, or, at least, would keep moving so slowly that no serious problems would occur.' This assumption was based partly on the curved shape of the sliding mass, which could suggest that it would eventually stabilise on its relatively flat base. But it was a gross assumption to make when millions of tons of rock were so precariously perched above a reservoir, standing in turn above a valley populated by thousands of people.

In July 1963 the reservoir was filled for the first time to over the level of 2300 feet (above sea-level), and the movement of the Mount Toc slope began to accelerate. By the end of September the movement was up to 1.2 inches per day, still not as high as the 1960 movement but enough to cause some concern, and the reservoir level was dropped back to 2300 feet, a level which would prevent a 65 foot wave overtopping the dam, and that was the maximum size of wave anticipated from any continued slow landsliding. But when the water level was dropped the mountain side continued to move and even accelerate, and on 1 October the animals which normally grazed on Mount Toc, more sensitive than man to minute ground vibrations, began to move away from the sliding area. The continuous monitoring revealed that by 8 October the whole slide area was moving as a single mass, and by the next morning the rate of movement was up to 8 inches per day. It rained really hard that day, and even though the villagers from below the dam became increasingly anxious, there was no evacuation or official action.

At 10:41 that evening, 9 October 1963, there was a series of loud cracks and the whole side of Mount Toc broke away in a massive landslide, in violent contrast to the slow creep of the previous years. Some 350 million cubic yards of rock hurtled at 70 mph down the mountainside, into – virtually through – the reservoir, and 400

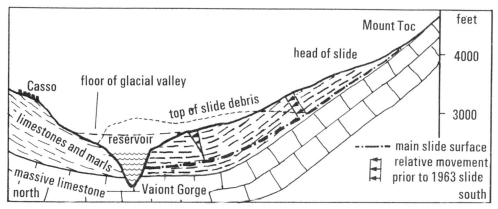

Labels within figure:
Mount Toc
feet
head of slide
4000
floor of glacial valley
Casso
top of slide debris
3000
limestones and marls
reservoir
-----·- main slide surface
relative movement
prior to 1963 slide
massive limestone
Vaiont Gorge
north
south

A cross-section through the Vaiont Reservoir landslide showing how slow movement was restricted in the foot of the slide mass until the rock suddenly broke across the bedding.

feet up the opposite bank. The rock ended up 1300 feet thick above the floor of the reservoir, and had displaced the water on a massive scale. To the east a 160-foot-high wave had swept up the reservoir and extensively damaged the village of San Martino. But worse was downstream. The water had washed an incredible 720 feet above the reservoir level, very nearly reaching the village of Casso – which did, however, have some houses almost blown apart by the enormous wind blast. Then the wave had crashed over the dam, without damaging it, to the credit of its designers. Every witness to this monumental wave died, but the extent of stripped vegetation and soil afterwards showed that the wall of water which went over the dam was more than 500 feet high. Forty million cubic yards of water crashed nearly 800 feet into the depths of the Vaiont gorge, and only two minutes after Mount Toc had failed, emerged as a 270-foot-high flood wave into the Piave valley. The town of Longarone stood directly opposite, and was promptly annihilated. Practically every building and structure was flattened to rubble, and almost every inhabitant died. Some of the people in the neighbouring villages heard the roar of the floodwave, and escaped to high ground. But the rapidly spreading water also destroyed their homes in Pirago, Villanova and Rivalta. In fifteen minutes the waters had drained away, but the Piave valley was left a sheet of rubble and flood debris in which lay the bodies of some 2117 people.

The Vaiont Dam stood almost useless. The landslide had not only half filled the reservoir but also acted as a natural dam for most of the water that remained. And the questions were asked – why had Mount Toc produced such a slide, and should it have been predicted? The dip of the bedding, the presence of marl layers in the limestone, the incision of the Vaiont gorge and the presence of the unloading joints had all pointed to the possibility of sliding, but the movement had been expected to be slow, with toppling of material at its toe even likely to increase its stability with time. Rainfall did not correlate with the monitored movement so it could not be blamed, and the heavy rain on the day of the disaster contributed only by adding its weight to the unstable rock mass. The reservoir filling, with the associated raising of the local water table and increasing of pore water pressures, was clearly instrumental in the slow creep of the slide which had continued for two years, but could not be associated with the sudden failure of 9 October. The ponded water had virtually buoyed up the lower end of the slide mass prompting its progressive deformation and loss of strength. But the reservoir levels never affected the upper parts of the slide, which, resting on the thin bedded limestone dipping at 30–45°, were essentially unstable and only supported by the nearly horizontal rock in the toe of the slide. The mechanism for the sudden movement of 1963 was revealed by two clues. After the slide took place, the main slip plane at the lower end was seen to cut across the bedding – indicating brittle fracture of the rock and not just sliding along bedding planes. In addition, monitoring of movement in a few boreholes before the October slide had shown that the surface zones were moving more rapidly than the rock at depth – in the lower end of the slide only, where the rock fracture was later recognised. This lack of movement at depth could therefore be correlated with energy absorption in that zone – energy which accumulated until the rock could be fractured and so instantly precipitate a rapid failure of the whole rock mass. The progressive discontinuous breaking of the rock at depth had not been recognised because it was replaced by steady creep in the surface layers, and so the sudden slide had not been anticipated. And while the reservoir engineers' interference with groundwater levels had undeniably influenced the steady creep of the Mount Toc hillside, it had been only a secondary factor in the catastrophic slide, which was probably inevitable anyway, given time. But in that case, the Vaiont Reservoir should never have been placed where it was.

Earthslides

Unconsolidated sediments and poorly lithified sedimentary rocks, such as clay, are weak and easily deformed even without the existence of the fractures and discontinuities which induce failure in solid rocks. Although a geologist may describe a weak and barely cohesive clay as a rock because of its age and geological history, a civil engineer would probably describe the same material as earth or soil on the grounds of its low physical strength and high plasticity. When the material is uniform it can be studied by the combination of laboratory testing and mathematical analysis which constitute the science of soil mechanics, and by these means slope stabilities in uniform materials are calculable today, so that there should be little remaining doubt or hazard. The problems in civil engineering arise where the sediments or rocks lack uniformity in ways which are not easily detected and severely limit the value of a mathematical approach. These losses of uniformity may be due to the existence of small fractures, minor structural changes across the bedding, or pre-existing failure surfaces originally generated and then made seemingly stable by environmental changes. The latter are particularly widespread, and yet are difficult to detect where associated with landslides that developed under the contrasting climatic conditions associated with the intermittent glaciations of the Pleistocene. Slides that moved in ancient permafrost conditions in an area like Britain may be stable in today's climate until disturbed by civil engineering construction works which may prompt renewed movement. It is, therefore, the responsibility of the engineer to ensure that he does not begin new slides or reactivate old ones. An ancient landslide mass moved during the 1950s and caused extensive damage in an area called Portugese Bend in Los Angeles. A court case, instigated by a group of aggrieved house owners, laid partial responsibility on Los

Angeles County, which had planned the buildings and roads of the area; the County lost the case and more than five million dollars.

Like rockslides, earthslides – which are in fact landslides in relatively uncon-solidated materials – commonly have separate mechanisms which act firstly as prime causes, and secondly as triggers. The basic cause is normally the lack of shear strength of the actual material, but the trigger may commonly be the activity of man. In the Menton district of southern France the clearing of olive trees in order to plant potentially more profitable crops of carnations caused earthslides through the loss of the tree roots' support, and was responsible for the deaths of eleven people. Ploughing of land previously used for grazing above the Czechoslovakian town of Handlova permitted an unprecedented rise in the local water table in the wet season of 1960 and a consequent loss of stability on the slopes. Forty million tons of soil started to slide down the hill, threatening the town. Emergency installation of drains stopped the movement inside two months, but not before 150 houses had been destroyed. Slope failures were similarly caused by deforestation of the edge of a 200-foot-high terrace in the city of Whitehorse in Canada's Yukon. When trees were cleared to give room for access roads, paths and services on to the terrace, many slips and mud-runs invaded the streets below, and were only stopped by a programme of drainage and revegetation.

Removing the toe of a potential earthslide, by cutting a steep slope into it, is the surest way of starting any movement. This may be done naturally, as in the case of marine erosion at the foot of cliffs in uncemented sediments or rocks. The cliffs at Barton, on the south coast of England, are cut in Tertiary clays and sands, and are subject to repeated landslips developed by shearing along certain bedding planes, and as a result a large number of houses on the cliff top are under permanent threat of destruction. Further north, the coastline east of Hull is well known for its rapid erosion which has been unabated since Roman times. The 40-foot-high cliffs of relatively homogeneous boulder clay fail in a continued succession of rotational slips, and roads and villages steadily disappear on to the foreshore. The ocean coastline of San Francisco is marked by cliffs 400–600 feet high just south-west of the city centre. The cliffs are formed in Pliocene-Pleistocene sands broken by numerous deep rotational landslips whose stability is hardly improved by the activity of the San Andreas Fault cutting their northern end. The slides were mainly related to relatively impermeable silt-clay layers in the succession, but also the strength of the sands is inadequate to survive in such a steep cliff under attack from the sea. The coast highway originally lay along a bench cut into the cliffs, but was a disaster from the start. From 1950 to 1957 it was closed seventeen times for a total of 174 days due to landslip damage, and was eventually abandoned after the 1957 earthquake. And even though landslides are accepted as a feature of the cliffs, urban development has been allowed to expand so close to the cliff top that many houses face only a short lifespan.

A famous succession of earthslides developed in the cutting walls of the Panama Canal when it was built by the United States between 1907 and 1914. The deep Gaillard Cut, through the watershed, was planned almost solely on the basis of topographical surveys, and was designed to have walls terraced to an overall angle of 56° from the horizontal. As excavation proceeded, the cutting walls in various volcanic rocks were found to be safe at this angle, but in the sedimentary rocks exposed the situation was disastrous. Worst were the weak uncemented sediments of the Tertiary Cucaracha Formation – shales with sandstones and conglomerates revealed in a broad syncline crossed by the Cut. As the excavations got deeper, the walls in these sediments failed persistently and uncontrollably. The 'rock' was so weak that some of it could not be sampled for strength testing, and in addition the entire thickness of the Cucaracha Formation was found to be moving on a failure surface at the top of the underlying calcareous sandstones. The slides continued moving, some of them for years, and the three largest were each more than 1500 feet square. All attempts at stabilising the slides proved fruitless; piles were just swept away, and the clay was so fine-grained that free drainage of it had little effect in reducing the weight of the unstable masses. Pore water pressures were not understood at the time, but the ditches dug to divert the surface water and stop it flowing into the fissures at the heads of the slides must have had some stabilising effect. In fact the slides were allowed to move, and the debris was continually excavated as it piled up in the canal. Today some of the slides extend over 1000 feet back from the canal, with an overall slope of about 11° – instead of the 56° planned – but groundwater levels are still not fully adjusted to the canal level, so that even further movement can be expected. Studies of the slides revealed three distinct types. Surface debris slips formed one group and were on a small scale causing relatively little trouble. A second group comprised large slides moving on pre-existing planes of weakness, such as bedding planes. Most of the slides, however, were of a rotational type, developed on new failure surfaces, involving uplift of the canal floor and progressive working backwards with the main shear surface related to the base of the Cucaracha clays. A modern site investigation and soil testing programme would have predicted the slides, and allowed a more realistic estimate of the cost than the American engineers had at the time; as it was, the problems were only overcome by a sustained and very expensive effort.

Both the slab slide and the rotational slide, of Panama experience, are recognised today and anticipated in studies on slope stability in clays. Clay slopes generally stabilise at an angle somewhere between 7 and 12° from the horizontal, given enough time. The range is due to varying geological factors – notably a higher silt or quartz content, or a greater age, generally give the higher figures – but laboratory tests on small samples can determine shear strength from which slope failures may usefully be predicted. Time is an additional factor, complicated by slow structural changes which take place in a strained, or loaded, clay. A laboratory test can reveal a clay to have a peak shear strength when it is subject to initial strain, but as the strain is increased the shear strength steadily declines to what is defined as the residual shear strength. The change is due largely to repositioning of the granules and also dilation with consequent increase in pore-water openings, and is important in clays as it encourages a slow progressive failure of a slope by one part failing and therefore passing its load to the next part which will fail under the increased strain. Added to this is the weakening effect of clay over a long period under strain. This is particularly important with overconsolidated clays – that is those which have been compressed by burial at great depth and, due to subsequent erosion, are once more located at the surface under less pressure, under which conditions they exhibit a great drop from peak to residual shear strength. The Tertiary London Clay has failed in a number of railway cuttings in the London area after long periods of time. One wall, in Kensal Green, failed 116 years after excavation, when its shear strength had fallen 60 per cent of the way from peak to residual, and another, at

Sudbury Hill, failed after 49 years due to an 80 per cent drop. From this experience it is possible to check the rate of change of shear strength and therefore calculate when a given slope is likely to fail in the London Clay – and it appears that many railway cuttings, dating from the peak of construction activity around the turn of the century, are now approaching their critical ages and will require extra strengthening.

The London Clay is now beginning to be understood properly, even though it does cause problems with its delayed creep and plastic movement. But at least it does not fail in the more violent manner exhibited by what are called sensitive clays.

Flow slides

A flow slide is a landslide in which the moving debris acts temporarily as a liquid, and there are a number of different ways by which this liquefaction can take place. One of the most common causes is the disturbance of sensitive clays, dramatically demonstrated at Nicolet in Canada.

Nicolet is a small town on the southern side of the St Lawrence Valley in Quebec, and it stands on a low terrace adjacent to the Nicolet River, a tributary of the St Lawrence. At one time the terrace at the town site consisted of 8 feet of fine sand overlying the Leda Clay, a thick stratified grey material; and a steep bank dropped less than 50 feet into the river. At just before midday on 12 November 1955, a large section of terrace slipped into the river, leaving a crater 600 feet by 400 feet and between 20 and 30 feet deep. The movement lasted only a few minutes and carried away a school, fortunately empty, and a number of houses. Three people died.

The slide debris behaved almost as a liquid – it was a classic flow slide – and its cause was the sensitive nature of the Leda Clay. The sensitivity of a clay is the percentage loss of strength due to remoulding or disturbance of the material, and materials such as Leda Clay, which can be described as very sensitive, or quick, have a sensitivity of around 90. This is enough to ensure that when disturbed, the clay acts and flows like a liquid. Samples of Leda Clay have been tested to an unconfined compressive strength of 2100 lb to the square foot, and yet they can be poured like a liquid after merely stirring, with no addition of water. The sensitivity may be due to its gentle deposition in a shallow sea adjacent to the glacier margin of the Last Glaciation. This gave the clay a composition in which more than 50 per cent of the uncoagulated grains were finer than two microns, and 50 per cent by weight of the whole material was water. In this state, the bonding of the grains was enhanced by the presence of the salt in the water. With postglacial uplifting of the clay it was exposed to rainwater seeping through it and thus steadily removing the salt from the interstitial groundwater. The reduction of salt content to around one tenth of its original value was parallelled by loss of bonding between the grains. In this leached state sensitive clays are prone, when saturated, to restructuring and fluidisation by almost any external disturbance. But salt leaching is only one theory in the controversial matter of explaining the causes of clay sensitivity. Other possible mechanisms include the addition of dispersal agents in the form of humus compounds from overlying peat, or the failure of unstable hydroxide cements, and indeed there may be more than one process contributing to the failure of any one clay deposit.

The basic cause of the Nicolet slide was that the underlying clay had progressively weakened until it was sensitive; the actual trigger to the failure was probably either the increased water pressures due to a fractured sewer, or vibration from road and sewerage repair works which had just started in the area. Unfortunately, when Nicolet was built, the properties of sensitive clays were not understood. Today they can be recognised on the basis of their geological history, grain-size distribution and water content, and they can also be revealed in laboratory testing, so that there is now no excuse for building on the crest of a steep slope in sensitive clay such as the site of Nicolet, where vibration from traffic and disturbance makes landslides inevitable.

Sensitive clays of Pleistocene marine origin are widespread in uplifted lowland areas of both eastern Canada and Scandinavia, and at least forty major slides have been recorded in recent history in these two areas. The most disastrous was in Norway in 1893, when 70 million cubic yards of terraced clay slipped in the Verdal valley adjacent to Trondheimsfjord. The failure of the sensitive clays was probably only due to time, but the consequent flow slide destroyed twenty-two farms and took 111 lives. The liquefied clay moved like a wave, at first very fast, and then slower, moving a total of more than 5 miles down the valley, in about 45 minutes, before stopping and solidifying. One family managed to ride the mudflow for nearly 4 miles on the roof of their farm, carried from the source area of the flow. But most people had no chance when their farms lower down the valley were swamped by the advancing wave of mud. At Surte in Sweden's Gota valley, vibrations from a pile driver triggered a slide in sensitive clay in 1950; in 3 minutes the ground moved up to 430 feet, destroying thirty-one houses, a road and a railway, and taking one life. The same clay beds failed again during December 1977 in an area thought to be safe. Over a hundred acres of ground formed a flow slide in the Göteborg suburb of Ture; 67 houses were carried away and eight people died.

The French Canadian town of Saint-Jean-Vianney, in Quebec, lay in a sheltered hollow surrounded by terraces in the now infamous Leda Clay. Only recently was the hollow recognised as the upper end of a massive flow slide which had occurred in the fifteenth or sixteenth century, and on 4 May 1971 part of this moved again. Animals were the first to feel the movements, refusing to go into some fields at 7 o'clock in the evening: three hours later, those fields were destroyed in a slide which lasted for four hours, rapidly expanding in a series of progressive slumps. Unfortunately, in the darkness little warning was received, and the most rapid part of the slide undermined a housing area. In front of the survivors' eyes, roads, a bus, cars and 40 houses disappeared into the crater, half a mile across and 75 feet deep, which was the source of the slide. The debris flowed in a wave 50 feet high down a small valley for 1.8 miles until it was swallowed by the Saguenay River. Thirty-one people died, and the town was subsequently evacuated because of the almost insuperable instability of the sensitive clay even under very gentle slopes.

Sensitive or 'quick' clays can liquefy under the slightest disturbances or even just due to their progressive alteration over time. Other materials can liquefy in the same way when a greater degree of disturbance compensates for a lower initial sensitivity. In this respect, earthquake vibrations are the most massive natural disturbances. The Bootlegger Cove Clay at Anchorage, Alaska, was only sensitive enough to liquefy when heavily vibrated, but the 1964 earthquake was all too effective in causing the massive landslides of Turnagain Heights and adjacent areas.

Similarly, flow slides are recognised in the San Francisco region as occurring mostly in well-graded, saturated sands which liquefy most easily under vibration. These two examples involve liquefaction due to support of the vibrated grains by intergranular water, but the same can happen with air support in materials such as loess. The catastrophic flow slides in dry loess during the 1920 earthquake in Kansu, China, in which nearly 100,000 people died when dozens of slides destroyed the loess teraces in which their cave homes had been carved, must rank as the world's most destructive liquefaction phenomenon on record.

Although liquefaction can be induced by vibration or increased sensitivity, the term was originally applied to the liquefying of sediments by the increase of pore water pressure until all the external stress on the rock is borne by the intergranular fluids. This in turn may be caused by externally produced rises in groundwater level; alternatively, internal restructuring without volume loss may transfer stress from the grains to the pore water with the same effect. There have been hundreds of liquefaction slides in the unconsolidated sands of Holland's Zeeland coast; most of them have occurred at very high and rising tides, and the sands, initially with surface slopes of around 10°, have only stabilised with slopes of 3 or 4°. Increased water also caused the many debris and mud flows in the Santa Monica region of southern California during the heavy rainstorms of January 1969. The slides developed in the soil cover on the steeply sloping sides of the many small villages in the area which provide such attractive but potentially hazardous home sites. A slide in Topanga Canyon was typical in that it occurred at the height of a storm, started in soil on a slope of about 40°, and once moving liquefied so that it rushed down without any warning on to and through a house, killing the three occupants.

A landslide that starts off as a relatively harmless slab movement of earth may develop into a fast and dangerous flow slide due to one or both of two factors. During failure, the head of a slide mass may load the toe of the slide so that the pore pressure is raised, thereby inducing liquefaction. Alternatively, the movement may induce a flow structure due to reorientation of the grains to offer minimum resistance to deformation which, under constant volume, results in an attendant increase in pore pressure. The constant volume is maintained either by a watertight seal around the porous sediment, or by the pore spaces being so small that permcability and escape of the groundwater is almost eliminated by surface tension. This was the root cause of the catastrophic failure in 1938 of the Fort Peck Dam under construction across the Missouri River in Montana. There the dam was a hydraulic fill type: fine sand and silt were laid hydraulically to form the bulk of the dam between two walls of coarser sand, and it was nearly completed when it failed. A massive flow slide developed and poured ten million cubic yards of the dam material into the partially filled reservoir. In three minutes the slide moved as much as a quarter of a mile, only stopping when it was nearly horizontal: into the liquefied mass had sunk many items of machinery, as well as eighty of the construction workers. It was later claimed that a slip failure in the shale which formed the dam foundation had resulted in displacement of the upstream wall of coarse sand, which had in turn allowed a shear movement and liquefaction in the fine silt of the dam core. In 1938 there was little understanding of shale slip and sand liquefaction, but the combination of the two potential hazards should be recognised easily enough to demand a more conservative design in any modern repeat of the Fort Peck situation. In fact the dam was rebuilt after the disaster with a thicker sand shell and a compacted internal fill.

Disastrous flow slides can also be the result of shearing after failure in materials accumulating on an over-steep slope – either naturally or artificially. Rapidly deposited volcanic ash forms impressive mud flows when slopes of it are saturated with rainwater, and the burial of Herculaneum by a flow of sodden ash from the slopes of Vesuvius in AD 79 is the most famous of many examples. Herculaneum's destruction involved the liquefaction of an ash, but the opposite process, namely the addition of debris to a flood to form a mudflow, occured on New Zealand's Ruapehu volcano in 1953. The flood originated from volcanic melting of snow, but picked up enough loose ash to form a highly destructive mudflow, which tore down the Whangehu River and swept away the Tangiwa railway bridge two minutes before a train was due to cross it. When the train hurtled off the end of the torn tracks, 154 lives were lost.

Almost as dangerous as volcanic piles of loose debris are man's comparable edifices in the form of mine or quarry tip heaps. Normally built to the angle of rest of the dry material, failures which have induced liquefaction by shearing of the saturated debris are not uncommon. Most have been on a small scale, where the flow slide has merely spread over ground already earmarked for the extending tip, and therefore caused little inconvenience. But tip slides which involve the buildings of mining communities have brought about some major disasters.

In the world of engineering and geology, the name Aberfan still provokes the greatest emotions of all. The failure in 1966 of the tip heap above the small Welsh mining village of Aberfan spread the name around the world, and now it has its sad place in every book on engineering geology. Part of its notoriety was earned by the extensive debate over the causes and responsibilities for the failure, but the disaster is also remembered because, of the 144 people who died in it, 109 were young children from the village primary school.

Aberfan lies on the floor of Taff Vale, one of the famous Welsh valleys cut 1000 feet beneath the Pennant Sandstone plateau. The valleys cut through these Carboniferous sandstones and their floors reveal the valuable Coal Measures. They are crowded with coal mines and their villages, and there is a permanent space problem over the disposal of mine waste. The tips from the Merthyr Vale Colliery were sited on the bleak upper slopes of the valley side, directly above Aberfan and some 300–600 feet higher up a 13° slope. These slopes consist of the Brithdir Sandstone, a massive sandstone which is the lowest unit of the Pennant Series; it is strongly broken by joints, widened by both valley cambering and mining subsidence activity, so that it is highly permeable. It dips at 5° to the south-east and overlies the non-productive Brithdir coal seam and its associated seatearth of impermeable clay. There is a thin superficial cover of sandy or clayey periglacial head on the upper slopes, but lower down this extends over a layer of still clayey glacial till which floors the valley. Small springs and seepages are a well-known feature of the regional hydrogeology, and many are concentrated along either the outcrop of the base of the permeable Brithdir Sandstone, or, where this is covered by impermeable till, along the upper limit of the till. The Aberfan slopes contained numerous springs from this sandstone, the largest emerging through the head just above the till outcrop.

The tip heaps above Aberfan were started in 1918 and Tips 1, 2 and 3 grew without any problems. In 1939 a tip in an almost identical situation failed at Cilfynydd, five miles to the south. In a pattern that was to be repeated twenty-seven

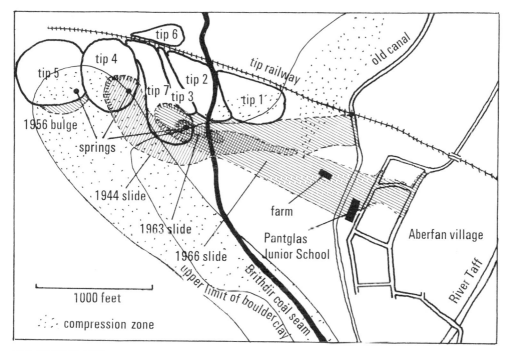

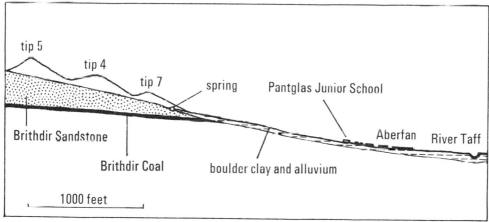

The tip heaps of Aberfan and the various landslides from them which culminated in the tragedy of 1966.

years later, a rotational slip developed into a flow slide which poured at about 10 mph for 1400 feet down a 10° hillside to bury the main Cardiff–Merthyr road 20 feet deep in debris. Fortunately no one was even hurt, and the event was soon forgotten, as the Aberfan tips continued to grow. Tip 4 had been started in 1933 and extended over a group of springs and seepages fed from the Brithdir Sandstone. It failed in a large but harmless slip and flow slide in 1944. Tip 5 was then started and grew across an open drainage trench; by the time it was closed in 1956 it had an ominous bulge on its lower side, but never actually slipped. Sited on dry ground to the north, Tip 6 was perfectly stable but was abandoned when it encroached on a neighbouring farmer's land. In 1958, the fateful Tip 7 was started in a convenient space between the existing tips even though it too extended over some springs. The tipped material was different in that it contained about 10 per cent tailings – very fine slurry from the coal washing plant which significantly reduced the overall permeability of the tip heap.

Tip 7 failed in 1963 with a large rotational slip, from the base of which emerged a small flow slide. Not only was this ominous warning ignored, but tipping continued in the worst possible way – straight into the hollow created by the slip, and no precautions against a repeat incident were taken except to stop the inclusion of tailings in the tip. The only 'inspection' of the site was in the form of casual visits by officials who looked at the area very superficially and were anyway not qualified to appraise the situation accurately. Starting in 1963, concern in the village led to a correspondence with the National Coal Board which produced an admission by the Board that there was a potential danger from slippage of the tips. But the few officials involved in these discussions thought that any slip would be slow enough to warn people to move away, and so they did nothing; and the officials responsible for the tip carried on in ignorance. They did not know what the local children, the farmers, and even the tipping gang knew – that Tip 7 was steadily extending over more springs. And the Coal Board had forgotten what had already happened to saturated tips.

Through 1966 there were many instances when the side of Tip 7 sank by a few feet or so at a time. At 7:00 am on 21 October 1966, there was a sinking of 10 feet. The tipping gang stopped tipping, moved their machinery back and sent word to the mine below. No danger to the village was anticipated by the few who even knew of the event. At 9:00 am the tip sank another 10 feet, and ten minutes later a flow slide developed at the base of the slipped mass. Slow at first, it gathered speed until it tore down the hillside at 10-20 mph making a noise like an express train – and heading straight for the village. In its 2000-foot-long run, the slide destroyed two farm cottages and then crossed the canal and railway to smother the end of the village in debris up to 30 feet deep. Survivors described it as a wave of black mud – the liquefied sediment had a density double that of water, and it flowed until enough water was squeezed out of it for intergranular contact to be regained, when it suddenly stopped. The outer edges of the flow were almost dry debris, but the bulk of it was a liquid powerful enough to smash the buildings, yet fluid enough to fill almost every corner of any surviving rooms. A few people outran the flow, a few survived under odd pieces of timber or in protected corners where they were trapped until dug out by rescuers; but 144 people died, including nearly every pupil at the Pantglas Junior School which caught the full force of the slide and was buried to its gables. By a freak of misfortune, all the children were gathered for morning assembly in the fated building, and the speed of the flow gave no time for escape.

The tragedy of Aberfan was that Tip 7 developed not just a small failure, but a classic flow slide, the mechanism of which demanded the coincidence of a number of geological features. The tip was saturated with water, particularly in its lower parts, due to its location on the springs and seepages from the highly permeable Brithdir Sandstone, and the content of tailings significantly reduced the permeability of the tip material itself – which was important in maintaining the fluidity of the eventual flow slide. The initial movement was a deep rotational slip, which was not unusual on tip heaps, and the failure surface almost certainly coincided with that formed in the 1963 movement. Liquefaction then took place to form the flow slide and this had two contributory mechanisms. It was initially due to shearing and collapse of the granular packing of the sediment so that, without its water escaping, the grains virtually floated and load was transferred to the pore water. Dry densities of the material ranged from 1.5 gm/cc in the tip itself to 1.85 gm/cc in the debris deposited by the flow slide – indicating the original material's capability of considerable volume change which is indicative of its high sensitivity and potential for liquefaction. In addition to this, the first rotational failure stripped the tip's underlying boulder clay off the bedrock, permitting trapped groundwater to flood out of the permeable sandstone. The flow of water from the sandstone was unusually high because the mining subsidence in the area had created two belts of compression in the rock just north and south of the tip complex. These compression zones had locally reduced permeability in the sandstone and funnelled the groundwater from a large area of highly permeable sandstone under tension, through a tension zone below the tips where there was therefore an unusually high groundwater pressure beneath the boulder clay seal. Much of this water was seen to emerge after the flow slide to form a mud run down its centre, but any that was ejected from the sandstone in the initial slip would have aided liquefaction of the debris.

With the origin of the slide reasonably well understood, at least in retrospect, the main questions following the Aberfan disaster were whether it could have been predicted and prevented, and how to avoid a repeat elsewhere. As the bad ground conditions were known to have caused the failure, the most distressing revelation by the official inquiry was that these had not been considered before or during the making of the tip. Phrases such as 'eight years of folly and neglect' and 'a tale of bungling ineptitude' were found at the inquiry to be fair criticism of the tip's owners, the National Coal Board. All the basic rules of site investigation had been ignored. The tip had been 'planned' purely on the basis of available untipped area, with no regard to the geology or hydrology. The springs had been ignored even though they were visible on site, well known to the local children and farmers, and clearly marked on generations of published maps. Lack of management co-ordination meant that the already recognised importance of drained ground for a tip site was not conveyed to those who were in practice responsible for the tipping. A publication dating from 1927, specifically implicating the Brithdir Sandstone and boulder clay coverage in tip failures, was ignored, as were reports of 1939 and 1965 blaming the Cilfynydd flow slide on a situation nearly identical to that at Aberfan. Air photographs of 1963, showing bulge and spring sapping of the tips, were also ignored. Precautions against slipping were talked about – but never followed by action. The warnings of Cilfynydd and the other tips which had failed at Aberfan were lost on anyone in authority. And the people who knew of the continued slipping of Tip 7 – the men of the tipping gang – considered that, despite doubts about the stability of the tip, their jobs were to tip, and to carry on tipping.

The lessons of Aberfan are clear: the vital importance of site investigation with respect to water conditions on tip heap sites, and the value of continued monitoring of tips. Before 1966 ungraded material such as that on Tip 7 was thought by many not to be prone to liquefaction, but now laboratory testing of sensitivity can be added to a programme of monitoring permeability, movement and the development of shear surfaces in tips. There can be no excuse for a repeat of the Aberfan disaster, and legislation has been introduced since 1966 to this effect. But it was too late for the children of the Pantglas Junior School.

Landslide prediction and control

It may seem trite to suggest that good site investigation and a thorough understanding of the geology are the ways to avoid disasters from landslides, but this is very much the case. Potentially hazardous zones should be recognisable if the geology is known well enough to identify any structural situations which can develop landslides and probably have done so in the past. The major problem normally is quantifying the hazard – in terms of time and magnitude – but a policy of avoidance in the case of doubt would have saved many lives from catastrophe in the past.

A first step towards prediction is the recognition of old slide debris, whether it is in massive heaps or just in the notoriously hazardous, semi-stable solifluction lobes dating from Pleistocene times. (Solifluction is the movement of saturated ground, faster than soil creep but not as fast as liquid). Slide material may be difficult to identify on the ground, for example, because of its occasional similarity to boulder clay, but its characteristically lobate form and hummocky surface make it very conspicuous on air photographs, which are therefore essential to landslide site investigation. The shear strength, and hence stability, of homogeneous soils can be determined by laboratory tests, and liquefaction potential can now be identified on the basis of measured sensitivity and permeability and not just anticipated in well-graded sands as was the case before Aberfan. The problem here is that failure commonly takes place not in the mass of the material, but at interfaces such as the rockhead, and the shear strengths of these are not readily determined in the laboratory. However, a combination of lithological considerations, data on slopes, drainage and groundwater movement, plus experience of past slips, can give a semi-quantified indication of hazards at any particular site. Landslide potential zoning based on these parameters is now successfully used in all planning and building in the Launceston area of Tasmania, where forty houses have been destroyed in recent landslides, but identification of the least favourable areas has reduced the incidents among more modern developments. A further aid to planning has been attempted in the Santa Monica area of California by predicting the recurrence interval for landslides at any location as a function of rainfall patterns once the physical properties – essentially slope, shear strength and permeability – have been measured. Success with this method can only be expected with shallow soil slides triggered by short-term groundwater level variations.

An alternative to avoiding recognisable hazard areas is the monitoring of movement in individual slopes in order to predict any sudden, rapid failure. The value of monitoring lies in the fact that any rapid slope failure, that is a landslide, is almost always preceded by slow creep over a period of time. This is particularly relevant where civil engineering works involve the introduction of slopes steeper than those formed naturally and therefore automatically involving an element of instability. The scale of this hazard was demonstrated during a three-year period in the 1930s when, throughout the world, thirteen failures of railway cuttings resulted in a total of 227 fatalities. Removal of the toe of the slope is the surest way of causing a landslide, and though monitoring may be expensive it can clearly be worth while in any dubious cases. Available methods of detecting slope movement include periodic surveying between marker points, listening for rock noise (i.e. vibrations due to deformation), measurement of seismic velocities to detect dilation, and the

29 (above) *A small earthslide on an over-steepened slope is enough to block completely this highway outside San Francisco.* 30 (below) *The unstable terrace of Folkestone Warren is crossed by the Dover railway — the concrete slabs on the foreshore are a key to the stabilisation of this notorious landslide.*

31 (above) *The Vaiont Dam stands useless, its reservoir filled by the enormous landslide which descended from Mount Toc (off the photo to the right).* 32 (below) *Villagers of the Piave Valley wander through the debris left by the enormous wave from the Vaiont Reservoir.*

33 *Rescuers search the remains of what was the village of Longarone before its destruction in the Vaiont Dam disaster.*

34 (above) *This apparently inadequate levee separates the Feather River, tributary of the Mississippi, from its inundated flood plain in 1955.* 35 (below) *The force of the floodwater swept this timber house clean off its foundations and deposited it on the local railway track at Norwalk, Connecticut.*

36 (above) *The subdued waters of the West Lyn River still follow the path cut by the flood torrents through the heart of Lynmouth village down to the junction with the East Lyn River, in the foreground. The old course of the West Lyn is now barely discernible between the buildings on the right of the picture* 37 (below) *Piled rubble and broken buildings are the side-effects of the new river route through Lynmouth.*

38 (above) *The gaping hole in the Eigiau Dam, North Wales, was knocked out in 1925 when the reservoir waters worked their way through the boulder clay floor and undermined the foundations.* 39 (below) *Debris piled against the famous Ponte Vecchio shows the height reached by the River Arno during the disastrous flooding of Florence in 1966.*

40 (above) *Los Angeles has the dubious distinction of having suffered two major dam failures. In 1928 all that was left of the St Francis Dam was a narrow central portion, both sides having failed almost instantaneously.*
41 (below) *Thirty-five years later the Baldwin Hills Reservoir began to leak slowly, and most people were evacuated from the dense suburbs below before the waters tore through the dam wall and poured into hundreds of homes.*

42 (above) *Little was left of the Malpasset Dam after the thin concrete arch failed due to ground movement under the far bank in 1959.*   43 (below) *The entire volume of water in the Malpasset Reservoir was emptied down the Reyran Valley in a single pulse when the dam failed, and the town of Frejus, lying directly in its path, suffered appalling damage.*

installation of such instruments as extensometers, borehole inclinometers, rock bolt strain gauges and groundwater piezometers. Inclinometers in short boreholes on the edges of unstable slopes are particularly useful in that they lend themselves to incorporation in automatic warning systems triggered when a slope creeps past a set limit; some of these have been established for many years in deep cuttings on Sweden's railways. Any acceleration of the movement or dilation can normally be taken as a warning of imminent failure, but there is still the problem of estimating at just what stage this will take place. With a background of extensive experience in similar conditions some slope failures in large opencast quarries have been predicted accurately enough for the events to be recorded and photographed. But without such comparative data, prediction is difficult where every piece of ground is different. Acceleration of the movement of the Mount Toc slopes was recorded, but its significance was not quantified enough to be able to avoid the Vaiont landslide disaster. In 1969 a Japanese experiment at monitoring a slope's movement induced by intentionally saturating it with water, led to the death of a number of the observers when a landslide developed earlier than anticipated. Perhaps this case, more than any other, serves to emphasise that slope stability is never completely predictable, even though today's level of knowledge should be able to avoid the repeat of some of the great historical disasters.

Construction projects commonly necessitate the oversteepening or toe-removal of slopes, and even when carried out in the light of soil mechanics studies, the critical angles of stability are often only discovered by experience on site. Slope stability can be improved in a number of ways, notably by thorough surface and underground drainage. On a small scale more direct techniques can be applied, such as the addition of heavy drained toe weights, rock bolting to enhance joint stability by keeping blocks firmly in contact with each other, grout injection, and even piling as long as sensitive clays are not disturbed during their placement. Before deciding on stabilisation or remedial measures, the probable mode of failure should be known. In some cases clays can have their liquefaction potential eliminated by compacting them under artificial vibration before their slopes are cut into. Clays can also have their cohesion increased through the replacement of sodium by calcium in their structure, by inducing base exchange from enriched groundwater solutions; but although this has been carried out with success, there is the possibility of the sodium removal increasing the sensitivity of some critical marine clays. When such remedies are inadequate or unsuitable it may be necessary to accept the creep and small-scale failure of a cut slope, but only as long as the absence of sudden large failure can be assured. The strictly short-term stability of some materials has been exploited by some Italian motorway engineers, who excavated very steeply faced cuttings, constructed tunnel linings in the open and then back filled on to them when they were in place. Even in open country, this was more economical than both bored tunnels and open cuttings with either very gentle or unstable slopes.

While the smaller landslides, for example those in engineering works, may be controllable by piling or total excavation, any of a larger size can only be stabilised economically by some form of drainage. This can entail surface drainage by both peripheral ditches and lined ditches on the slide material itself, and also underground drainage by either adits or nearly horizontal boreholes lined with perforated pipes. But gravitational drainage of relatively impermeable clays or silts is inadequate. Stabilisation of a wet clay slide may therefore necessitate drying it out by either electro-osmosis, as has been done successfully in sensitive clays in Norway and Canada, or pumping hot air through boreholes, as was first tried in California in 1932. Freezing of wet sediments is a well-known technique of stabilisation, but is only applicable in the short term such as on temporary cuttings on a construction site. The success of even the less esoteric drainage methods of landslide correction have been demonstrated all over the world. A slide of tip material at Pentre, in the Rhondda Valley in Wales, was halted in 1916 by a drainage system above and below ground which produced nearly two cusecs of water. In the United States landslides occurred along much of the 1500 feet length of a massive road cutting in unconsolidated sediments at Sear's Point in northern California during 1950, and they were stabilised by the insertion of 6250 feet of bored drains in addition to some slope reduction. Hastily installed drains, boreholes and adits drained the Handlova earthslide in Czechoslovakia enough to halt it in two months during 1960. These successfully stabilised slides are all quite small, and it is unfortunate that large slides are proportionately more difficult to control, proving an almost constant battle for engineers.

Just east of Folkestone, on the south-east coast of England, a zone of rough ground beneath the high chalk cliffs is known as the Warren. It is an undercliff area, formed on the contorted ground of a whole series of landslips which date back thousands of years but are still continuing today. Along two miles of coast the Warren forms a zone about 1200 feet wide and ranging between 50 and 150 feet above sea level. Its lower margin is a low sea cliff, and its inner edge is overlooked by the High Cliff – white chalk cliffs which rise another 300–400 feet.

The geology of Folkestone Warren is very simple. The Cretaceous chalk is over 500 feet thick where it forms the High Cliff, and rests on the Gault Clay, with the contact cropping out roughly along the back of the Warren. The Gault is a strong, overconsolidated, grey clay between 140 and 160 feet thick, resting in turn on permeable sandstones still of Cretaceous age. In detail, the stratigraphy is complicated by various thin marls and sandstones which develop local, perched aquifers, but have little effect on the Warren landslides. The whole sequence dips at about one degree to the north-east; at the western end of the landslip zone the chalk escarpment swings inland, and at the eastern end the chalk–Gault Clay contact is beneath sea level and incapable of influencing the stability.

Major landslips were recorded on the Warren in the years 1765 and 1800, but the overall instability of the area was soon forgotten. The Folkestone to Dover railway was laid along the Warren, and opened to use in 1844 – making it a classic example of where not to build a railway. The designers of the railway did not really appreciate the hazards of their chosen route, but they can be partly excused in that they had little alternative: the relief of the chalk Downs precluded a reasonable inland route, and the four mile long tunnel necessary to avoid the Warren would have been a major expense. In fact the railway has rarely been troubled – with one major exception – and the success of remedial works on the landslips has now eliminated the need for a by-pass tunnel, which was authorised but never started during a state of moderate panic in 1934. Over thirty major landslides have been recorded in two hundred years, and those since 1844 have been studied in some detail. A major slide in 1877 caused the collapse of 106 yards of the Martello Tunnel and though fortunatlcly it did not catch a train, the railway was closed for a time. Not so lucky were the passengers on a train of December 1915, which had its coaches

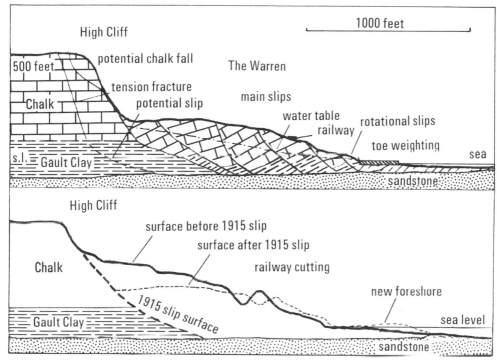

The Folkestone Warren landslides. Above, the structure of the slides, and below, the profiles through the centre of the slide before and after the 1915 movement.

thrown from the track by the worst landslide recorded. Almost the whole Warren moved in one massive slide; the head scarp ran nearly the whole way along the foot of the High Cliff. The railway was moved up to 165 feet towards the sea and lost 20 feet in altitude, the ground displacement lifted the foreshore to form a promontory 400 yards out to sea, and chalk falls from the High Cliff buried part of the railway. The train was caught on the southern edge of the slide mass and was derailed by the 15-foot-high step which suddenly developed in the tracks. The line was not reopened until 1919, partly due to the priorities of war. Since then the Martello Tunnel had its lining cracked in a slide in 1937, but neither that slide nor the slide of 1940 affected the railway to any great extent.

There are three types of slide movement currently active on the Warren. Falls of chalk from the High Cliff are on a relatively small scale and tend to develop in two stages. They are initiated along tension fractures roughly parallel to the cliff face and then develop a curved slide surface; as they move first they rotate backwards, so closing up the tension fissure and 're-locking' the rock temporarily before failing again at a later date. The first stage results in a subsidence along the cliff edge which may drop up to 5 feet along a line 20 yards or so back from the face. The main movement of the Warren is in the form of large multiple rotational slips developed mainly in the Gault Clay. These are not circular slips, for the head scarp runs up through the lower chalk beds near the foot of the High Cliff, and the main movement surface then runs along the base of the clay. This develops in a montmorillonite-rich zone in the clay, which has a much lower shear strength than

77

the higher calcite-rich beds; its location has been proved by finding in boreholes slickensided (scratched) surfaces concentrated at this one horizon in the clay, whereas that same level is not slickensided in the clay outside the Warren area. The 1915 failure of the Warren was of this type. The third type includes the much smaller circular rotational slips which develop in the outer edge of the Warren, and were responsible for the movements of 1937 and 1940.

The third type, of small rotational slips, is simply due to erosion and undercutting of the sea cliff, but the chalk falls and big multiple slips are largely a feature of the unstable situation of the chalk overlying the clay within the overall height of the cliff. Any coastal cliff with this geology would be prone to slip, but the Warren movements are spectacular due to relief expansion of the overconsolidated Gault Clay. Buried to such a depth that it must have borne an effective pressure of 40 tons per square foot during Tertiary times, the clay is now restrained from upward relief by the chalk overburden, but is freely able to move towards its eroded edge in the sea cliff. This movement is concentrated in weak montmorillonite-rich beds and develops the horizontal shear planes beneath the Warren; it also accounts for the opening of the fissures in the chalk as the outer blocks are literally torn away from the main mass. The movement is also aided by temporary increases of pore water pressures in the slipped masses. All the rotational slips recorded since 1844 have occurred during the period December to March – precisely the season of highest piezometric levels, which are normally only just below ground level, in the slipped chalk and clay. There is no such correlation with long-term water level variations in the chalk, which is freely drained close to the cliff, nor with water heads in the underlying sandstone which are normally close to sea level anyway, due to the outcrops in the sea bed.

All the information on the nature of slip surfaces and the hydrology in the Warren came from a comprehensive and well-planned programme of borehole investigations, which have since made possible a constructive approach to the problem of stabilising the area. Sea defences, in the form of groynes and imported shingle, were begun in 1896 to minimise toe erosion, but they were not very successful as they did not remedy the root cause of the movement. Drainage of the landslips was clearly essential, and though this was started after the 1877 movement it was on an inadequate scale, and most of the drains were broken by the 1915 slip. Since then they have been restored and added to, so that there is now an adit every 200 yards or so along the Warren. These start at about 25 feet above sea-level and some go back under the Warren for over 800 feet. In addition, since 1948 massive concrete toe weights have been built along the foreshore.

The success of the various operations can be judged from the striking decrease in the number of movements during the present century. So while the disaster of 1915 was a fine example of the consequences of ignoring unsuitable geology, more recent events at Folkestone Warren have shown how thorough investigation and understanding of the geology can successfully control such a problem.

The future

Aberfan, Vaiont, Frank, Nicolet – four notorious landslides which between them killed 2340 people. Each slide has been studied and analysed, and, with the benefit

78

of hindsight, the failure mechanisms have been understood. But have the lessons been learned?

Perhaps the best known and in some ways the most horrific of the four was Aberfan. News of the disaster flashed round the world, and in its wake came a series of official reports, procedure modifications, and re-examinations. In the United States all mining tip heaps were checked for potential instability. As the cause of the Aberfan disaster was seen to be the saturated nature of the tip debris, one American tip carefully examined in late 1966 was that in West Virginia's Buffalo Creek, which also acted as a dam to impound a small settling pond. It was deemed adequately safe.

But some memories, it seems, are just too short. Three years later a new and larger tip in Buffalo Creek was founded on wet sludge and built up to such a height that it retained a considerable reservoir behind it. The outlet for this reservoir, almost unbelievably, was by seepage through the tip heap. On February 26 1972 a large slip developed in the front face of this makeshift dam. The remaining section of the tip heap was then overflowed by the reservoir; it was rapidly scoured out and a massive floodwave swept down the valley, killing 118 people. The main reason for the failure of the tip heap-cum-dam was that it consisted of non-adhesive mine debris saturated with water that had built up a considerable pressure inside it. Even though the flood at Buffalo Creek provided a different means of destruction from the slide at Aberfan, the cause of the disaster was almost identical. And Buffalo Creek was six years after Aberfan.

It is a sad situation that, even with the knowledge of hindsight, man can still cause the needless deaths of so many of his fellows by imitating his past follies. The details of the Frank and Vaiont landslides have not yet been repeated, although a month after the April 1903 slide at Frank, the village was reoccupied and the mining (which had been the cause of the disaster) was recommenced; only eight years later, after stronger and stronger warnings of danger, was this precariously hazardous mine closed down completely. Almost a carbon copy of the Nicolet flow slide occurred sixteen years afterwards at Saint-Jean-Vainney, and killed another thirty-one people. Hundreds of other landslides have occurred in every country of the world. And there are plenty of hillsides standing today which have geological structures similar to those that have failed in the past. Man has the technological ability to control at least some potential slides – as the case of Folkestone Warren has shown.

But will it be just hundreds, or thousands of people who will die in future landslides? Part of the problem is that although specific geological studies may successfully reveal numerous potential landslides, for the mechanisms are now understood, such investigations are lengthy and costly. In terms of saving human life, can they possibly cost too much? There are hundreds of thousands of people who live or work beneath steep hillsides, knowing nothing about their stability or instability. Even in the light of past experience, how many of these think that 'their' hillside is safe, and do nothing? Unfortunately some of these people will be proved wrong – and landslides have a nasty habit of being fatal.

WATER

On the night of 31 May 1889, the people of Johnstown in southern Pennsylvania were suffering from the third day of exceptionally heavy rain, and the high level of the Little Conemaugh River was threatening the lower parts of the town. An even greater cause for concern was the South Fork Dam, nine miles upstream, which held back a reservoir full to the brim. The dam was an old rock-fill type in bad condition – its inadequately small spillways were partly blocked with vegetation and debris – and consequently the waters rose till they swamped the spillway, and then overflowed and eroded the main embankment. The easily scoured rock fill yielded almost instantly to give a wide breach for the whole 75 feet height of the dam and the reservoir emptied in a massive floodwave. The flood swept down the valley, overran the flood plain and almost annihilated Johnstown; in the tumbling mass of water, rocks and broken buildings, 2209 people died.

Water is unique both in its great abundance, and in being so essential to life and yet at the same time capable of such appalling damage when it gets out of control. The Johnstown flood provides a fine example of the destructive power of water, and it is clear enough that a reservoir restrained by an inadequate dam is about as welcome as an undated time-bomb to anyone living in the valley beneath it. When a dam fails, it is usually in one of three ways. It may be structurally inadequate for its task (which is normally the responsibility of the designer of the dam) and, while simple structural failure of a concrete or masonry dam is a rare event, internal erosion of earth dams has been and still is all too common. Secondly, a dam may be overtopped and then, particularly if it is an earth dam, eroded so rapidly that it appears as an almost instantaneous failure. This was the case at Johnstown's South Fork Dam, and here the responsibility is split between the fields of hydrology and meterology, and structural design concerning spillway capacity. The third cause of dam collapse is failure of the foundations, and though it is probably the least common of the three it is a direct function of geology. The technology of civil engineering has today reached a stage where a structure can be placed in just about any geological environment, but it is in the field of dam construction that relatively obscure details of the geology can still have the greatest influence on choice of design, as a number of dam failures so spectacularly demonstrate. The other feature of the Johnstown disaster was the location of the town on the flood plain of the river downstream from the dam – and flood plains are by their very nature the sections of land most prone to inundation by floods, whether they be man-made or natural. While river flooding is largely controlled by the details of the topography, geological and geomorphological studies play a vital part in the prediction of hazard areas subject to periodic flooding which is on such a long time-interval that there are no immediate historical records available to act as guidance.

Water can be the enemy of man in many other ways besides flooding. Lack of it, whether due to the whims of climatic variation or the artificial diversion and reorganisation of natural sources by man, can also be disastrous. Both the contamination of water, particularly groundwater supplies, and the silting of reservoirs can lead to hydrological problems, which have a significant element of geological control in their nature and extent. But dam failures, poisoned water supplies, or any other disasters due to man's interference and inability to control water properly, all pale into insignificance when compared to the scale of perfectly natural flooding events in which man just happens to be involved.

Flood plain inundation

The flood plain of a river is a clearly definable physical feature of its valley, being the almost flat area which borders the river and which is built up of layers of sediment deposited by the river when it periodically overflows its normal banks. Steep narrow valleys in mountain regions have no flood plain at all, but a large complex system of converging rivers in a lowland region may have a flood plain over a hundred miles wide. There is a natural tendency for a river to deposit sediment in its channel during times of low flow, so that an equilibrium is arrived at where the river comfortably fills its main channel under normal conditions. Therefore the river will spread out automatically on to its flood plain during periods of high flow – after all, flood plains are for floods.

Unfortunately sites on river banks have always been attractive locations for towns. Being close to high-quality farmland on the flood plains, convenient for water, and acting as a focus for routes at a bridging point, towns tended to develop first on bluffs or terraces close to the river. London, Paris and Washington all lie on series of river terraces above their present river plains. With the town safely on a terrace, the periodic flooding of the farmland on the flood plain could be a distinct advantage – the fertility of the silts deposited by the annual Nile floods are well known. But expansion of the towns soon forced them to spread out – all too commonly on to the flood plains, where they were immediately in danger. It is estimated that in the United States alone there are currently ten million people living in areas subject to flooding.

The scale of flood hazard can vary enormously, and it is some of the rivers of Asia which provide the most spectacular examples. China's great Yangtze Kiang River floods at infrequent intervals, and the 1871 flood reached a height 275 feet above its normal level in the gorges downstream from Chungking. This phenomenal rise can be appreciated by considering the river steamer which was caught on a rock as the flood subsided and was left 120 feet above the river. In the Yangtze's 1954 flood it was claimed that ten million people were evacuated from their homes in the lower valley – though this figure may represent some politically motivated exaggeration. Across northern India the River Ganges has formed a vast flood plain in which the sediments are up to 35,000 feet thick. The monsoon pattern of rainfall ensures flooding every year, but this is not too serious because of the continued subsidence of the region and its consequently slightly curved cross-section. But the same does not apply to the delta area which is shared with the Brahmaputra River and occupies most of the country of Bangladesh. In November 1970 flooding due to a combination of high river levels, high tides and a powerful on-shore cyclone, caused the inundation of 4000 square miles of the delta area and a death toll of over a million.

The Ganges floods to a certain level just about every year, but less frequently much higher floods occur. Long-term records of river levels show that there is some sort of relationship between flood levels and intervals of recurrence – level increases are roughly proportional to the logarithm of the interval. Consequently hydrologists can speak of a '50-year flood' as being one unlikely to recur in that interval of time. This concept can be invaluable in planning construction in river valleys. While the significance of the area inundated by the annual floods on the Ganges is patently obvious, it is also clearly uneconomic to build, for example, a house with a life expectancy of a hundred years on the plain of a twenty-year flood. The likely recurrence of floods should therefore be used as planning guidelines for any particular types of building or land use on flood plains, though in Britain the hazard line is often drawn at the level of the 1947 meltwater floods (which were mostly at around the 100–200 year mark).

The frequency and ferocity of floods is clearly most directly controlled by local and regional weather and climate patterns; but it is also strongly influenced by factors such as vegetation cover which absorbs water, slope steepness which encourages run-off, and channel patterns which may either disperse or superimpose the effects of individual storms. Heavy rain at the onset of winter can have an unduly severe effect when it lands on clay soils which have been baked to a hard crust during a long, hot, dry summer. In Southern Spain 150 people died in 1973 during floods of just this type, which overflowed channels and destroyed houses which had stood safe for over a century. Flash floods are generated in much the same way by isolated storms in semi-arid regions. Rapid City in South Dakota was hit by a 2000-year flood in 1972, when water swept down a canyon and caused enormous damage in the town, as well as 237 deaths. Since then much of the river's flood course has been left undeveloped as open parkland.

Bedrock can have an enormous influence on flooding, particularly regarding the absorption capacity of rocks such as sandstone or limestone. While these permeable rocks may minimise flood hazard, the extreme event can be very serious when in a limestone region normally dry valleys are suddenly swamped by more water than the underground drainage can accommodate. The 1968 floods on the Mendip Hills in Somerset demonstrated the erosive power of rivers in valleys which have no riverbed and are crossed by unbroken field walls and road embankments. An unusual geological situation exists above the town of Caraz in the Peruvian Andes, where a lake is dammed by a natural barrier of a semi-permeable glacial moraine through which the lake's outlet steadily filters. Should the input to the lake ever exceed the moraine's permeability the barrier could be topped and rapidly eroded to give a unique but massive flood downstream – where Caraz lies on the flood plain.

With the world's flood plains so densely populated, flood control has become an important aspect of civil engineering, and there are many ways in which it can be executed. Flood-control reservoirs are designed to stand part empty so that they can catch a flood and release the water at a lower rate over a greater length of time. Clearly there is a limit to the size of flood that can be handled in this way, but today nearly a third of the reservoirs in the United States are primarily for this purpose. The inadequacy of the flood-control dams on the Brisbane River in Australia was demonstrated in 1974 when Brisbane itself was heavily flooded. Even worse was the mismanagement during the flooding of Florence in 1966, when after two days of exceptional rain, water was released from two flood-control dams too early, and arrived in the city on the peak of the flood. The most obvious way of controlling rivers is to build artificial levees or heighten natural ones. Except in some urban areas levees are normally just earth embankments high enough and spaced wide enough apart (maybe 10 miles or more) to keep any flood within them and so protect the rest of the flood plain. The Mississippi now has 2200 miles of levees controlling its lower course, and in addition many towns and sites have their own encircling levees. Unfortunately levees can be overtopped, and then their erosion and the flow of water down on to the lower flood plain can make the local flooding from a levee breach worse than if the levee had never been built. The 1973 Mississippi flood was the highest ever known, and although damage amounting to $420 million was recorded it is estimated that the levees nearly halved the potential damage of the flood.

Many other flood-control methods have been practised on the Mississippi. Meander cut-offs can shorten the river length, so steepening the gradient and encouraging a flood on its way; and in 1933–6 the lower part of the Mississippi was shortened in this way by 13 per cent. Emergency flood routes can vary greatly in size, though all have the same purpose. Concrete-lined storm drains, dry most of the year, are a common feature in tropical cities, and contrast with the Mississippi's enormous diversion channels into the Atchafalaya distributary and Lake Pontchartrain. On a catchment area smaller than the Mississippi's, planning of land-use and vegetation can also make a significant reduction in flood propagation at source. One disadvantage of flood-control measures is that they themselves generate their own hazards. The breaching of high levees has already been mentioned, but there is also the danger of overestimating the security which levees can provide. More directly, in the Los Angeles area there is now the threat of earthquakes causing the failure of the many flood-control dams in the canyons around the city—this very nearly happened with potentially disastrous consequences at the Van Norman reservoirs in the 1971 San Fernando earthquake.

The complement to flood control is hazard zoning of flood plains. For most rivers historical records are accurate enough to delimit the extent of a forty-year flood, but to go beyond this becomes more hypothetical, especially in steeper valleys. Detailed geomorphological mapping, aided by aerial photography, can search for features such as terraces, meander scrolls and river sediments which can help to identify flood plain occupancy by a river. Hazard zoning can then be used not for relocating old towns but for planning new development. Shrewsbury in Shropshire straddles the River Severn and has over five hundred buildings on the flood plain, though few date from later than 1947 when planning regulations were tightened in the light of England's great floods of that year. In Shrewsbury, the 1946 flood, a 120-year event, was even higher and is now used to determine the hazard zone. Within it parkland and sports grounds are developed, and any new buildings have floors above the 1946 flood level.

An even more important aspect of flood planning is to minimise encroachment – where buildings are allowed to restrict a flood flow, and thereby increase the ponding effect of the water. In New Jersey buildings have to allow unrestricted flow of a 25-year flood, and in other American cities high buildings on flood plains have parking lots with no walls on the lower floors for just this purpose. While some industrial development may have to be on active flood plains, housing and buildings such as hospitals should never, in theory, be sited in such hazard zones. In practice the situation may be different – as can be demonstrated by two examples at opposite ends in terms of size.

Lynmouth is an attractive village, popular with tourists, which stands on the North Devon coast, just tucked into a narrow Y-shaped valley at the confluence of the East and West Lyn rivers. The catchment areas of both rivers consist of steep, narrow ravines in the almost impermeable slates and grits of Exmoor – and flooding is transmitted downstream so rapidly that there is hardly any warning. In August 1952 the ground was already wet from two weeks of rain, and on the fifteenth of the month there was an exceptional storm on Exmoor which averaged 5.6 inches of rainfall over the whole 40 square miles of the Lyn catchments, with the highest concentration in the West Lyn basin. On the peak of the flood the flow at Lynmouth was 18,000 cusecs (comparable to a very strong flood on the River Thames). The village was overrun by the water and extensively damaged, and thirty-four people were injured.

The disastrous consequences of the flood were essentially due to the constricted and neglected river courses through the village. In such a narrow valley it is barely realistic to speak of a flood plain, but there is a recognisable zone that must become flooded by any given flow rate once the normal channel is overtopped. Houses and hotels had been allowed to encroach on the river so that it was left in a totally inadequate channel, and, worst of all, the West Lyn bridge had an arch which proved only half the size needed to let through the flood which occurred. All this had been done even though there were records of great floods in the years 1607 and 1769 – the latter probably higher than the one in 1952. The result was predictable. The rivers flooded into the village and the West Lyn cut a new course from behind the bridge restriction. In just the few hours that the flood lasted, entire buildings were swept away, as were the bridges and roads, and thirty-four people were injured. Boulders weighing up to 10 tons and more were carried down the steep river beds and smashed into the houses – boulders covered most of the village when the flood retreated – and the flood damage was intensified by surges of water from the collapse of temporary dams formed from tree or boulder jams and landslides in the untrained river courses.

After the disaster the village of Lynmouth was rebuilt, on its same very attractive site, because there was really little alternative in the narrow valleys of that coast. But the village looks different, for it has large clean-cut channels right through its heart. Though the rivers are normally almost lost in the bottoms of the channels, these are the long-term safety factors which now make Lynmouth a much safer village.

Hwang Ho translates from the Chinese as Yellow River, but throughout the world it is also known by another name – China's Sorrow. This amazing river has the dubious distinction of being responsible for more human deaths than any other individual feature of the world's surface. The cause for this is the river's unique morphology. For nearly 2500 miles it flows through the mountains and plateaux of northern China, and on its route through the easily eroded loess lands it picks up an enormous quantity of silt. The flow of the river may be 40 per cent yellow silt (which gives it its name) when it arrives at Kaifeng. From there it travels another 500 miles to the sea across the great Yellow Plain – essentially a massive alluvial fan, sloping more steeply than a true delta – which is also 500 miles wide and spreads both sides of the mountains of Shantung which must once have been an island. The river gradient across the plain is a little over a foot per mile, far higher than in a normal delta, but the Hwang Ho is still unable to carry its sediment load, and the plain is made of redeposited silt.

From Kaifeng, fifteen channels radiate across the plain, and each time the Hwang Ho tops one of these it causes enormous floods before resuming a single channel. The floods have drowned unbelievable numbers of people on the crowded plain, and the destruction of crops results in famine and yet more deaths. A chronology of just the major events of the river's history tells its own story:

2356 BC	After a great flood the river channels were cleared out and the river drained to the Chihli Gulf at Tientsin.
602 BC	The worsening flooding prompted the first of the levees to be built, but in this year the river changed to an outlet together with the Hwai Ho into the Yellow Sea.
AD 69	Although the levees were now forming a unified series right across the plain, the river reverted to various courses in between its present one and its most northerly outlet at Tientsin, all into the Chihli Gulf.
1324	Reverted to its southerly route into the Hwai and Yellow Sea.
1851	Turned north again and occupied its present course.
1887	A massive flood killed two million people by drowning or starvation.
1931	The worst flood ever claimed a total death toll of 3,700,000.
1938	The levees were breached intentionally in order to forestall an invading Japanese army. The new course of the Hwang effectively restrained the invaders but also caused around half a million deaths in the local population.
1947	Repairs of the levees returned the river to its present course.

The scale of this flooding is difficult to conceive. Each major change in the river course involved altering between mouths that were 270 miles apart. They were equivalent to the Thames suddenly entering the North Sea at Newcastle, or the Columbia flowing into the Pacific through northern California. The 1933 flood was not the highest on record, but it still reached a flow of 825,000 cusecs and deposited 60,000 million cubic feet of silt on the flooded plain.

The levees, which were started over 2500 years ago, have had to be constantly raised, by the labour-intensive methods for which the Chinese are famous, for there is nothing to build them with except the silt. The constant raising means that the Hwang Ho now crosses its plain about 25 feet above the surrounding countryside, between inner and outer levees which form a belt 12 miles wide. The silt is the cause of the problem, for it is constantly deposited in the river channel, so that the river rises to yet higher levels and the Chinese are left with a literally never-ending task of building the levees higher still. Because of this the Hwang Ho now has no tributaries for over 400 miles, and millions of people live below river level with the

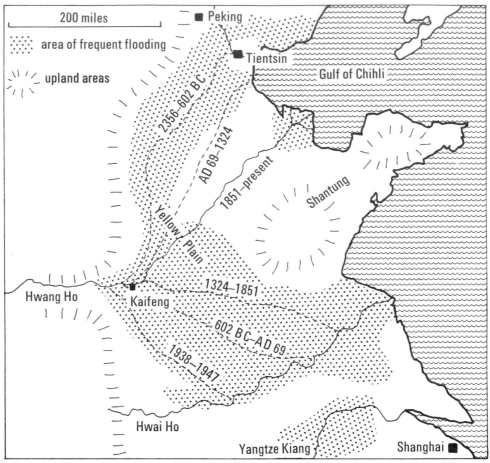

The lower part of the Hwang Ho River, showing the various courses it has taken in historic times across the Yellow Plain.

constant threat of flooding. There are no hills in the plain, no escape routes in the event of a flood. And the average area flooded each year is 3200 square miles. As the plain is below river level it cannot drain, and regions stay flooded to the horizon for a year at a time. When a major levee break once lets the river completely escape it occupies a braided course perhaps 15 miles wide for up to ten years before it settles itself into a new channel. Lesser breaks in the levees of both the Hwang Ho and the other rivers of the Yellow Plain are made difficult to repair because stone has to be transported hundreds of miles and then bound with wire to resist the erosion of the escaping water.

There are clearly enormous problems and dangers in living in an area of almost total flatness except for a ridge along the top of which runs a flood-prone river. Until about 2000 BC the Hwang Ho stood at plain level, but the frequency of its floods encouraged the building of levees and from then on the vicious circle could not be broken. Now the threat is permanent, and the long-term plans for flood-control reservoirs are plagued with the problem of the silt content of the river. Not only did the Hwang Ho build the Yellow Plain but it will continue to dominate it – whether man is there or not.

Hazards of water management

The cycle of water seems an enormous and unchangeable process, but its often incredibly delicate balance can be revealed all too easily when man tries to modify, use or abuse it. On the large scale it is difficult to appreciate just what effect man may have on natural processes, because the time scale is so great that feedback of information on changes arrives only after a long interval and then probably too late. But water usage, land use, vegetation patterns, evaporation rates, local climate effects and large-scale climatic effects are all linked in a chain reaction which could feasibly be triggered by man. There is a school of thought which suggests that overpumping of groundwater, together with intensified cropping and overgrazing, in the Sahel – the belt of marginally productive land south of the great Sahara Desert – may have caused the appalling repeated droughts of the region which are allowing the true desert of the Sahara to expand southwards. There is also concern over the large-scale climatic effects of the schemes under consideration by the Russians for diverting the waters of their great rivers flowing into the Arctic Ocean so that they can be used for irrigation in the Caspian Sea area; water movement on this scale could be capable of altering climates over entire continents.

With smaller schemes of water management, not only do the effects become more easily recognisable, but also the geology becomes more significant. One of the most famous river management schemes is that on the Colorado in the south-western United States. Though it has virtually transformed southern California and Arizona from a desert into an economically valuable region, there have been problems, especially in the lower reaches. Soon after river water was diverted at the Imperial Dam westward into canals, it broke free from its dykes and from January 1905 until February 1907 poured into a dry desert basin to form the Salton Sea – which has ever since been maintained as a salt lake by drainage water accumulating more rapidly than it can evaporate. But the more serious problems have been back in the main river, where the extensive removal of good-quality water has lowered the flow into Mexico so much that the input of land drainage water has made the river too salt to be of use even for agriculture. Because of the high evaporation rates, salty groundwater has to be continually pumped from the sandy soils before it builds up to the level of crop roots; this water, mainly from the Gila valley, now has to be canalised for considerable distances so that it only re-enters the Colorado below the last of the irrigation extraction dams. Additionally it is a bone of political contention that the Mexicans living in the poorer areas of the Colorado delta have now been deprived of almost their entire sweet water supply.

Contamination is also a problem with some groundwaters, partly at least because of the popular belief that water from the ground must be purer than from a river. This is in fact only true where the groundwater is adequately filtered on its journey through the aquifer rocks. It will not hold where the underground journey has been very short through rocks with large open voids which have negligible filtration capacity – such as gravel or limestone. The movement of water and impurities in gravel is controlled by the local hydraulic gradients, but in the case of fissured or cavernous limestone, or even chalk, the local geology has an even greater influence. Water supply springs at Ashwick Grove in the Mendip Hills were badly contaminated with phenols in 1969. The source was found to be silage liquids which had poured from a farm into a sinkhole over a half a mile away, and had passed through the cavernous Carboniferous Limestone. The same limestones were responsible for a gruesome situation at Ballymacelligott, near Tralee in Southern Ireland. The exploration there in 1962 of a few sinkholes and interconnecting caves revealed that the stream at The Rising 'is used by cattle, a farm, several cottages and a creamery as a water supply, after already having been used twice by cattle for drinking and other activities and once as a lavatory sewer during its course underground.' The problem is exacerbated because not only does limestone freely transmit all impurities but the course of water within it is notoriously unrelated to surface indications.

The limestone plains of the southern and central United States have long suffered from contamination of groundwater supplies by underground sewage disposal – merely because all water and sewage ends up underground in this sort of terrain. Steep-sided collapse sinkholes make very convenient garbage dumps where they are surrounded by endless flat country, but in the state of Missouri a horrifying number of cases have been proven of direct flow of unfiltered water from such dumps to springs used for water supply. The city of Horse Cave, in the Kentucky limestone plain, normally obtains its water from numerous wells, but in the drought of 1930 so many wells dried up that water was taken from the underground stream in Hidden River Cave. It was not at the time realised that the cave stream did in fact catch nearly all the drainage from the many local sewage operations which had to feed into the limestone. The result in 1930 was an outbreak of typhoid in the town. After that water was no longer extracted, but the sewage got worse and worse in the cave stream, and Hidden River Cave eventually had to be closed as a show cave in 1944 because of the foul odours underground. Since then, further accidental or 'unplanned' contamination of sinkholes has been shown to polute water supplies at distances of five miles and more. In both gravel and limestone, sewage drainage and water extraction schemes must quite clearly be kept well apart, and in the case of fissured limestone the safe scale of separation may only be assessed after extensive water tracing tests, using dyes, have revealed the patterns of groundwater movement.

Man's disturbance of the natural movement of water can also bring its special problems when reservoirs are impounded by dams. On limestones reservoirs may only have a chance of survival after very extensive ground treatment with grout to render the rock watertight. The success of such grouting can be judged by the number of reservoirs on limestone in countries such as Jugoslavia and France, but failure is assured if the geological problems are not recognised before construction. Missouri has a number of examples of mainly small and old dams which failed to live up to expectations, because of the nature of limestones buried beneath thin covers of inadequately impermeable superficial sediment. The sequence of events at the Dean W. Davis Reservoir, near the southern edge of the state, may be guessed from the fact that its dry basin has been renamed the Dean W. Davis Wildlife Area.

A problem with reservoirs that is not restricted to limestones is their filling up with silt to the eventual exclusion of any water. It is unfortunately unavoidable that reservoirs act as perfect settling ponds along the courses of silt-laden rivers, and rivers that flow through regions of easily eroded sediments such as loess, clay or poorly consolidated sandstone give reservoirs rather restricted lifetimes. Even the enormous Lake Mead, impounded by the Hoover Dam in the western United States, will be filled in about four hundred years from now with the huge amounts of silt and sand carried in by the Colorado River. Pakistan's vast new reservoirs in the soft-rock terraines of the Indus Basin have severe silt problems, and the vast Tarbella Dam will probably be holding back silt, not water, within about a century; the nearby Mangla Dam has been designed so that it can be heightened in the future to keep pace with silting. Many ancient dams in the Near East are now completely full of sediment, and for modern dams the record probably goes to the Austin Dam in Texas, whose reservoir was 95 per cent silted up within fifteen years of completion. Although little can probably be done about silting on a really massive scale, the history of the Macmillan Reservoir on the Pecos River in the western United States is encouraging. Rapidly filled with silt to half its capacity, the introduction of tamarisk grass on the upper Pecos catchment virtually eliminated silting, and the reservoir survives. Failing such control, periodic draining and scouring of the silt may be the only way to avoid complete fossilisation of impounding dams; indeed scour valves are incorporated deep down in many modern dams so that silt can be removed easily with high velocity water.

While silting or leakage may be disastrous economically for individual reservoir schemes, a far greater hazard is their threat of failure. The floods released from failed dams may be rare events, but in their awful scale and complete lack of warning they can be catastrophic where the downstream valleys contain villages and towns.

Geological problems in dam foundations

The Dolgarrog aluminium works in the Conway Valley of North Wales are fed by an adjacent hydro-electric power station which uses the water of the Afon Porth-Llwyd, a tributary to the Conway. A constant flow from the Porth-Llwyd was assured by two small lakes higher up the valley. The upper one was retained by the Eigiau Dam. Completed in 1911, this concrete-wall dam was 3523 feet long with a maximum height of 35 feet. The local bedrock consists of strong and impermeable slates and volcanics, but the dam was founded only in the thick blue glacial clay which mantles the hillsides. Thin layers of peat and weathered clay were removed before the dam was set in a trench in places only a couple of feet deep into the blue clay. Two and a half miles downstream the smaller Coedty Reservoir was held back by a different type of dam. This was an earth dam, built in 1924 of the local glacial moraine, with a thin concrete core wall; it stood 36 feet high and had a total length of 800 feet.

The Eigiau Dam had stood satisfactorily for nearly fifteen years – until 9:15 on the evening of 2 November 1925. Then the water broke through underneath the dam at one point, and rapidly scoured a channel 70 feet wide and 10 feet deep which was bridged by the intact concrete wall of the dam. It was estimated that the flow of water out of the Eigiau Lake was 14,000 cusecs. This poured down the valley, rapidly filled the much smaller Coedty Reservoir, and soon overtopped that dam – the Coedty spillway had been designed only for normal floods and not the emptying of the Eigiau Reservoir. As soon as the Coedty Dam was overtopped, its earth embankment was easily scoured away and the unsupported core wall then failed. The result was the almost instantaneous emptying of the Coedty's 11 million cubic feet of stored water, and this far greater flood pulse descended on Dolgarrog village. By a stroke of fortune it was the evening of the weekly film-show and the well-attended cinema was located safely on high ground, so despite extensive damage to the village only sixteen people died.

Although the destruction in Dolgarrog was caused by the floodwave from the failure of the Coedty Dam, there was nothing unsatisfactory about this dam – and it has since been rebuilt on the same site. The real cause of the trouble was the Eigiau Dam, and here the undermining and failure was quite simply due to inadequate foundations. No attempt had been made to tie the dam to the solid rock beneath the glacial drift, and the dam's footing just a couple of feet into the glacial clay took no account of the fact that its upper layers were weathered and that there were also pockets of boulders within it – some indeed just beneath the point of undermining. In addition the summer of 1925 had been extremely dry, and the clay beneath the dam had probably been further weakened by the development of desiccation fractures when the lake bed was exposed. The combination of weathering, boulders and shrinkage fractures was enough to allow water to move through the otherwise impermeable clay underneath the dam – where it rapidly developed pipes all too easily scoured to form a full-scale channel. In the light of modern experience with clays, the failure of Eigiau was quite predictable, but without that experience the builders of the dam were misled by the apparent impermeability of the glacial clay.

It is a sad fact that there have been hundreds of dam failures around the world, each with its own consequent flood which has ranged from spectacular to catastrophic. The great majority of failures, including those of the South Fork and Coedty dams, have been caused by overflowing due to the inadequate capacity of the spillway. The second most widespread cause of failure has been the internal structural failure of earth dams. Both these causes are design features, and geological problems take only third place in failure responsibility. To some extent the distribution of failure causes is historical, because engineers recognised the importance of good foundations before they really understood the mechanics of clay soils inside dams or the predictability of flood magnitudes. Nevertheless, the geology of dam foundations is of fundamental importance because the forces involved in impounding a deep reservoir are greater than those met in any other civil engineering project; there are many locations where the geology rules out certain types of dams, and many other sites can only be used after very extensive, expensive exploration and treatment of the rock.

Massive, unweathered, barely fractured granite offers ideal foundations for even the most daring designs of dams. Similarly, thick uniform clay is known to be incapable of bearing the stress concentrations of a concrete dam but probably competent to support an earth dam provided due precautions are taken over pore-water pressures and consolidation. These two situations are comparable, because they involve uniform rock lending itself to mechanical analysis to yield figures which can be applied to design considerations. The problems arise where geological irregularities are so unpredictable that quantitative analysis becomes extremely difficult. China clay veins in granite, and faults and weathered zones in any rock, represent major structural weaknesses which normally have very unmathematical patterns, as do solution cavities in limestone or gypsum. Sedimentary bedding and partings of shale, metamorphic cleavage and schistosity, and joints due to unloading or valley cambering may have recognisable patterns but still need to be investigated in detail because certain orientations of them may be very significant for dam design. All these problems have been recorded at various dam sites: when recognised early they have in some cases resulted in the abandoning of a particular location; when recognised late they have involved the considerable extra expense of remedial work. Some have resulted in failure. The Bouzey Dam, near Epinal in eastern France, was built in 1881 but was poorly founded on fissured and permeable sandstone. When it failed in 1895 its floodwave resulted in eighty-six deaths, and though the cause was essentially a structural design failure the inadequacy of the foundation sandstone was found to be contributory because of its proneness to rapid scouring.

The Austin Dam, in southern Texas, was built in 1894 and failed in 1900. It was in an appalling location, on practically horizontal limestones, clays and shales, all well fractured and thinly bedded. A masonry gravity dam, it was only 65 feet high, but it sat on the valley floor with no cut-off trench or keying to deeper rock layers. During some high floods, water flowed through the limestone beneath the dam, partly dissolving the rock, but more significantly saturating the interbedded layers of clay. Heavy rain in April 1900 caused a flood to top the dam and scour the bedrock immediately downstream, and the dam then failed when its middle section slid bodily some 30 feet downstream. It was subsequently found that partial, selective solution of some limestone beds had aided the underflow and the weathering of the clay – and the dam site was only viable when this had been stopped by a cut-off trench and 'grout curtain' (a cement seal injected through lines of boreholes) placed beneath the dam when it was rebuilt.

Permeable rock is particularly hazardous for the foundations of earth dams, which can be eroded from the inside by excessive amounts of seepage. Britain's worst dam disaster was the failure of the Dale Dyke above Sheffield in 1854, which resulted in 250 deaths. This was an earth dam which was piped and eroded essentially due to an inadequate clay seal within it, but a contributory factor was the permeability of the Millstone Grit sandstone bedrock which transmitted water into the core of the dam.

Unconsolidated alluvium is now known to be so suspect, both in terms of strength and permeability, that it is normally completely removed so that any dam is founded on bedrock. The consequences of building on alluvium were shown by the Puentes Dam on the Rio Guadalentin in south-eastern Spain. Completed in 1791, it was a masonry dam standing 165 feet high, but it failed when first filled in 1802 and was therefore the first high modern dam to fail. The floodwave from it was on a proportionately large scale, and 608 people died in the town of Lorca 12 miles downstream. Most of the dam was founded on good rock, but during construction a deep alluvium-filled, buried channel had been discovered, and instead of replacing the fill with masonry, the builders had merely placed wooden piles deep into the alluvium and supported the dam on them. Even with a masonry cap on the alluvium, when the reservoir was filled the water pressure in the alluvium was enough to blow it out. A hole was blown right through, beneath the base of the dam which remained like a bridge while the flood escaped beneath it. The effect of pore-water pressure underneath reservoirs had been all too clearly demonstrated, and yet almost a repeat situation was allowed to develop a century later at the Eigiau Dam in Wales before the dangers of unconsolidated sediments were fully appreciated.

Old mine workings have required the relocating of a number of small dams, but a more serious problem is posed by the threat of subsidence damage when modern mining passes underneath a dam. Normally a pillar, of a size dictated by the depth of working and locally applicable angle of influence, is left to support a dam, even though reservoirs in South Wales have been safely worked beneath where adequate clay ensured that leakage would not develop. A slightly different problem was encountered at the King's Mill Reservoir near Mansfield in Nottinghamshire, where coal mining subsidence caused one of the streams feeding the reservoir to reverse its flow and no longer contribute. That earth dams can withstand a considerable amount of deformation was shown in California by two dams astride the San Andreas Fault when it moved during the 1906 San Francisco earthquake. Neither dam failed, because their clay cores were plastic enough not to fracture when the movement of 12 feet along the fault line at right angles to the dam axes put double-bends in them. A concrete dam could not withstand such a displacement, and in that situation would fail. The 1954 Orleansville earthquake in Algeria resulted in the Ponteba Dam being cracked and tilted, fortunately without subsequent failure. Dams can even be the cause of earthquakes, as a result of rock being deformed by the weight of a reservoir and also by being excessively weakened through the increased pore-water pressures. So far no dam has destroyed itself in this way, as the resultant quakes are mostly quite small, but the Hsinfengkiang Dam founded on faulted granite in southern China developed a huge crack in its concrete upper structure as the result of a self-induced earthquake of magnitude 6.1 in May 1962.

Alluvium, earthquakes, rock permeability, shear structures – all can offer massive pitfalls for dam builders. Thorough previous examination of the geology is a necessity in dam construction, and as each case is different and so often can only be treated in a qualitative, or at best semi-quantitative way, a few examples of classic failures can at least demonstrate the hazard potential.

The St Francis Dam, California, achieved permanent record in the annals of engineering geology because from the moment it was built its eventual failure was inevitable. This was due simply to the appallingly unsuitable geology of the dam's location – and its planning, by the Los Angeles Bureau of Water Works, was classic because no geological advice was ever sought. The dam was built on a constriction in the San Francisquito Canyon, 45 miles north of Los Angeles and 9 miles upstream of where the canyon opened into the Santa Clara Valley leading westwards to the sea. The purpose of the reservoir was to store water fed by aqueducts from the east before it was distributed in Los Angeles. The reservoir was completed in 1926, and the main structure was a simple gravity dam 700 feet long and 205 feet high at its centre, with a low wing wall on the west bank which was as long again as the main dam. It is almost beyond belief that the dam was ever built at a location where the geology was so unsatisfactory. The dam was founded on schist and conglomerate straddling the faulted contact between the two rock types. Mica schist with a well-developed flaky schistosity and numerous shear planes formed the eastern flank of the dam site. The rock was not prone to weathering or disintegration in water, but it did contain small quantities of the mineral talc which gave very little frictional resistance across the shear planes in which it was concentrated. Although the schist

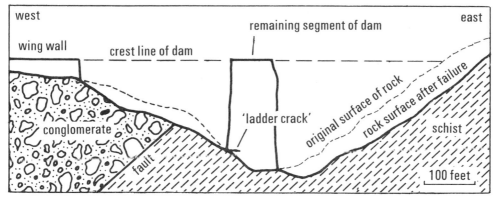

A cross-section of the St Francis Dam after its disastrous failure in 1928 – a failure made inevitable by the rock on which it was built.

was strong in compression, it slipped like a pack of cards when load was applied other than perpendicular to the schistosity. The direction of the schistosity could not have been worse, with a dip to the west of around 50° so that it was nearly parallel with the east slope of the canyon, which was consequently very unstable. Landslides occurred in the schists both before and after the dam construction, though the rock was firm enough in the canyon floor.

On the opposite side of the canyon, the western end of the dam was founded on red conglomerates, with some interbedded siltstones and standstones, of Oligocene age. The fragments in the conglomerate ranged in size from silt up to pebbles eight inches across, and some of them were fractured in shear zones which laced the rock. At best, the conglomerate could be described as poorly lithified with its feeble matrix of clay and gypsum; its crushing strength was no more than 500 lb a square inch just a quarter of the consequently superfluous design strength of the dam concrete. But this strength was of dry rock. When wet the clay cement expanded and disintegrated while the gypsum was rapidly dissolved, and the cementless conglomerate became merely a muddy sand – it could no longer be described as rock. A hand specimen of the conglomerate placed in a beaker of water completely disaggregated in less than fifteen minutes; unfortunately this simple test was not done till after the dam failure, but the results were clearly to be seen in the state of the 'rock' on the shores of the reservoir.

The conglomerate–schist boundary passed beneath the dam part-way up the western bank. It was a thrust fault, dipping westwards nearly parallel to both the metamorphic rock's schistosity and the conglomerate's bedding. The fault was described as inactive, and indeed there has still been no movement recorded on it. Even so, the building of a concrete dam on any fault in an active earthquake region such as California must be regarded as foolhardy; the nearby San Fernando earthquake of 1971 originated on a fault previously described as inactive. More directly significant was the 5-foot-wide band of plastic clay-like gouge within the fault, together with the zones of sheared, brecciated and veined material on its immediate flanks. When wet the fault gouge was like an uncohesive paste.

Filling of the St Francis Reservoir began in 1927, but the water first rose to top level on 5 March 1928. By then seepage through the conglomerate beneath the dam was causing some concern and engineers from the Los Angeles Department of Water and Power went to inspect it. They found the seepage water running clear, indicating that it was not scouring out the rock, so they issued no warnings of danger; but the water was high in sulphate, due to the solution of the gypsum cement in the rock, and its flow was increasing, and on the morning of 12 March was actually surging due to internal break-up of the conglomerate. Two minutes before midnight on 12 March the dam failed.

Unfortunately there are no witnesses alive to tell of the failure – but it must have been spectacular indeed as the water was released almost instantaneously. The first pulse of the flood must have had a flow of over 800,000 cusecs, and it swept down the canyon as a wall of water nearly 130 feet high. Five minutes later it demolished the powerhouse a mile and a half downstream. Everything manmade or alive in the canyon was destroyed, and the flood then swept into the Santa Clara Valley where it spread out sideways, losing some of its power but little of its ability to kill. There were few survivors in the upper part of the valley – only those who had freak escapes on tall trees or floating debris. By the time the flood hit the coastal plain it was a rolling, dirty wave 2 miles wide moving at a fast walking pace. Behind it lay 50 miles of drowned valley. At one time there were fourteen timber-frame houses floating around on the flooded school playing-fields at Santa Paula. And over 600 people had died. Back in the canyon, the reservoir lay dry – it had emptied in less than an hour. The middle section of the dam still stood, although slightly moved from its original position. The eastern end had broken into a dozen or more massive blocks which had been strewn about by the floodwave, and most of the western wall had disintegrated, though the low wing extension still stood. Up to 35 feet of rock was missing from the foundation sites on both sides of the dam.

The amazing thing about the St Francis Dam failure was that, even ignoring the unrealised threat of fault movement, there were three separate aspects of the geology which could have been responsible. The conglomerate could have crumbled, the fault gouge could have been scoured, and the schists could have sheared. Design of the dam, with insignificant cut-off trenches, no grouting and no deep anchoring took none of these hazards into consideration. After the failure different geologists and study groups blamed individually all three structures, and the official inquiry ascribed the disaster 'wholly to the unsuitability of the material on which the dam was built'. In the event there was little evidence that the fault gouge had been responsible for the failure, and the previous seepage concentrated the early investigations on the inadequacy of the conglomerate. The lack of strength of the wet conglomerate was undeniable for the section of dam on that rock had been destroyed, and a later survey showed that the wing wall was up to 4 inches higher than it had been when built. Clearly the conglomerate had expanded as the clay minerals in its cement had absorbed water from the reservoir, and such a reaction would be paralleled by a total loss of cohesion.

The real culprit of the disaster lay however on the east bank, unsuspected by the engineers examining the west bank seepages just before the failure. Flood debris above reservoir level proved that there had been a landslide of the schist into a full reservoir, and this must have been followed by the massive lateral slip which took so much of the schist away from under the dam itself. That this side of the dam failed before the conglomerate side was proved by a freak event. After the failure, a ladder was found jammed and crushed in a crack in the western side of the base of the

94

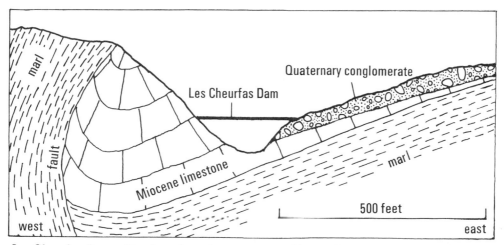

Les Cheurfas Dam, Algeria, where the young, unstable conglomerate was mis-identified as being part of the limestone succession.

remaining central segment of dam. This could only have beeen the result of that segment being pushed over to the east, partly by the swelling conglomerate, into the void from where the schist-founded side of the dam had already gone. That movement would have caused too great a strain on the side of the already weakened conglomerate, and the western side of the dam would therefore have failed almost immediately after the eastern side – so soon after that only one massive flood pulse was recognised. So the root cause of the failure was a slip in the easily sheared schist; how much movement took place will never be known, but it was enough to strain the dam beyond breaking point, before the floodwave scoured away all the slipped bedrock.

It is an understatement merely to say that failure of the St Francis Dam was predictable. It is obvious that the geology of the site was unsuitable, and it is hard to believe that the properties of the wetted conglomerate were not appreciated during construction. But even if workmen or individuals said anything, the management was blind to the geological hazards. No outside geological advice was sought, yet the fault was marked on published maps, the schist and conglomerate in all their weaknesses were well exposed, and the engineer in charge was reckoned to be something of an amateur geologist. At least the St Francis Dam failure encouraged the disciplines of engineering and geology to move a little closer to each other, and it did provide the perfect example of 'how not to do it'.

Like the St Francis Dam, the Les Cheurfas is a geological classic because it failed due to unsuitable foundation geology. But whereas at St Francis the geology was simply ignored, at Les Cheurfas the failure arose from an error in geological interpretation. Situated not far inland of Oran in western Algeria, the dam was completed in 1885, impounding 72 feet of water.

At the dam site the bedrock was a thick Miocene limestone containing some recemented breccias, dipping to the west into the core of an overfolded syncline. The limestone overlay a series of marls with thin limestones and sandstones which cropped out high on the west bank. Overlying these were Quaternary clay, alluvium and conglomerate which were patchily distributed over the valley floor, but were locally 100 feet thick. Most of the Quaternary was unconsolidated, but some of the conglomerates were locally cemented, as often occurs in surface debris of limestone fragments, particularly in hot regions with high evaporation rates. The west end of the dam was founded on the Miocene limestones, which though prone to leakage were structurally sound. But the eastern side was founded, due to an error in identification, on a cemented conglomerate in the Quaternary sequence which was little more than a brittle crust overlying unconsolidated material. Consequently, when the reservoir was first filled and permitted to overflow, on 8 February 1885, the eastern half of the dam was washed away and the reservoir emptied in a floodwave which inundated the town of St Denis-du-Sug 12 miles downstream.

The failure was directly due to the inadequacy of the Quaternary sediment as foundation material. The western half of the dam, founded on the limestone, was unharmed and was incorporated in a rebuilt dam completed in 1892 and founded entirely on the limestone; this dam still stands today, though a grout curtain down to the marl had to be added to prevent leakage through the limestone. The blame for the disaster, as revealed by the subsequent inquiry, lay with the confusion of the Quaternary cemented conglomerate for a breccia layer in the Miocene limestone. Though there were similarities between the two materials in that they both consisted of mainly limestone fragments, there were pebbles of non-calcareous material in the Quaternary which distinguished it under close examination. Admittedly weathered and broken outcrops of both materials were very similar; but any engineering geologist should be aware of the possible formation of hard but thin surface crusts in such regions where calcite is readily available, easily transported and rapidly deposited as a cement, and he must be prepared to make a detailed enough examination. The Les Cheurfas failure demonstrated only too clearly the consequence of not recognising a buried layer of unconsolidated sediment.

Geologically, failure of the the Baldwin Hills Reservoir in California was unusual in the initial obscurity of its precise cause, though much has since been learned about the mechanisms involved. The failure was also unusual in that it gave a recognisable warning and therefore allowed a successful evacuation of the danger area. This was particularly fortunate because the reservoir was perched on the Baldwin Hills some 350 feet above densely populated suburbs of Los Angeles. The urban sprawl of Los Angeles surrounds the hills, and the reservoir was sited there to act as a distributor source for the expanding south-western district of the city.

The reservoir was built between 1947 and 1951 by excavating sediment from a shallow ravine and using it to form the main dam 130 feet high across its mouth and also a series of low dykes on the surrounding ridges and cols. The result was a nearly square reservoir with sides of around 1000 feet, 70 feet deep and with a capacity of 300 million gallons. The clay sediments so excavated were not used in the main dam wall, but were retained and then rolled on to the floor and inside banks of the reservoir to form a layer 10 feet thick, thinning to half that at the tops of the walls. Covered with a 3-inch-thick asphalt layer, this formed an impermeable lining, and was laced with efficient underdrains to prevent seepage water building up to dangerously high pressures within it and the dam wall. Also incorporated were large gated drains which could in an emergency empty the reservoir in less than twenty-four hours.

Bedrock at the reservoir site was only barely consolidated Pliocene and

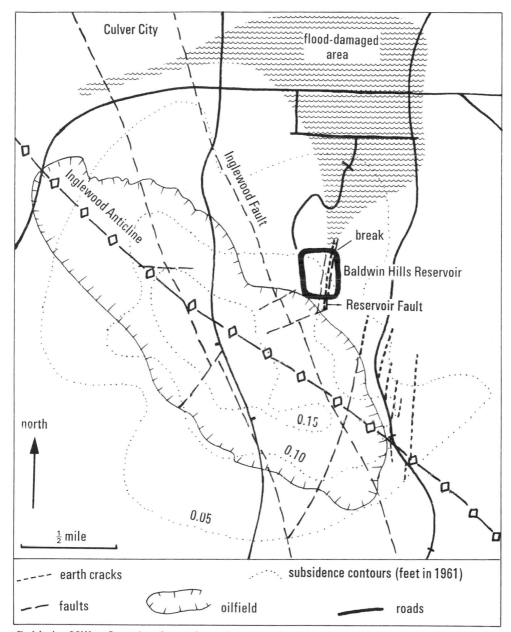

Baldwin Hills, Los Angeles, where the reservoir failed in 1963 on account of ground movements associated with the oilfields in the Inglewood Anticline.

Pleistocene sediment. They were mainly sands and silts, with some clays, the upper layers being mainly very friable and some capable of being crushed by the bare hands. The lower, Pliocene, beds could be described as moderately consolidated, with some beds partially cemented. The permeability and easily eroded nature of these materials had given some cause for concern. A geological report commissioned in 1941 suggested that the site was suitable for construction of the reservoir, but a

97

second report in 1943 reversed that conclusion. When a third report stated that the reservoir could be built, 'with a conservative design', and it was considered that there was no alternative site, construction went ahead.

The site geology was further complicated by the regional structure. The Baldwin Hills are formed on an anticlinal dome developed in 12,000 feet of oil-bearing Tertiary sediments over a basement of Mesozoic schist. The anticline axis is west of the reservoir, and on the same side but only 500 feet away the Inglewood fault has a lateral displacement of 1500 feet and has been the origin of a number of recent earth tremors. Two minor faults were revealed on the reservoir site during construction, the larger one to the east now being known as the Reservoir Fault; it bore a clay gouge up to 4 inches thick, with slickensided surfaces, and was conspicuous enough to cause the resiting of the outlet tower away from it. The domed Inglewood anticline was a significant producing oilfield, with hundreds of wells sunk into its Tertiary sands since 1924. The oil exploration had revealed many faults associated with the Inglewood Fault at depth, and one of these was thought to have been the continuation of the Reservoir Fault. The extraction of oil from the sediments made the Inglewood anticline the centre of an active subsidence bowl, which has seen 7–9 feet of vertical movement in its centre between 1917 and 1963. The reservoir site had settled nearly 3 feet in the same time, and was also in the ring-shaped zone of lateral movement where the ground had moved, over a period of 29 years, a maximum of 2.49 feet in towards the centre of the subsidence bowl.

During the lifetime of the reservoir there were plenty of signs of continuing earth movements. Minor cracks were found in the concrete of the inspection galleries, and there were even small cracks in the reservoir walls, while surveys revealed the progress of both subsidence and horizontal displacement. The most significant result of the repeated surveys was that between 1947 and 1962 the reservoir site and dam had been stretched 5 inches along a northeast–southwest diagonal. In May 1957 major earth cracks began to open in the area south-east of the reservoir, and in the following years further cracks got even closer. These were open fissures up to 2500 feet long with no lateral movement, inclined steeply to the west and parallel to the minor faults in the area. But there were no signs of damage to the reservoir until 11:15 on the morning of 14 December 1963, when the caretaker found the reservoir underdrains spouting water at high pressure. Realising this meant that reservoir water was breaking through the asphalt lining into the clay bed, he raised the alarm.

By 12:20 pm a start had been made on emptying the reservoir, but at one o'clock water began to seep out from near the foot of the eastern end of the dam. With the dam now being eroded from the inside it was realised that the reservoir was doomed. Television and radio announcements and helicopters equipped with loudspeakers were used to order a rapid evacuation of 1600 people from their homes immediately below the dam. By two o'clock the seepage was enough to generate a whirlpool near the edge of the reservoir, and ninety minutes later this developed into a massive hole through the base of the dam. At 3:38 pm the upper part of the dam collapsed into the hole leaving a gash 90 feet deep and 75 feet wide at the top. The water poured out through this initially at a flow rate of 4300 cusecs and in just over an hour the reservoir was empty. The flood caused five deaths, a number greatly reduced by the success of the evacuation, as it roared down the ravine and spread out up to 8 feet deep on the plain below. It destroyed forty-one houses and damaged nearly a thousand more, leaving thick mud everywhere over the wrecked streets and torn-up services. Total damage ran to nearly $15 million.

With the reservoir empty, the villain of the piece was clearly visible – a crack, right across the asphalt floor and into the breach in the dam, lay along the outcrop of the Reservoir Fault. The movement on the fault was like that on the earlier earth cracks to the south-east in that it had opened up by 4 inches and thrown down on the west by nearly double that. Water had poured through the cracked asphalt, swamped the underdrainage system and continued down into the fault, scouring the weak sands and silts beneath the rolled clay bed. It had eventually worked its way beneath the reservoir and out under the dam, and then with an efficient outlet established had rapidly piped beneath the dam; the dam had not ruptured in the fault movement, and had even bridged over the leak until finally collapsing into it. The cause of the fault movement was clearly the tensional development associated with subsidence in the Inglewood anticline, but here the confusion began. The subsidence was not due to water withdrawal, as there had been none, nor was it related to landslides in the area or to earthquakes, as none had been recorded on the day. Some claim was made that the movement was due to oil extraction in the Inglewood oilfield which would have resulted in subsidence, yet movement around the oilfield had markedly decreased since 1957, when oil production had moved into the stage of secondary recovery with brine being pumped into the rock to force the oil out. This raised the question of why there should suddenly be renewed movement in 1963. One suggestion was that the movement was of deep tectonic origin, but there was no recorded movement on the Inglewood Fault and the tectonics would tend to favour uplift, not subsidence, of the anticline area, hence compression, not tension, in the reservoir area. The balance of feeling after the event may be judged by the oil companies' payment to the city and its insurers, in an out of court settlement, of the sum of nearly $3.9 million – around 25 per cent of the total damages. The official investigation was summarised thus: 'Sitting on the flank of the sensitive Newport–Inglewood fault system with its associated tectonic restlessness, at the rim of a rapidly depressing subsidence basin, on a foundation adversely influenced by water, this reservoir was called upon to do more than it was able to do.'

Only later was the significance of the secondary recovery operations in the oilfield appreciated for its part in the failure of the Baldwin Hills Reservoir. This operation involves driving the oil out of some wells by injecting water or brine down other wells, to increase the fluid pressure in the rocks at depth. It is now well known that such increases in pore-water pressure can result in the effective lubrication of fault planes – and indeed have been responsible for triggering minor earthquakes in a number of cases. In this case it triggered movement along the Reservoir Fault which had been stable until its water pressure was raised. The proof of this theory came in the correlation of the rates of brine injection in the Inglewood field with the opening of earth cracks on its margin, and also with the loss of fluid into the fault planes as recorded by the oil companies.

Although the designers of the reservoir had made allowance for resistance to both earthquake tremors and movement through subsidence, they had unfortunately made two errors. They had assumed the Reservoir Fault to be only minor and shallow, whereas it penetrated deep enough to intersect major fields of stress in the subsiding anticline, and they had not anticipated the inevitable lubrication effect of subsequent oilfield operations. It is an open-ended question as to whether the oil companies or the Department of Water Resources were responsible for the disaster, but it is undeniable that in the Baldwin Hills situation the oilfield and the reservoir were incompatible.

Whereas the failures of the St Francis, Les Cheurfas and Baldwin Hills dams were predictable if only the geology had been correctly appraised, Malpasset was different. The failure of the Malpasset Dam was a geological one, but the mechanism was not known before or at the time of failure – it was only revealed by research after, and partly prompted by, the disaster. The dam, completed in 1953, impounded the River Reyran just 5 miles north-east of the town of Fréjus, at the western end of the French Riviera. It was a thin-arch concrete structure, 217 feet high, with a curved crest length of 732 feet, and it retained a reservoir 4 miles long with a capacity of 880 million cubic feet.

The geology of the site appeared to be almost ideal, with bedrock of strong Carboniferous gneiss and only thin alluvium which was entirely removed during construction. The gneiss contained pegmatite veins which did not represent any weakness, and also a dense network of microfissures which did not appear to have any regular pattern. Any concern about these was alleviated when the grout acceptance of the foundation rock was found to be minimal. The foliation banding in the gneiss contained mainly mica, but also significant amounts of calcite and sericite especially in a zone on the east bank of the site. The surfaces of the silky sericite were prone to slip, particularly when wet, but the angle of the foliation at the dam site was so much steeper than the valley slope that there was no danger of the loaded dam sliding. A small fault, entirely in the gneiss, was not found during the initial site investigation but was only revealed by the scouring action of the failure. Had it been noticed it would not have caused any concern, for though it cropped out just downstream of the dam and dipped at 45° to pass about 50 feet beneath it, the loading of the dam would not have stressed the fault to form any potential danger.

After completion of the dam in 1953, the reservoir was progressively filled, but, due to demand for water, it only approached top level in late November 1959. Until then measured deformation and movement of the dam had been well within acceptable limits. On 15 November the keeper reported seepage from the west bank about 65 feet downstream of the dam and this continued into and through a period of very heavy rain which started on 27 November. When the dam failed just after nine o'clock on the evening of 2 December, there were no witnesses. The keeper in his house nearly a mile down the valley heard a series of loud cracks and then saw the doors and windows of his house blasted out by a sudden wind. Clearly the failure of the dam was instantaneous and the resultant floodwave was of mammoth proportions. It swept down the narrow Reyran valley and then spread out across the plain below, causing immense damage and over 400 deaths in the town of Fréjus – it was a national disaster for France. Little was left of the dam. A rib of the structure remained on the west bank, but opposite there was only the extreme end of the dam, and this was shifted 7 feet horizontally from its original position. A huge chunk of the gneiss on the east bank had been ripped out, partly by the plucking action of the escaping water.

It was significant that among the debris in the valley, fragments of concrete still bonded to the gneiss revealed that the contact had not been the cause of failure. The

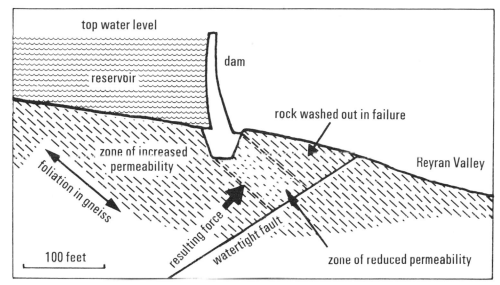

A cross-section of the Malpasset Dam shows how the orientation of the fault and the compressed zone of gneiss caused the critical build-up of water pressure.

Inquiry Commission appointed after the disaster found nothing wrong with the dam design, the concrete or the lack of grout in the almost impermeable gneiss: it ascribed the failure to buckling of the thin concrete arch due to movement in the rock foundation. In the absence of the guilty section of rock, which had been scoured out during the failure, there was then much debate on whether the rock had failed by deformation or sliding. Although neither of these mechanisms eventually proved to be responsible for the failure, there were two very pertinent results from the discussions. The first was the comment that engineers and geologists did not seem to be speaking the same language, with the result that they could not understand each other's problems. The second was a plea for more and better *in situ* testing at full scale of the foundation rocks, particularly on the surface layers, instead of relying on laboratory tests and site tests carried out in adits as was the common practice.

Only some years later did a group of French engineers discover the real cause of the Malpasset disaster, when they carried out a series of laboratory tests to relate permeability to prevailing stress in a series of rocks. They found that permeability was greatly reduced in some rocks when they were under compression, and the greatest reductions were found in microfissured rocks such as gneiss. Similarly, tensile stress resulted in an increase in permeability, and, of all the rocks tested, the Malpasset gneiss proved to have the greatest of all stress-dependent changes in its permeability, varying as it did across three orders of magnitude. When viewed in the context of the dam, the significance of this discovery became clear, as did the importance of the little downstream fault. The force from the loaded dam compressed the gneiss and reduced its permeability to about a hundredth of normal in a zone below the dam and down to the underlying fault. The fault itself contained an impervious gouge, and there was therefore an almost watertight barrier beneath the dam. The tensile zone in the gneiss beneath the end of the reservoir had increased permeability and efficiently transmitted the full pore pressure from the hydraulic head in the reservoir down into the rock. This then acted against the nearly watertight gneiss under the dam to give a consequently immense force upwards – parallel to the weakness offered by the fault, and tending to force the gneiss out at right angles to the weakness in its foliation. The result was that the pore-water pressure in the gneiss just lifted the dam and then blasted the rock out from beneath it. Almost certainly the failure had been triggered by the final filling of the reservoir, which had strained the dam and rock that little bit more and opened up fissures in the reservoir floor to enable even more effective transmission of the water pressure down into the rock.

The safety of the Malpasset Dam could only have been assured by the installation of drains in the rock beneath the dam to relieve any build-up in pore-water pressures – such drains are now features in the design of many similar dams. Even though the failure mechanism at Malpasset appears almost obvious with the advantage of hindsight, it would be unfair to attach any blame to the design engineers who worked, at the time, in total ignorance of the principles involved. And in this respect, Malpasset must have the final word; for, while there can be no excuse for some of the geological blunders that engineers have made, they can still be at a severe disadvantage in that the geological sciences have not yet mastered all the problems involved when enormous forces are applied to natural materials such as water and rock.

The future

In how many ways can a dam fail? And does each variation on the theme have to be demonstrated by a catastrophe before man can understand the dangers involved? The Malpasset and Baldwin Hills failures could both be ascribed to mechanisms 'not appreciated at the time', and foresight is admittedly a lot more difficult than hindsight. The ludicrous errors of St Francis and Les Cheurfas are way back in history. And yet in June 1976 the Teton Dam in the United States failed – a ludicrous error, or the discovery of another way that a dam can fail?

The cost of the Teton failure was eleven lives, 25,000 people homeless and damage claims which approached $400 million. But on the credit side, the Bureau of Reclamation, which designed both the Teton Dam and over 300 other successful dams, has encouraged a full investigation into the failure. The earth dam was piped and then scoured away as the reservoir was being filled for the first time. Though the real cause is still under debate, it appears to have been rooted in the foundation rock. This was a rhyolite tuff so heavily fractured that it was locally used as an aquifer into which a number of wells had been sunk. Incorporated into the dam, therefore, was a grout screen and deep cut-off trench on an unprecedented scale. The floor of the cut-off trench had been grouted and sealed by hand – and here, through lack of communication, lay a crucial error. The designers assumed that such grouting would render the rock surface watertight. But the construction workers carried out the grouting only to ensure a good footing for the dam; the stiff cement grout was poured into all significant fissures in the rhyolite, but cracks less than half an inch across were ignored. The silt and clay dam was then laid on this surface, and, as the reservoir filled, it seems that water was forced along these cracks in contact with the base of the dam. The water scoured the silt–clay mixture – a material not as suitable as a self-sealing clay, but one which had been used successfully elsewhere. The result was a water route under the dam, but over the grout curtain in the foundation rock: once such a route was established, failure was inevitable.

The Teton failure may ultimately be ascribed to the communication gap – an adequate design that was divorced from practice. It is tragic how often this communication gap is the cause of disasters. Will the lesson be learned at Teton?

Geological causes for dam failures normally make their presence known rapidly, and if a dam survives the first filling of the reservoir it normally means that the geology of its foundation at least was satisfactory. But the same cannot be said for other works where water is concerned. Until the year 1818 the upper course of the Rhine, between Basel and Karlsruhe, in West Germany, meandered naturally across a wide flood plain. But in that year a scheme of control was started which is still being added to today. This involved shortening the river and building dams, canals, levees and so on to make it into the transport artery which it has now become. One sad result of all these works, instigated by a host of non-coordinated independent authorities, is that the river is now deprived of its flood plain, so any floodpulses from spring meltwater in the Alpine catchment areas are rapidly swept downstream. The city of Karlsruhe is now in an unenviable position. In 1955 it was heavily damaged in the spring floods – but the result of river works since then would increase the flood level by 35 per cent should the same conditions occur in the Alps in 1978. The best way of preventing this is to recreate the pre-1818 flood plain which would dissipate the floodwaters over open countryside instead of pouring them into Karlsruhe. Such a scheme exists on paper. But will it be put into practice? Or will it have to wait till Karlsruhe suffers yet more damage – due not to the river, but to man?

SUBSIDENCE

In 1965, a truck was drawn up at a building site in the town of Lexington, Kentucky, cement pouring from the truck straight into the formwork for the foundations of a house. Suddenly there was a low rumble and the ground opened up beneath the cement truck – without any warning, it dropped into a gaping hope 12 feet deep.

At Lexington the bedrock is limestone which contains a number of caves, and the collapse of the roof of just one, quite small cave had seen the disappearance of the cement truck. The event can hardly be described as a major catastrophe, but it was none the less disturbing. People tend to regard the ground as solid and immovable, and when it collapses and disappears down holes it leaves them with little to believe in.

Ground subsidence can take place in a number of different ways. It can affect only a very small area suddenly, perhaps just enough to undermine a single support of a building, or it can result in entire cities slowly sinking – Venice is the best known example of this. Although the subsidence may be a perfectly natural process, it may also be the direct result of man's activities; the most obvious cases of the latter are collapses into old mines. It is significant that a great proportion of land subsidences are at least indirectly related to man's interference with the natural stability of ground.

On the premise that the art of civil engineering has now reached such a state that almost any problem can be overcome, as long as the nature of the problem is known, subsidence need rarely provide insuperable difficulties. Many cases of subsidence involve small and manageable areas, but the real problem is predicting it; natural cavities in the ground, limestone caves for example, are notoriously difficult to find without very expensive programmes of closely spaced boreholes. Regional subsidence, involving larger areas, has at least the advantage of being generally more predictable, and it now seems to be technically feasible to arrest the subsidence of an area the size of Venice, though admittedly at incredible expense. Perhaps the one type of subsidence which will always be beyond man's control is crustal warping, in which the movement may involve the entire thickness of the Earth's crust. Only when associated with earthquakes does this reach catastrophic proportions, as normally the movement involved is extremely slow, taking perhaps many hundreds of years to show noticeable effect. With this last exception, ground subsidence is in theory predictable or controllable; in practice though it has been notoriously unpredictable.

Subsidence due to solutional removal of rock

Limestone, gypsum and rock salt are significantly soluble in water under natural conditions. Of these, limestone is by far the most common, and the least soluble. It also differs from gypsum and salt in that it is normally a very strong rock, and the result of its underground solution is the formation of caves, usually with perfectly stable roofs. Subsidence and collapse are common in limestone regions, and the processes are invariably related to the caves. In contrast, salt is a much weaker rock, besides being more soluble, and subsidence hazards on it are very common, though they rarely involve the formation of caves. Gypsum is almost an intermediate case between limestone and salt.

Calcium sulphate is highly soluble in water, and yet it forms two minerals which are both common enough to form thick beds of rock in various parts of the world – gypsum is the more widespread hydrated form and anhydrite is the rather less common anhydrous form. Both materials underlie large areas in the United States, Germany, France and Russia, to name but a few countries, and solution has given rise to subsidence problems in each of these countries. An additional problem with anhydrite is that when it first comes into contact with groundwater it reacts with it to form gypsum, and this involves a considerable expansion in volume. This expansion can result in a dramatic uplift of the ground. Over a number of years explosions were heard in north-west Texas as the ground lifted violently due to anhydrite expansion. Then in September 1955, near the town of Novica, an explosion heralded the vertical uplift by 18 feet of a piece of ground a few hundred yards across; soil and rock mushroomed into the air, the debris hitting a man who was standing half a mile away. However, the more common type of ground movement over gypsum is downward subsidence, with its solutional removal. The famous Roswell Bottomless Lakes on the edge of the Pecos Valley in New Mexico are a series of steep-sided, water-filled collapse features formed by solution of the gypsum bedrock. No further collapse of them has been recorded in historical times, but the largest of these features is now 300 feet across and up to 120 feet deep. Of similar but more recent origin are various sinkholes in the gypsum of the Kootenay Mountains in British Columbia. In 1967 a vertically walled shaft 70 feet in diameter developed overnight in the floor of a gypsum quarry at Windermere – fortunately without doing any damage. In Europe the most extensive gypsum beds are found in northern Germany; the small town of Bad Frankenhausen is just one which has suffered subsidence damage, with many of its buildings twisted and leaning where the underlying gypsum has been dissolved Paris is probably the largest city affected by gypsum subsidence; large areas in its suburbs provide constant problems for engineers as cavities are repeatedly discovered in the bedrock.

Although it is not as widespread as gypsum, rock salt (sodium chloride) is much more renowned for subsidence because it is so much more soluble. Subsidence therefore takes place on a greater scale. In February 1954 a collapse hole suddenly developed at Windsor, Canada; it was more than 300 feet across and 27 feet deep, and it rapidly filled with water. Material damage was extensive, including the total loss of two buildings. The cause of the collapse was solution of an underlying salt bed, though it was probably helped along by nearby brine pumping and the collapse of ancient deep mine workings. But the sudden collapse at the village of

Runjh in northern India in 1970 was entirely unaided by man's activities. In the early hours of the night of 21 November of that year, the villagers were rudely awoken by a deafening rumbling as their houses vibrated. Rushing outside they found a deep gaping hole in the middle of a field which the previous evening had held a bamboo grove. The hole was about 60 feet in diameter, and 40 feet deep to a mass of rubble itself thick enough to bury all the 50 foot high bamboos which had completely disappeared. The rock on which Runjh is built is volcanic lava, but at a depth of a few hundred feet this is underlain by a bed of salt. Groundwater seeping through that salt over many years had dissolved a cavern in it. The roof of the cavern, formed of the overlying lava, had then collapsed into it, and this collapse had worked progressively upwards, each bed in turn falling into the void below. Eventually the collapse had reached the surface, and swallowed the bamboo grove.

Perhaps the collapse at Runjh is only the foretaste of greater ones to come, for in Canada there is good evidence of far more spectacular collapses in the geological past. The Prairies in Saskatchewan are underlain by vast deposits of salt – the main bed is 400–700 feet thick and lies at a depth of up to 5000 feet. Solution of the salt by naturally circulating groundwater has caused the local collapse of the overlying beds. Crater Lake, 100 miles north-east of Regina, lies in such a collapse depression. It is almost perfectly circular, about 700 feet in diameter and now only about 50 feet deep due to the accumulation of sediment. The geological structure reveals cylindrical faults around the lake margin with a vertical displacement of about 200 feet, and the distribution of surface sediments indicates that this movement took place during the various Ice Ages of the last million or so years. Even older, with a clearly pre-glacial origin, is the subsidence at Rosetown, 100 miles south-west of Saskatoon. Glacial deposits have filled in the Rosetown collapse so that there is now no sign of it on the surface, but it is on an enormous scale. The downward movement was 380 feet, affecting a nearly square area over 12 miles across! Deep boreholes have revealed that the salt beds which lie 5000 feet below the surface are missing immediately under Rosetown, and where they should be, the drillholes found only great masses of broken collapsed rock.

On 26 March 1879 a steep-sided collapse hole some 200 feet in diameter was found directly across a cattle trail in Meade County, Kansas. Wagon tracks left three weeks earlier were clearly visible on each side of the hole, which was yet another example of the effect of underground solution of salt. The same cause accounted for the overnight disappearance of the railroad station at Rosel, also in Kansas. The Rosel collapse hole was 70 feet deep and an acre in extent; it immediately filled with water, hiding any trace of the station and several other buildings. These two collapses were entirely natural processes, and as such would have been extremely difficult to predict from any geological evidence. Rather more predictable are collapses which have been triggered by man's interference – notably the pumping of brine groundwater from beds of salt – but even then the precise geography of the collapse is hard to predict. The pumping of salty groundwater from wells during oil production in the Sour Lake region of Texas must undoubtedly have accelerated underground salt solution. On the morning of 9 October 1929, a large collapse hole developed. It started as a gentle depression, but then the sides broke into steps and within five hours it was 90 feet deep.

The most famous of all salt subsidences are those connected with the salt mining in Cheshire, England; these were truly catastrophic. The Cheshire Plain is a

44 *All too often the subsiding city of Venice is flooded by an* aqua alta *which allows the gondoliers to row straight across St Mark's Square.*

45 (above) *Digging the foundations for a warehouse was enough to disturb the ground on this construction site in Birmingham, Alabama, so that a sinkhole developed as the surface sediments were washed down into the cavernous limestone below.* 46 (below) *A man is almost lost in the bowl of the huge subsidence hole which developed at Meade, Kansas, due to solutional erosion of an underlying salt bed in 1879.*

47 (above left) *The Leaning Tower of Pisa – the bell tower on the cathedral.* 48 (right) *The leaning tower of Bristol – the Temple Church. Both owe their distinctive leans to differential compaction in the laterally variable unconsolidated sediments beneath them.* 49 (below) *Originally there were two chicken houses in the garden of this house in Bishopriggs, Scotland, but during a winter night in 1947 most of the garden and one chicken hut collapsed into a forgotten and inadequately capped old mine shaft.*

50 *This excessively bad subsidence damage in 1972 is due to coal mining beneath a jointed sandstone supporting the unrafted foundations of the house in Hucknall, Nottinghamshire. The building has since had to be demolished as it was beyond repair.*

51 (above) *Earth fissures and a ruined house indicate the extent of the subsidence in Bank, South Africa, in 1972. There is no sign on the surface of the cavernous dolomite far below into which the surface sediments were washed when mining activity changed the local drainage patterns.* 52 (below) *Subsidence caused by salt mining in Cheshire was all too common on this scale, but because the threat was recognised the buildings had timber frames and could often be jacked back into level positions.*

53 (above) *The roadway of Jacqueline Close, Bury St Edmunds, is barely recognisable with the gaping collapse holes which developed as the saturated and liquefied chalk drained into the old mine workings below.* 54 (below) *This great crater in the wet peaty ground of an open field was formed when the peat ran into the upward heading from the Knockshinnoch Colliery (in the background) and trapped over a hundred miners underground in 1950.*

55 *This classical glaciated valley – Gasterntal – has a flat floor which is clearly on a sediment layer of unpredictable depth. In 1908 the Lötschberg Tunnel was driven into these sediments over 600 feet below the woods in the centre of the photograph, and the inrush of sand and water killed 25 of the tunnellers.*

56 (above) *Mud, boulders and wrecked mine equipment half fill the main roadway in the Lofthouse Colliery after the disastrous inrush from old workings in 1972.* 57 (below) *This enormous sinkhole, some 300 yards across, in the dumped tailings from Zambia's Mufulira mine occurred suddenly in 1970. Nearly 2000 feet below the sediment and water poured out of the cavernous limestone and swept into the mine workings.*

monotonously flat region which extends 20 miles or so between the hills of North Wales to the west and the Pennines to the east. The local relief seldom exceeds 50 feet, though a large number of small lakes are scattered across the plain – they are known as meres and are regarded as water-filled subsidence hollows caused by salt solution at depth. Linear subsidence hollows are also a feature of the plain; they are shallow troughs, maybe 600 feet or so wide and up to 30 feet deep, which extend for miles across the countryside regardless of valleys and hills. They too are the result of prehistoric subsidence. Dramatic instances of collapse subsidence have been reported regularly since 1533, when one developed at Combermere. The salt beds were first discovered in the area in 1670 (during a search for coal), and since then a major salt extraction industry has developed, centred mainly around the towns of Northwich and Winsford.

The surface geology of the Northwich area consists almost entirely of sands and boulder clay of Pleistocene glacial and interglacial origin. This layer of uncon-solidated sediment averages about 50 feet in thickness, completely obscuring the underlying Keuper Marls of Triassic age. The Keuper is around 4000 feet thick, consisting mostly of soft siltstones, clays, shales and then sandstones. Salt occurs in two bands known as the Saliferous Beds, which occur within the Keuper. The Upper Saliferous Beds are over 1000 feet thick and the lower average about 600 feet. All the Triassic rocks are gently inclined, and they are folded into a shallow syncline plunging to the south; they are also somewhat faulted. But the salt is so soluble that the Saliferous Beds are not found in the zone of wet ground immediately beneath the Pleistocene cover – instead, down to depths of around 250–450 feet, the salt has been removed. The subseqent collapse is responsible for both the meres and the linear subsidences. Below this level the salt is present but is saturated and in process of solution (wet rockhead), while at greater depths, due to the imperme-ability of most of the Keuper succession, it is normally completely dry (dry rockhead).

Clearly any subsidences in the Cheshire Plain are directly related to the removal of the underlying salt, and it is significant that this has taken place in a number of different ways. Perfectly natural drainage has resulted in underground water flowing along the salt beds and eventually emerging on the surface as powerful brine springs. This must have been happening for about 10,000 years (since the last glacial retreat) and has accounted for the linear subsidences. The brine springs were used for salt manufacture from pre-Roman times, but they dried up in the seventeenth century with the onset of brine pumping.

Salt mining started in 1682, and hundreds of small mines were sunk, many into wet rockhead, mainly in the eighteenth and nineteenth centuries. Mining practices were very poor, as the small mines were designed to be abandoned after only a short working life; in many cases an inadequate 10 per cent of the salt was left behind as roof support, making collapse inevitable. Wild brine mining started in the seventeenth century. This was done simply by sinking a borehole into the wet rockhead and pumping out the brine – salt saturated groundwater. It was soon found that the most successful wells were those sunk into the natural brine 'streams' where the brine was already flowing across the top of the salt beds, along the line of the linear subsidences. Even more successful than the wild brining was 'bastard brining', started in the mid-nineteenth century. This entailed pumping brine from flooded abandoned mine workings, and while very profitable for the brine operators, it resulted in the rapid corrosion of the few pillars left in the mines and brought about considerable collapse.

These cheap but dangerous methods of mining and brining have now been largely superseded by more modern techniques. Since 1930 controlled brining has been carried out, notably at Holford; it entails pumping fresh water in, and brine out, of a cavity dissolved in otherwise dry (and therefore watertight) salt. The size of the cavity is carefully controlled, water leakage is minimised by even lining of the boreholes, and when a safe maximum size of cavity is reached it is filled by waste solids, mainly lime from nearby chemical works. The maximum total amount of salt extraction is only 25 per cent, so there is no danger of subsidence. Since 1928 a salt mine has been developed at Meadowbank, near Winsford, which operates on a pillar and stall working. With at least 30 per cent of the salt left behind as pillars for roof support there have been no collapses.

It is not surprising that the uncontrolled mining, wild brining and bastard brining carried out mainly between about 1780 and 1930 led to the most extensive subsidences and collapses. Individual mines were nearly all on a small scale and each one was worked until the roof started to fall in. The mine was then abandoned. It soon filled with water, which then corroded the pillars and led to the collapse of the roof rocks right up to the surface. The collapse crater on the surface then filled with water, creating an additional hazard to adjacent mines. The last major subsidence of a salt mine occurred in 1928 with the collapse of the Adelaide Mine, the last working mine at Northwich.

The lakes which suddenly develop in subsidence hollows are known locally as flashes; they are the direct result of wild brining, though it is fair to add that they are only a vastly accelerated variety of the linear subsidences which develop over natural brine streams. The Witton Flashes which developed in the 1790s at Northwich and the Top and Bottom Flashes formed in the 1820s at Winsford were the largest flashes; both extended to over 100 acres. Their relentless expansion, as more brine was pumped from beneath them, was aided by the low relief of the region. The Witton Flash was especially troublesome as it grew in the middle of the main industrial area of the period. This particular flash could hardly have been unexpected, surrounded as it was by numerous wild brining operations, but flashes could also develop miles away from the scene of pumping. The subterranean brine streams that are tapped in the wild brining process are fed by water which leaks down from the overlying Pleistocene sediments into the salt beds. This may happen far from the scene of pumping, as the maximum amount of salt solution is obviously produced by the fresh water where it first enters the salt beds. The best example of this 'distant subsidence' is at Billings Green, where a hundred acres of farmland has subsided and flooded since 1900. In a similar fashion various transport routes have been badly affected in the region. A number of canals traverse the salt field, and subsidence damage to them has involved almost continual maintenance problems. Subsidence caused the failure of a canal embankment at Northwich on 21 July 1907, with the result that the canal was completely drained, stranding a number of barges on it at the time. The Crewe to Liverpool railway line was built on level ground through Winsford in 1866, but continuous settlement and corresponding track adjustment meant that by 1882 it was on an embankment 30 feet high.

Concentrated into smaller areas, but with far more catastrophic effect, were the dramatic ground collapses over the areas most heavily mined and then bastard brined. The most extensive damage was in the Dunkirk suburbs of Northwich, which were badly undermined in the second half of the nineteenth century. Dunkirk was the centre of mining and pumping activity at the time. Subsidence was noticed in the previous century, and by 1830 the Witton Flash was well established and kept topped up by Wincham Brook. Houses, roads, canals and the salt works themselves continued to be damaged or destroyed, till in 1880 the area could merit the following contemporary descriptions:

> Houses overhang the street as much as two feet, whilst others lean on their neighbours and push them over.
> A district extending fully one thousand feet in length by as many in breadth, sank rapidly to a depth of forty or fifty feet in the centre.
> Nearly 400 houses and other structures of the value of over £100,000 were more or less seriously injured by subsiding of the ground.
> The area of the mischief is extending yearly.

On the north side of Dunkirk, Platts Hill provided a typical example of the subsidence. The first indication of trouble was on 9 December 1892 when the level of the brine in the shaft at Winnington, not far to the west, rose overnight by 30 feet and continued to rise dramatically over the next two days – clearly some major changes were taking place underground. More brine level changes were recorded, then on 26 May 1893 subsidence developed near the Wincham Road over an area 90 feet by 15 feet. Seventeen days later the subsidence, by now known as Platts Hill Hole, was 132 feet deep and flooded. By the autumn of 1894, the Hole was still growing: its sides were still steep, land was slipping into it, water was still going down it, and it had cracks all around causing yet more damage to adjacent buildings. On 28 July 1896, Platts Hill Hole was measured as 285 feet across and 165 feet maximum depth; it was still growing. Damage to adjacent roadways, buildings and salt works continued on into autumn 1897 as the Hole progressively expanded before it began to stabilise once more.

Not really so typical of the subsidence, but of the same basic origin and rather more spectacular, was the Great Subsidence, which took place at Dunkirk on 6 December 1880. At six o'clock in the morning local people were awakened by a great rumbling noise, and the ground started to heave and shake over an area nearly half a mile across. Air and gas were forced out of cracks in the ground. This was most impressive at Ashton's Old Rock Pit Hole lake where mud geysers spouted 12 feet into the air. Clearly all this air expulsion was due to massive collapses of the old mines and inrushes of water. Then the source of the water was found – a great crack had opened across the course of the Wincham Brook and its entire flow was going underground. At nine o'clock another rift developed in the bed of the stream, damaging part of the adjacent salt works, and the downstream section of Wincham Brook then developed a reverse flow, partly draining a sizeable lake and also diverting most of the flow of the River Weaver into the hole in the ground. The sink itself developed into a great whirlpool with the centre of the vortex 12 feet below the rim. People gathered to watch as the banks were torn away and carried into the depths. At four o'clock there was a great explosion in an adjacent pool, and the crowds scattered as a geyser of mud and water shot 30 feet into the air. Clearly another collapse had taken place, but this seemed to slow down the events of the day, as if it had blocked some underground channel. The whirlpool abated and less water was lost below. An hour later a tall chimney collapsed at the salt works as a saucer of subsidence spread outwards, then at six o'clock in the evening a block of land 500 feet in diameter around Ashton's Old Rock Pit Hole suddenly subsided; two deep holes engulfed two brick kilns and various other parts of the salt works. The next day all was quiet.

The conclusions to be drawn from the Cheshire salt subsidences are fairly straightforward. Natural salt solution and subsidence will always be a problem, even though a relatively small one, in Cheshire. Some prediction can be made as to where natural subsidence will take place, because many of the brine streams are already established in the salt beds and maximum solution takes place where fresh water first enters the salt – perhaps many miles away from the springs. The courses of many of the brine streams are along the strike of the beds, towards the springs, and they appear to be guided by lateral variation in the rock salt, though other brine streams are probably guided by faults. Where Pleistocene sands overlie the dissolving salt beds the ground subsidence is uniform and gentle; where the stronger marl beds overlie there are more sporadic, but more spectacular, collapses, as the marl beds have a limited ability to bridge voids.

The early methods of mining and the bastard brining clearly had disastrous effects on the Northwich area, but these practices have now ceased, as there was no way in which they could be made safe. Wild brining merely exaggerates the effects of natural salt solutions, but it can lead to unpredictable ground failure. It now accounts for less than 10 per cent of Cheshire salt production, and will continue to decrease in importance. Wild brining has not resulted in loss of life since 1930, and the Brine Subsidence Compensation Board now effectively deals with damage to land and buildings due to salt extraction. The Board, which originates from 1891 but only received major powers in 1952, also advises the construction industry on the hazards of ground failure and on precautions against them. Fortunately its activities are ever decreasing, for the modern methods of controlled brining (75 per cent of current output) and mining (15 per cent) do not lead to dangerous subsidences. Salt is now extracted the safe way: the lessons of uncontrolled extraction have been learned.

Subsidence on unconsolidated sediments

Compaction is a perfectly normal, natural process whereby sediments sustain a loss of volume, most frequently due to pressure by layers of overlying sediment. Most sediments are laid down in or by water and they undergo compaction as part of the process that slowly turns them into solid sedimentary rocks. (It should be noted that while geologists refer to this natural volume loss as compaction, civil engineers refer to it as consolidation – hence the term 'unconsolidated sediments' for those which are loose, friable and not yet compacted. To an engineer the term 'compaction' refers to artificial methods, such as rolling or vibrating, of inducing the shrinkage which he calls consolidation. In the following paragraphs 'compaction' will be used in the geological sense.) Almost any sediment will compact to some degree, and those laid down on land commonly form tracts of level ground suitable for development by man; hazards therefore arise when the compaction takes place after development, and particularly when it involves those sediments which sustain maximum shrinkage.

The extreme case of sediment compaction involves the layers of matted vegetable material known as peat. It is difficult to quantify peat compaction, as it is a process which can continue for millions of years until the peat is eventually transformed into coal, but to give an idea of magnitude, peat can be regarded as compacting down to less than 10 per cent of its original volume. The great majority of this shrinkage is due to the removal of water, as it is in the case of most sediment compaction, and consequently it is very easily affected by man's activities. The Fenland region, south of The Wash in eastern England, provides the classic case of peat compaction and land subsidence due to drainage – for peat soils make high-quality agricultural land. An iron pipe was embedded in the underlying rock in 1848 and since then has provided a visible record of the surface lowering. By 1932 the land had subsided 8 feet 10 inches and the thickness of the peat had been reduced to 11 feet 4 inches. Compaction to 56 per cent of the undrained thickness of the peat had taken place in less than a century. Even in 1848 the lower layers of peat would already have been substantially compacted due to the weight of the overlying layers, and compaction is still continuing today. Once water has been removed from peat, further shrinkage takes place due to losses of material by oxidation, and on thin peat layers this can eventually result in insufficient thickness for agriculture. The United States provides examples of peat subsidence, notably in the Florida Everglades. There the ground level drops under cultivation by about one foot per decade, and it has been found that the maximum subsidence is near the drainage channels. The Sacramento Delta in California is a vast region of peat which has been drained for agriculture; it has consequently subsided to below sea-level, with the result that periodic breaks in the artificial river levees cause disastrous flooding.

Peat is not the only material to compact so spectacularly. Dutch engineers have found that drainage, related to the land reclaimed from the sea in Holland, has resulted in the compaction of clays by 25–50 per cent, depending upon grain size and silt content. Compaction of clay does not involve either the amount or the chemical alteration of peat compaction and it is therefore rather more predictable. Temple Church in Bristol, England, was built in the fourteenth and fifteenth centuries, before foundation problems were recognised. Sited on wet ground on the alluvium of the River Avon it barely stood a chance, and the tower now leans 4 feet out of true although it still stands. In a more enlightened age, an industrial estate was recently built in Nottingham, England, on a geologically similar site on the alluvium of the River Trent. Compaction and subsidence were anticipated and allowed for, and a number of large factories have been built and have subsided with little damage, but extra problems have involved the tilting of some small outbuildings sited within the bowl of subsidence created by the larger buildings.

Chronologically in between these two cases was the building of the Transcona grain elevator in central Canada between 1911 and 1913. This was sited on a basin of very fine silty clays originally deposited in a glacial lake. A concrete raft foundation was poured into an excavation 12 feet deep, at which level loading tests had indicated that the clay could bear the necessary load, though no other site investigation was carried out. But when the grain silos were first filled in October 1913, the elevator subsided suddenly by one foot; within twenty-four hours it tipped over sideways to an angle of 26° from the vertical. Fortunately there was little damage to the concrete structure. It was subsequently discovered that while the upper layers of clay were strong enough, the lower layers, from 20 to 40 feet down, were wetter and very much weaker – it was these layers that had not been previously tested and which failed under loading. The elevator was later jacked up, and with foundations put in to a depth of 52 feet on to an unyielding limestone it is still in use today.

Deltas are areas of major sedimentation where subsidence takes place not only due to compaction of the sediment itself but also through other causes. The Mississippi Delta in the United States has been extensively studied, and it is estimated that sediment compaction accounts for an average of more than 0.29 of a foot of subsidence per century. On top of this is crustal warping – that is, sagging of the basement rocks of the earth's crust due to loading by the delta sediments – which accounts for 0.07 feet of movement per century. Also, there is an overall sea-level rise of 0.32 feet per century which affects the delta, as it does all parts of the world. The subsidence figures are only averages, and when one allows for local variation depending on the type of sediment, the prospects for the delta area appear bleak. The town of Balize on the Louisiana side of the delta was abandoned in 1888 during a fever epidemic; just fifty years later the streets were 4 feet below water.

While removal of water is a major cause of sediment compaction, the addition of water can have a similar effect on some sediments. Loess is a very fine wind-deposited silt which occurs in many parts of the world. When it is wetted for the first time it undergoes hydrocompaction – that is, intergranular reorganisation takes place to permit a considerable degree of shrinkage. Problems are therefore encountered when irrigation projects in arid or semi-arid regions run into loess. An area west of Fresno in the Central Valley of California has experienced extensive hydrocompaction subsidence. Irrigation canals have brought water into the area so that the land has been wetted for the first time; the result has been subsidence of up to 15 feet with consequent damage to buildings, roads, pipelines, wells and the canals themselves. The subsidence of part of a canal is particularly unfortunate; more recently this problem has been solved by temporary flooding of the land to allow hydrocompaction to take place before the canal is built.

It can be said fairly that a little subsidence need not be a disadvantage, at least on an inland construction site. But subsidence is serious if it is not uniform for any single building, and differential compaction of ground materials can easily cause this. A terrace of houses built in Nottingham, England, in the early part of this century, provide a good example of this. Many years after the houses were built the end wall of the last house subsided so badly that the house had to be abandoned. Looking for a cause of the subsidence, searchers found an old map which predated the building of the houses; it showed a small quarry, the edge of which underlay the damaged house. The quarry had later been filled, probably at least in part with domestic waste, and no trace of it had remained on the surface. The builder of the houses had not even carried out the first step of a site investigation – the checking of available records and maps. Consequently the house, with one side founded on rock and the other on compactable debris, was doomed. Such tilting and damage to buildings is not only caused by differential compaction as at the Nottingham site.

Any building sited on a weak, plastic clay is really on a delicate balance, and only a very slight unevenness will have a marked and self-generating effect when a building starts to subside. While it can hardly be called a catastrophe, being now such a successful tourist attraction, the Leaning Tower of Pisa takes pride of place in any study of ground failure. The ancient city of Pisa has grown on a wide flat plain, almost at sea-level, overlooked by the mountainous ridges of the Apennines. Although the flatness of the plain has contributed to the growth of Pisa, the soft sediments of which it is made up offer a most unsuitable foundation for any major construction.

The Leaning Tower is actually the bell tower for the adjacent cathedral. Constructed in the eleventh century, the main building of Pisa Cathedral suffered noticeable subsidence soon after it was completed, but due to its more stable height–width ratio it has not significantly tilted. Building of the bell tower started a century later on what was known to be poor ground, with incredibly inadequate foundations. Work started in 1173; a few years later and three storeys higher the tower had already developed such a tilt that the architect abandoned the project and left Pisa. With no further weight being added to it the tower stabilised and movement ceased, so that in 1275 a second builder thought it safe to continue the work after correcting the tilt by merely adding extra layers of masonry on the subsided side – in other words, putting a bend in the tower. But tilting continued, and it was only after a third architect and more one-sided layers of masonry that the tower was finished in 1350. Since then the tilting has continued unabated and the tower is now more then 17 feet out of true.

The technical term to describe the movement which the tower has undergone is 'differential settlement'. Total settlement, or subsidence, of the tower is around 6 feet the entrance doorway is now reached by a flight of steps going downwards – but this is a mean figure; due to the tilt there is about 9 feet of subsidence on the south side and 3 feet on the north side. The differential nature of the subsidence was initially due to a very slight variation in the underlying sediments; once the tilt was established, the shift of the tower's centre of gravity away from its centre of support imposed a turning moment on the building which is increasing as the tilt increases. Immediately beneath the surface is a layer of silts and clays of Pliocene age which is partly volcanic in origin. This layer is about 15 feet thick, and is very plastic and highly compressible. A simple laboratory test of the physical strength of these sediments would make compaction and subsidence under the weight of the tower completely predictable. The foundations of the tower consisted of no more than a ring of masonry 60 feet in diameter, laid just a few feet below ground level. The tower is 180 feet high, making it three times as tall as it base is wide. When such a structure is made to sit on top of the very weak silts and clays, movement is inevitable.

The surface layer beneath the tower grades down into a bed of sand, extending between depths of about 15 and 30 feet. The sand is virtually uncompressible and very much less mobile than the clay–silt beds, and though it does not provide a completely adequate foundation base it has almost certainly played a large part in keeping the rates of subsidence and tilt of the tower to comparatively low levels. What is more, the 10 feet or so of clay and silt between the tower foundations and the sand must now have gained strength due to draining and slow compaction under load, which is why the tower has survived for nearly 700 years. However, the sand bed 15–30 feet down does contain thin zones of clay and silt which are thicker towards the south, and their greater compressibility accounted for the initial tilt of the tower. What is more, beneath the sand there is more weak plastic clay extending to a depth of 130 feet, where at last a substantial lower bed of sand is met. Continued movement in the top three layers – the clays and silts, the upper sand, and the lower clay – is bound to take place, and therefore the lean on the tower must increase due to its already established turning movement.

What is the future of the famous tower? Modern engineering techniques are quite capable of stabilising it, in its present position, by underpinning it with foundations keyed to the sand layer 130 feet down. Injection of the underlying sediment with liquid cement grout has already been tried – with no noticeable effect. Something else as bold as underpinning is required, and there is naturally some concern about working beneath such a delicately balanced structure. Plans have been made for many years and there are still more in hand. With luck they will be carried out, successfully; because without help from man, given another century or so the tower will fall over.

Subsidence due to withdrawal of ground fluids

Compaction of soft sediments, leading to ground subsidence, is almost impossible to prevent if the material is loaded by the construction of some large building. The precise mechanisms of the compaction are varied but in many cases involve the squeezing out of intergranular water. Sand is virtually incompressable and water is not easily squeezed out from it. If however the intergranular water is pumped from sand, and adjacent silts and clays, the loss of support from the hydrostatic pressure of the groundwater can result in significant compaction and consequent ground movement. The worldwide importance of sands, particularly uncemented or poorly consolidated varieties in mixed sediment sequences, as high-yield aquifers, means that their groundwater has been extensively pumped – in many cases with pronounced effect on surface levels.

The San Joaquin Valley in central California receives very little rainfall; its intensive agriculture owes its existence to irrigation water, much of which has been pumped out of the sediments beneath the valley floor. Sands and coarse silts, in some places more than 2000 feet thick, floor the valley. They have been heavily pumped for most of the present century, resulting in ground subsidence affecting areas of many hundreds of square miles, with a maximum movement of over 28 feet. The subsidence corresponded to the lowering of the artesian head and the consequent loss of hydrostatic support, and on average for every 20–30 feet that the artesian head was lowered the ground settled one foot. As this is an inland region of agricultural land, such subsidence, even with the ground fissuring which accompanies the distortion of the sediments, need not be of any great consequence. It is ironic that the main damage in the San Joaquin Valley has been to the various components of the irrigation schemes which initially caused the subsidence. Ground movement has destroyed many of the wells (well damage cost around a million dollars per year over the worst period), and irrigation canals, with their very low gradients, have had to be continually repaired. Long embankments have been necessary to carry the canals through the subsided areas without flooding them. Clearly the answer to the San Joaquin Valley subsidence problem is to stop pumping the groundwater. The partial replacement of underground water supplies by water imported from the mountains has allowed the rate of ground subsidence to slow down considerably.

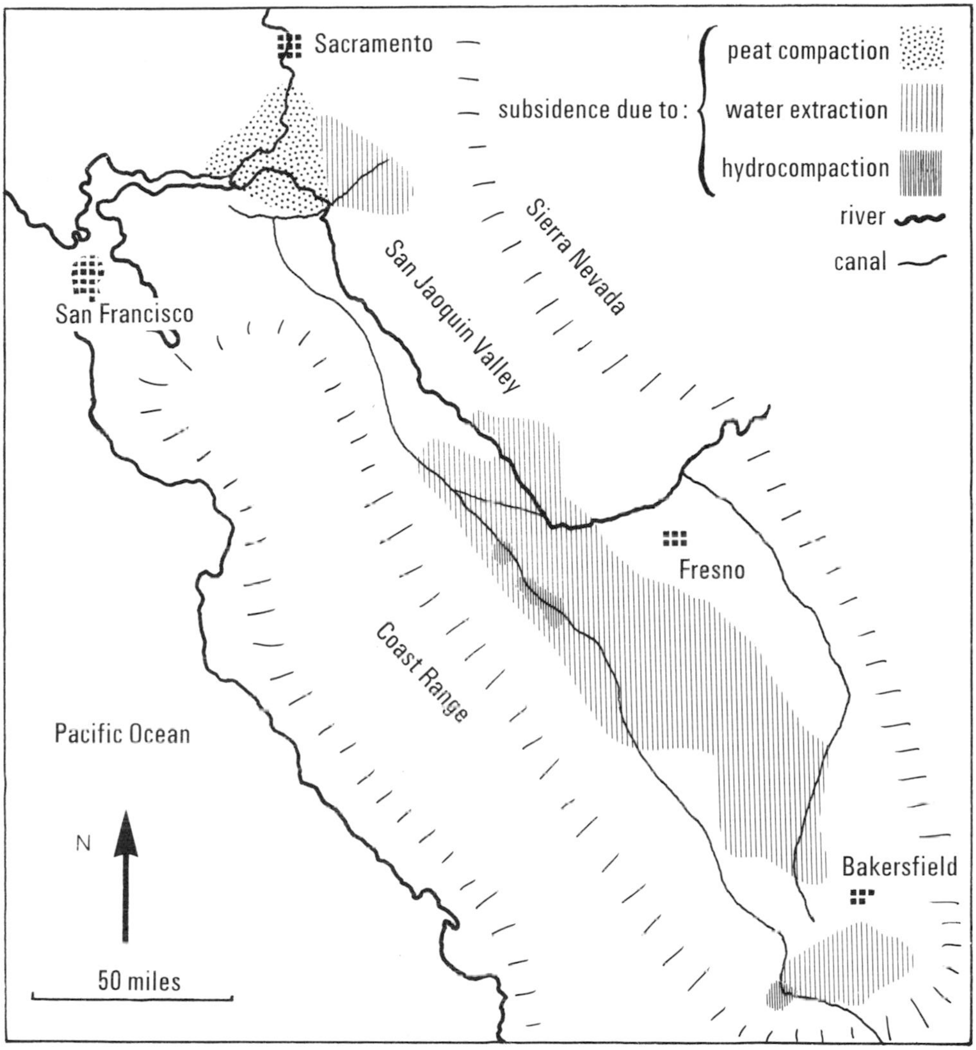
Sacramento
subsidence due to:
peat compaction
water extraction
hydrocompaction
river
canal
San Francisco
Sierra Nevada
San Jaoquin Valley
Fresno
Coast Range
Pacific Ocean
N
Bakersfield
50 miles

The Central Valley of California which has suffered serious ground subsidence from three different causes.

Comparable land subsidence in urban areas, particularly those which are critically close to sea-level, can have a far more damaging effect. A large part of the city of Tokyo has suffered subsidence, at one time at a rate of 6 inches per year, due to water extraction from underlying silts. Many of the larger buildings were founded on deeper layers of sound rock, so that they appeared to rise from the ground as the surrounding surface subsided. The movement was so great that by 1961 some 15 square miles of suburbs were below sea-level – protected only by large and expensive sea-walls. In China, the city of Shanghai has had similar problems. With 1000 feet of unconsolidated sediments containing many overpumped aquifers, the total amount of settlement in the dockyard area has been 8 feet between 1921 and 1973. Increasingly frequent flooding of the docks area prompted efforts to reduce the rates of subsidence, and these have included pumping water back into the boreholes during the wet seasons in order to maintain water-table levels even when the groundwater is pumped in the dry seasons.

It is not only sands and silts that may settle with groundwater extraction. In London, water has been extensively pumped from the chalk which underlies the city, with the result that the artesian head has dropped by hundreds of feet. The chalk itself is still in the saturated zone and has not compacted at all, but the loss of pore-water pressure in the overlying London Clay has resulted in compaction of this bed. Fortunately the resultant ground subsidence is no more than one foot, and this has not been enough to have any significant effect, even where the centre of the subsiding basin is crossed by the River Thames.

Subsidence of the area around Savannah, Georgia, has also been attributed to groundwater extraction, and in this case the rock concerned is a limestone. Most limestones are adequately strong, even when highly fissured aquifers, to support any weight without movement, but the Tertiary Ocala Limestone beneath Savannah is a very porous, poorly consolidated variety, and does compact when its pore-water pressure is reduced. Not far to the west, the Houston–Galveston region in Texas has also subsided very seriously. Only monitored since 1943, subsidence had locally exceeded 5 feet by 1964 and was still proceeding at a rate of 3 inches a year. While most of the settlement is undoubtedly due to water extraction from the various sand aquifers, some of it is due to removal of another liquid – oil, which is taken from deeper-lying beds of permeable sediments. Unfortunately, the extraction of any liquid from an inadequately consolidated sediment may cause compaction and ground subsidence. The city of Niigata in Japan has suffered disastrous subsidence, in some parts to below sea-level, due to the extraction of methane-bearing brine solutions. But after water, oil has provided the most subsidence problems, and Los Angeles provides a spectacular example.

The port area of Long Beach, at the southern end of Los Angeles, lies directly above the highly productive privately owned Wilmington oilfields. Large quantities of both oil and water have been pumped from a gentle dome in the 6000 feet of sediments. The result is an elliptical bowl of subsidence 6 miles across, with the same plan shape as the underlying geological structure. In the centre of this bowl, the vertical subsidence has totalled 29 feet in the period 1928–71. Horizontal movement on the sides of the bowl has locally been as much as 9 feet. The cost of damage in the city area has exceeded a hundred million dollars, and one of the worst sufferers has been the great Naval Dockyard, much of which is now well below sea-level and surrounded by high concrete walls which had to be continually built up as the sea threatened to overtop them. By 1957 the situation was so bad in Long Beach that the US Department of Justice stepped in with injuctions against the operators of the oil wells. The result was a mammoth scheme to pump millions of gallons of water back into the ground through two hundred wells. Not only would this re-pressurise the sediments and therefore counter the subsidence, it would also pump more oil out of the other wells still used for extraction. Water injection is in fact a standard method of increasing recovery in an oilfield, though this was really a secondary benefit at Wilmington. The operation was so successful that by 1963 the subsidence had been largely stopped, and in places reversed.

Although uplift of the ground by water injection has taken place in the Wilmington oilfield, the possibility of complete recovery to the pre-subsidence levels is almost nil. There are many factors to be taken into consideration in such a subsidence prevention scheme, and the Wilmington dome provided a relatively simple situation. Unfortunately, water injection is not the simple answer to this type of problem, which is significant for two other cities still suffering from subsidence – Venice and Mexico City.

Famous throughout the world because of its almost unique situation, Venice is not only a major city but also a work of art, and it is in very real danger of being destroyed as it sinks steadily beneath sea-level. Founded more than 1300 years ago, the city lies almost in the centre of a great lagoon 35 miles long and 6 miles wide. The lagoon is separated from the Adriatic Sea by a long series of sand bars which were reinforced with sea walls as long ago as the eighteenth century, leaving three open channels into the lagoon. Inland a wide plain of sediments extends for many miles westwards all the way up the Po Valley, and northwards to the foothills of the Italian Alps and the Dolomites.

Venice has long suffered from subsidence and inadequate foundations. In 1902 a bell tower, the Campanile of St Mark's Cathedral, collapsed in a heap of rubble. But few buildings have made such a dramatic exit; instead there has been a gradual gnawing away at foundations as the whole area steadily subsides. Approximately 70 per cent of the city is at a height no more than 4 feet above mean sea-level, and this height is regularly exceeded by flooding. Known as *acqua alta* (high water), the periods of flooding are due to a combination of wind, tide, large-scale oscillations in the Adriatic Sea, rainfall and lowered atmospheric pressure. The worst *acqua alta* was in 1966, when damage ran to a total cost of £30 million. The flooding is becoming more regular; around the turn of the century it averaged once every five years, but by 1930 it was an annual event, and since 1960 it has occurred three times a year. The submergence of St Mark's Square is now barely a newsworthy event. The increasingly frequent flooding is the most obvious sign of the unmitigating subsidence of this unique city.

The buildings of Venice have been constructed on wooden piles sunk into the floor of what were the very shallow parts of the lagoon. The sediments which floor the lagoon are unconsolidated materials of Quaternary age which have a thickness of 2650 feet, and beneath them is more unconsolidated sediment dating to the Pliocene. The Quaternary sediments are made up of approximately 50 per cent sands, 35 per cent silts and 15 per cent silty clays. With such foundations in a marine deltaic environment, subsidence must be expected; in Venice there are a variety of reasons for it.

Archaeological explorations have revealed that subsidence of the lagoon area since prehistoric times has been locally as much as 20 feet, and since Roman times has totalled between 6 and 10 feet. This gives an average annual amount of subsidence of 0.04 inchs during these earlier centuries – a rate that would be expected in any deltaic region where sediment is accumulating. The main Po delta is not far south of Venice and deposition there will induce crustal warping as the bedrock subsides under the accumulated load. In addition, the fact that all the half-mile-thick Quaternary sediments are of shallow water origin indicates that subsidence over that period must have also been in the order of half a mile. At the same time these sediments must be compressed as they are progressively buried, but laboratory tests on material from boreholes beneath Venice have shown that such primary compaction is not a significant contributor to the city's subsidence.

During the twentieth century the rate of subsidence has increased dramatically, as these figures for the average subsidence per year show:

1926–42	0.09 inch
1943–52	0.14 inch
1953–61	0.20 inch

Clearly some new factors have become involved, and the most important is groundwater extraction. Venice's water has always come from shallow wells sunk into the many aquifers within the Quaternary succession, but since the turn of the century there has been an ever-increasing demand for water. Since 1930 the Marghera industrial development, just a few miles west of Venice, has sunk over 7000 wells into the sub-lagoon sediments. Heavy pumping has lowered the artesian head by over 60 feet beneath Marghera and more than 25 feet below Venice; the resultant loss of pore-water pressure must have initiated considerable subsidence. Furthermore, it has been discovered that most of the sediment compaction beneath Venice has been taking place between depths of 350 and 1000 feet, and the majority of the Marghera wells are to aquifers at depths ranging from 600 to 1000 feet. Venice has been fortunate in that the groundwater removal has resulted in much less compaction than has been recorded in other parts of the world. Subsidence at Venice has averaged about 0.2 inchs per foot of fall in the artesian head, while California's Central Valley has recorded rates six times as high, and at Mexico City settlement has been as high as 2 inches for every foot of artesian head lowering.

There have been other factors to account for the steady sinking of Venice. The extensive construction in the lagoon region in the present century has imposed a greater loading on the sediments, and this must have had some effect. Natural gas was pumped from the Quaternary sediments beneath the Po delta from 1935, until pumping was banned in 1955 because of its subsidence effects. More recently, it has been suggested that the gas extraction only caused sinking in a zone well south of Venice itself. Then, on top of all the different types of land subsidence, there has been the additional rise in sea-level. This is a worldwide phenomenon due to gradual melting of polar ice as the world's mean temperature steadily rises; it has accounted for an extra 0.06 inches per year.

The sinking of Venice therefore comes down to two causes – a small amount of natural subsidence combined with the natural rise in sea-level, and the much greater subsidence induced by groundwater extraction. Subsidence due to the latter can of course be prevented, but it was only the disastrous flooding of 1966 which prompted government action. In 1973 the Law of Venice was passed, setting aside over £200 million to preserve the city. The main result was a ban on pumping water from beneath Marghera, compensated for by the building of an aqueduct to bring water from the River Sile to the north. Due to this move, the artesian heads have started to rise in the sediments beneath Venice and the subsidence in the last few years has been greatly reduced. It has not altogether stopped, because of the continuing natural processes. More must be done; two schemes stand out as possibilities from the many proposals that have been made.

One of these is to place enormous movable barrages in the channels between the lagoon and the Adriatic. In high-water conditions these barrages could be closed to prevent excessively high water-levels in the city. One disadvantage of this scheme would be a great reduction in tidal scour in the canals of Venice; at present this is all that keeps the city from fouling up with sewage, which is just dumped in the canals. An extra cost in this scheme would therefore be the construction of a modern sewage system for the whole city. While this plan would take care of high-water conditions, it would not prevent subsidence, and future subsidence would lead to more and more frequent closing of the barrages and the eventual isolation of the lagoon.

A second, and bolder, scheme involves actually lifting the whole city. A wall 400 feet deep and 8 miles long would be sunk into the lagoon floor completely surrounding the city. It would therefore isolate the various sand aquifers in the sediments immediately beneath the city from their lateral continuations beneath the rest of the lagoon, because the sand beds are essentially horizontal and are sealed off downwards by impermeable beds of clay. Water could then be pumped back into the aquifers, increasing the pore-water pressure and literally raising the city as the sediments re-expanded to and beyond their original volume. Problems have been envisaged with frictional drag against the sunken walls, causing a doming of the city site, but this scheme does seem to offer a more permanent answer than the barrages, and the results of the water injection in Los Angeles suggest that it may work. If it doesn't work, Venice will slowly disappear beneath the waters of its famous lagoon.

Mexico City has an impressive situation, lying in a broad flat-floored basin at an altitude of 7400 feet, surrounded by towering mountains. The basin is over 50 miles long by an average of 15 miles wide, and is crossed by many small rivers. The flat floor of the basin is due to the thick layer of sediments which underlies it and distinguishes it from the older limestones and volcanic rocks of the surrounding mountains. Essentially the sediments are coarse sands overlain by fine clays, but some details of the succession are very significant, and the main beds are as follows:

		depth below the surface
	silts, sands (and some artificial fill)	0–20 feet
Upper Pleistocene lacustrine deposits	upper soft clay	20–110 feet
	coarse cemented sand	110–125 feet
	lower soft clay (with some sand layers)	125–170 feet
Lower Pleistocene sands and gravels		more than 170 feet

The lower series of sands and gravels, which extends to depths of at least 1700 feet, consists mainly of river-deposited fragments of volcanic andesite, which are highly productive aquifers. Above these the two thick units of Upper Pleistocene clays are similar, and may best be described as bentonites. This is because they consist mainly of the clay mineral montmorillonite, together with smaller proportions of other clay minerals and quartz silt. Though all clay minerals have some ability to attach water to themselves with weak electric bonds, montmorillonite exhibits this property best of all. When magnified thousands of times and viewed in an electron microscope, the crystal structure of montmorillonite can be seen to consist of hollow tubes, rather like macaroni, which give it great water-absorbent properties. The net result is that the upper clay which underlies Mexico City has an average porosity of 88 per cent, while the lower clay has a porosity of about 82 per cent. In other words, 88 per cent, or seven-eighths, of the 'upper soft clay' consists of water, and only 12 per cent of solid mineral matter. The fact that the water is bonded, even though very weakly, to the clay minerals means that the material is not just a liquid slurry but a very soft plastic clay. Nevertheless, it is clearly a bad foundation for a major city, unfortunately established long before the days of reasonable site investigation.

Subsidence was first noticed in Mexico City late in the nineteenth century; the time coincided with the expansion of well pumping, taking water from the excellent sand aquifers below the depth of 170 feet. By 1959 most of the city had subsided by 13 feet or more, and the worst affected areas were down by 25 feet. The actual rates of subsidence had shown a marked change as more water was pumped out to support a rapidly expanding city. From 1898 to 1938 subsidence averaged 1.6 inches per year; for the next decade the figure was up to 6 inches per year, and over the period 1948–52 the average subsidence of the city was 1 foot per year, and locally over 2 feet. By 1948 it was recognised that water extraction was the cause of the subsidence of Mexico City, yet for many years after that there were more than 3000 wells supplying the expanding city and at the same time eating away its foundations.

The artesian head within the main aquifers was roughly at ground level before pumping, but by the late 1950s it had fallen between 65 and 110 feet below the surface. Clearly the loss of supporting hydrostatic pressure was instantaneous in the sands and gravels, but the very low permeability of the overlying clay layers meant that the water was slow to drain from them – the bonding between the clay and the water did therefore have one advantage. This was fortunate because it was the loss of pore-water pressure in the clays which was causing the ground subsidence, which therefore took place slowly, with a delayed reaction. One spectacular effect of the ground subsidence was that the many well casings protruded from the ground because they were sunk down to the sands below the clays. One well was sunk to a depth of 300 feet and left with its steel casing level with the ground. By 1954 the area in which it was sited had subsided 20 feet, and the well casing stood 18 feet above the ground – showing dramatically that almost all the subsidence was due to compaction within the top 300 feet of sediments, essentially in the layers of very compressible clays.

Protruding well casings were unfortunately not the only effects of the subsidence. Buildings were damaged, and water transport systems and drainage channels suffered badly, especially where there was differential subsidence induced by variable loading. Perhaps the most spectacular consequences were suffered by the magnificent Palace of Fine Arts, right in the middle of the city. Construction of the palace started in 1904, but did not finish until 1934. Its only foundation was an inadequate 10 foot thick mat of concrete laid with its top at surface level. Even before building had started, the concrete mat had noticeably sagged in the middle, and as construction continued it sank even further into the ground. By 1908 the partly constructed building had sunk over 5 feet, and two years later a crack appeared in the foundation mat. The year 1910 saw an attempt at stabilising the palace, when 70,000 bags of cement were injected as grout into the underlying clay. But the fine-grained nature of the clay did not permit a uniform distribution of the grout, and instead of cementing and stabilising the sediment, the grout settled in patches and merely added to the weight loaded on to the clay – probably hastening further subsidence. Five years later, steel sheet piling was sunk in a loop around the palace to stop what was thought to be lateral migration of the clay under loading; but this was also a waste of effort because the clay was only compacting due to downward movement of its pore water. However, construction continued, and the completed palace sank further into the ground. It has now settled over 10 feet below the level of the surrounding streets – the differential subsidence is due to its enormous weight. Flights of steps lead downwards into the palace, and access to the first floor is easier than to the ground floor. The lighter door archways have sunk less and have consequently broken from the main building, and the surrounding streets are cracked and tilted towards the palace.

Underpinning – the insertion of adequate bearing piles put down to a suitable foundation, namely the sand layer 110 feet down – would easily stop the subsidence of the Palace of Fine Arts; it is quite a feasible engineering project. Deep piling has been used on many of the modern buildings in the city – which like the well casings have ended up above ground level as the surrounding streets continued to subside. This was not, therefore, the complete answer to the problems of Mexico City. Instead the subsidence would have to be stopped at its source, by curtailing groundwater extraction. In 1952 water began to be imported into the city; groundwater pumping was stopped, and the following year water was pumped back into the overdrawn aquifers. The result was that by 1974 subsidence of the city was down to less than an inch per year, which is quite manageable. A fine example of the understanding of the engineering problems involved in the city's subsidence is the Tower Latino Americana. This forty-three storey office block, completed in 1951, was founded on piles 110 feet deep to the sandstone bed, and surrounded by the now unpumped and uncompacting clays. It is only one block away from the Palace of Fine Arts – and its entrance is at street level.

Subsidence and collapse on cavernous limestone

Limestone is one rock known throughout the world for its likelihood of containing caves. Such completely open voids within rock obviously present a hazard to the stability of the ground surface, and indeed when the layers of rock overlying a cave do fail, the resultant subsidence tends to be abrupt, in complete contrast to the slow settlement encountered with subsidence on soft sediments. On the other hand, limestone is commonly a very strong rock (it is frequently used as building stone) and is therefore capable of bridging over quite large voids. Natural cave chambers occur with diameters of up to 800 feet. There tends to be a partial collapse of their ceilings until stable domed shapes are arrived at, though they are essentially stable as long as there is an adequate thickness of roof rock. Most cave passages and rooms are much smaller than this, and even in the most highly cavernous regions the ratio of cave to remaining rock is extremely small. Even in weaker, heavily fractured limestones, underground collapse is normally quite small scale and localised.

The strength of limestone, the extreme slowness of rock solution processes and the limited size of most caves all combine to make the collapse of a cave roof a comparatively rare event. Florida contains vast areas of limestone, and the central part of the state experienced a cave collapse a few years ago. A steep-sided hole 100 feet deep and about 110 feet in diameter developed overnight in open country, without any warning; it appeared to have been caused by the collapse of the thin roof of a fairly sizeable cave. Chalk is a fine-grained variety of limestone with a distinctively low strength, and it floors very large areas in southern England and northern France. In France, not far from Troyes, a collapse hole opened overnight in a cabbage field in the late 1960s. The result was a shaft 50 feet deep and 30 feet in diameter with vertical walls of chalk and a debris floor.

While most other cases of limestone cave breakdown have been on a much smaller scale, there have been instances of potential dangers with construction schemes. In 1956 it was proposed to erect school buildings on an area of open ground at Pen Park, in Bristol, England. Local historical records made reference to a large cave with a vertical entrance which had been blocked in a century earlier, after a man had fallen to his death. The roof of the main cavern was claimed to be within 20 feet of the surface. The entrance was reopened and the cave accurately surveyed – as a result of this investigation the school was resited.

Limestone is not the only rock to contain caves. Gypsum and rock salt may both be cavernous, as mentioned earlier in this chapter, but their higher solubility rates and lower strengths mean that the process of subsidence will be different. Subsidence in basalt lava, however, is comparable to that in limestone. Lava flows produced by a volcano consist of molten rock which cools and solidifies most rapidly on the upper surface. With very fluid basaltic lavas, this may then result in lower layers of lava flowing away beneath a solidified crust, leaving a lava cave. The distinctive feature of lava caves is that they are nearly always close to the surface, and their thin roofs are prone to collapse. This represents an obvious hazard where roads and houses are built in lava cave regions, such as the Mount Hood region in Washington, DC, or many regions of Iceland. In Iceland, the main road south from Reykjavik was discovered in 1970 to cross over the Raufarholshellir lava cave; a thickness of no more than 13 feet of crumbly basalt supported the road over a cave passage 25 feet in diameter. The possibility of collapse is obvious, though whether it will take place next year or in ten years' time, nobody knows. At present the rate of roof collapse is monitored by regularly checking the amount of debris on the cave floor – a rather inadequate way of assessing the current strength of the jointed rock arched over the cave; and the road remains where it was.

While the collapse of rock due to its failure to bridge across a cave is a rare occurrence, the subsidence and collapse of softer sediments lying on top of pitted and cavernous limestone is all too common. A great proportion of the world's very extensive limestone outcrops is covered by some form of young unconsolidated sediment – mostly river-borne alluvium or glacial boulder clay. Both of these materials tend to be semi-permeable, so that water soaks down through them and into the limestone beneath. Where the limestones are fractured, solution results in open fissures through the rock. The water then washes the finer material out of the overlying sediment and down through the fissures, leaving cavities in the limestone bridged over by the unstable, uncemented, coarse fraction of the sediment. Eventually collapse takes place as this material drops into the limestone fissure, and the result is a conical depression on the surface known as a subsidence doline or, particularly in America, a sinkhole. This kind of sinkhole formation tends to be abrupt, although there is another kind of sinkhole resulting from solution over a long period of time: this usually leaves a very irregular surface on the top of the limestone, and when covered by younger sediment a smooth ground profile may hide greatly differing thicknesses of sediment sitting on the pitted and pocketed limestone. Compaction of the thicker pockets of sediment may then result in shallow subsidence depressions on the surface, which are frequently accompanied by sinkhole collapses as downward leaching takes place simultaneously.

Subsidence dolines, or sinkholes, formed in limestone regions are common natural events, and in many cases the limestone cave beneath is opened to the sky. In 1944 on Ireby Fell in the English Pennines, a 10-foot-thick layer of boulder clay collapsed and revealed a shaft in the limestone 25 feet in diameter and 40 feet deep with a cave passage leading off at floor level. Twenty years later a collapse hole developed on the Salem Plateau, Missouri, and even though it was 42 feet in diameter and 65 feet deep it had formed entirely in the sediments above the limestone. In 1966 another sinkhole opened up in the bed of Sycamore Creek, also in Missouri; it was 60 feet deep and 25 feet across but was rapidly filled with stream-washed gravels. Two years later a similarly large shaft opened up at Manor Farm in the Mendip Hills. The collapse of a huge plug of surface debris during a long heavy storm revealed a deep shaft reaching down into the limestone. Fortunately none of these four unpredictable natural collapses caused any material damage.

The prediction of such collapse depends on being able to locate the relevant cavity in the rock. Where some part of the cave is open to the surface, direct exploration is possible. A closely spaced grid of boreholes will of course locate any cave, but this is an exceptionally expensive operation. Research into predicting the location of caves from geological considerations has only shown that they are largely unpredictable. Various remote sensing techniques have been tried, but the results have been rather mixed. Gravity surveys can locate very large chambers or buried sinkholes, but they do not work to fine enough detail for most cases. Similarly, seismic geophysics has not been able to pinpoint caves, though it can be used to identify the floor shapes of filled sinkholes. Electrical resistivity surveys have successfully located zones of heavily fissured limestones, and even pinpointed the individual cave passage at Pen Park Hole in Bristol prior to its re-excavation. Ordinary air photography has had very limited success in locating caves or filled sinkholes, but infra-red photography and microwave radiometry (the latter more successfully) have been able to detect variations in ground temperature and water distribution which in turn relate to cave patterns in some cases. On the whole, cave detection and collapse prediction is difficult, and this is doubly unfortunate in light of the increasing frequency of sinkhole collapse, when the natural balance is disturbed by man's activities.

So many projects – road construction, building-site excavation, land drainage or groundwater extraction – result in changes in patterns of water movement, and beds of unconsolidated sediment overlying cavernous limestone are particularly susceptible to movement with such change. Removal of water increases the drawdown into the limestone, and therefore the compaction, and an increase in water flow results in more washing down of sediment. Either way, subsidence is the consequence, and the nature and effect can be devastating.

The region around Birmingham, Alabama, is underlain by thick dolomitic limestones covered by a blanket of clay between 2 and 70 feet thick, due to the irregular erosion of the top of the limestone. Sinkholes were almost unknown in the area until drainage in two quarries lowered the local water-table during the late

1950s. Throughout the 1960s numerous collapses occurred as the clay was washed down into the limestone fissures. Factories, roads and service systems were damaged on an industrial estate, and in one spectacular case a totally unpredictable sinkhole developed in the middle of a construction site soon after foundations were laid. The Frisco railroad was also damaged, and 150 sinkholes of varying sizes opened up along Interstate Highway 459 and its immediately adjacent land. Only the raising of the local water-table (and consequent flooding of the quarries), or the installation of very expensive and efficient drainage systems could save the continuing undermining of the region. Even more disastrous was the fate of a road bridge near Tarpon Springs in the neighbouring state of Florida. A sinkhole collapse developed beneath the bridge one January night in 1969 – the collapse of three of the bridge supports was so abrupt that traffic was unable to stop and one person was drowned.

Not far from Tarpon Springs, at Weeki Wachee, a sinkhole opened up and engulfed a drilling rig in September 1974; again clay was overlying fissured limestone. The drill was 200 feet down in the limestone when it hit a fissure and the sudden rush of water triggered the failure of the clay. The ground rumbled and cracked and the drilling crew had to leap to safety. As the hole opened up, the truck-mounted rig fell into it, followed by a second truck with a water tank, pumps, tools and even pine trees. Within ten minutes, $100,000 worth of equipment was lost irretrievably in a hole 150 feet across and 75 feet deep, filled nearly to the brim with water.

Hershey Valley lies in the Appalachian Mountains in Pennsylvania. It is floored by steeply dipping Ordovician limestones and bounded on either side by shale and sandstone; a layer of unconsolidated sediment and soil sits up to 60 feet thick on most of the limestone. The town of Hershey, including the large Hershey chocolate factory, stands on the valley floor. The location of the factory was partly determined by the presence of strong permanent springs nearby. Two miles to the north-east, a quarry and underground mine operated to extract a very pure band from the steeply inclined limestone. When the mine deepened its operations in 1949 enormous quantities of water were pumped out of the cavernous limestone, resulting in a major lowering of the water-table (which had previously stood only 30 feet below most of the valley floor). The effect was immediate. Wells dried up, spring flows declined for the first time ever and eventually dried up, streams ceased to flow – and sinkholes developed. Within five months there were a hundred sinkholes in the valley floor; they were mostly cylindrical collapse holes 5–20 feet across and up to 25 feet deep. Bridges, buildings and roads were lost and damaged, though fortunately no lives were lost. The sinkholes had obviously been caused by the flushing down of sediment into limestone fissures, prompted in turn by the increased drawdown with the lowering of the water table. Most of the sinkholes occurred where the water-table had dropped by 50 feet or more. As the area of sinkhole development extended towards the chocolate factory, the Hershey Chocolate Corporation, realising that groundwater changes were the cause of the trouble, started injecting water into their boreholes, thereby raising the water table again. This succeeded in slowing the subsidence, but also involved even more pumping in the limestone mine if it was not to be flooded. Consequently, in 1950, the chocolate company and the mining company became involved in complex litigation with each other. The result was that a cement grout screen was injected into the limestone around the mine, isolating it hydrologically and permitting mining to go on while surrounded by a

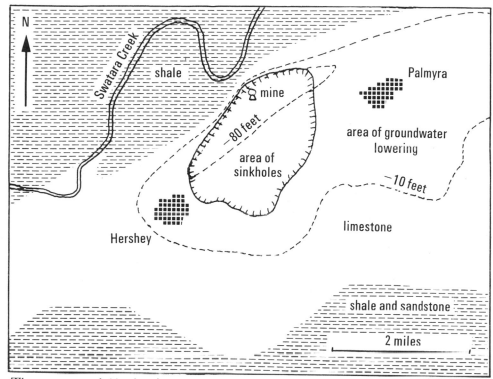

The area around Hershey in Pennsylvania where drainage of the limestone by a mining company promoted sinkhole development far beyond the confines of the mine.

high water-table in the valley. This was a complete success and mining continued without associated sinkhole development until 1953 when the mine was purchased by the chocolate company and allowed to flood.

The construction of a building or road will always interfere with groundwater movement, however efficient the drainage installations may be. The results of this can be seen in countless places in the form of sediment overlying fissured limestone. In August 1910 three sinkholes more than 50 feet across engulfed parts of four buildings in the town of Staunton, Virginia. During 1950 a series of holes opened up in roads in the middle of Bridgend in Wales. One house was destroyed and three more damaged when a sinkhole 80 feet in diameter developed in the town of Castleberry, Florida, in 1965. Then in January 1964, after a period of particularly heavy rain, a sinkhole opened up beneath a house in Farmington, Missouri; the hole was 75 feet deep, and the basement of the house disappeared into murky waters, followed by the 300 truckloads of rubble needed to fill it up. All these cases involved the collapse of sediment into totally unpredicted limestone fissures. Slightly different was a case at Akron, Ohio, in 1969. A section of foundations for a two-storey department store had been laid on soft clay and silt, filling in a buried sinkhole which lay in an irregular surface of limestone just below ground level. The sinkhole did not collapse, but the clay compacted and settled just enough to distort the building, the rest of which was founded on solid limestone. Consequently the building collapsed, injuring ten people and killing one. Clearly, the pre-

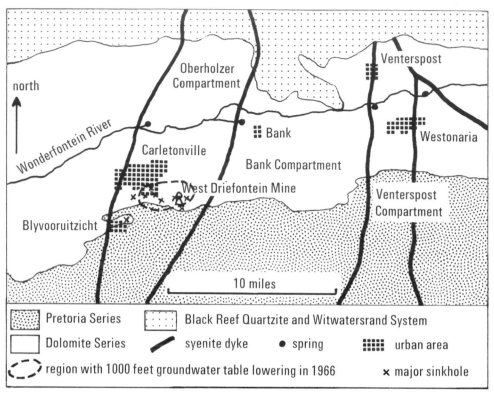

A geological map of the gold mining region in South Africa's Rand where disastrous sinkholes were the direct result of dewatering the dolomite bedrock.

construction programme of drillholes had not been spaced closely enough to locate the sinkhole in the conditions prevailing at the site. The building has since been reconstructed – on a concrete raft.

Of all the known cases of man-induced subsidence, the largest, most extensive and most catastrophic have occurred in the gold mining area of South Africa. The Wonderfontein Valley is a broad shallow valley some 5–10 miles across which lies at the western end of the Rand region centred on Johannesburg. Mining is one of the major industries in the Rand area. It currently produces nearly four-fifths of the free world's gold, and the richest gold mines are located in the Wonderfontein Valley. Within the valley a series of towns, mainly clustered around the mines, house 150,000 people. Although the first mine in the valley was only opened in 1938, one at Carletonville now reaches to a world record depth of 12,600 feet.

All the gold is found in thin beds of quartzite and conglomerate in the Witwatersrand Series – an early Pre-Cambrian sequence, mainly of quartzites and shales. However, the main gold-bearing beds (or reefs as they are called) reach only about 3000 feet below the surface because they are unconformably overlain by a series of later Pre-Cambrian rocks. These have the thin Black Reef Quartzite at their base, followed by the 4000-foot-thick Dolomite Series which consists of massive cavernous dolomitic limestones with variable amounts of insoluble chert. Above these are the Pretoria Series shales, quartzites and lavas. All these beds dip south at between 6° and 12°, so that the outcrops of the different rocks occur in roughly east–west bands, parallel to the valley. The dolomites floor most of the valley, while the Pretoria Series crops out on the hills to the south and the Black Reef Quartzite rises to the north. Deposited over all are the thick sandstones, shales and coals of the Karoo Beds, which have since been mostly eroded away and remain only in patches. Youngest of all the sediments are the various sands and gravels of Quaternary age.

The dolomites are rarely exposed at the surface because of the thick veneer of unconsolidated sediment. This is rarely less than 30 feet thick; it often exceedes a few hundred feet and in places reaches a depth of over 500 feet. This material consists of the Quaternary sands and gravels and the very deep weathered zones of Karoo sediment and dolomite – the latter containing mostly chert debris, with associated sands, clays and manganese wad. One other important element of the geology is the series of syenite dykes, vertical sheets mostly 100–200 feet thick which are oriented north–south across the valley.

Hydrologically the Wonderfontein Valley is probably unique. Surface drainage is westwards, but the dolomites are extremely permeable aquifers so that there is also an enormous amount of groundwater movement. The cross-cutting syenite dykes divide the dolomite very efficiently into hydrologically independent blocks, known as compartments – consequently groundwater builds up within each compartment until it overflows at the lowest point where the down-valley dyke is exposed at the surface. The result is the series of powerful springs, known locally as eyes, which occur just upstream of each dyke close to the course of the Wonderfontein River, and within each compartment the water-table has naturally stabilised at a level very close to that of its own eye.

The vast quantities of water within the dolomite have presented a constant difficulty to the mining of the gold from the underlying beds. For many years the mines simply maintained pumping programmes to keep pace with the water draining down into the Witwatersrand quartzites and then into the mine. But then in the 1950s a start was made on major programmes of dewatering the dolomites – pumping out all the water to remove the ever-present threat of flooding the mines beneath. The watertight nature of the syenite dykes allowed each compartment to be dewatered independently and the sequence of events over the next twenty years tells the story.

1955	The dewatering of the Venterspost Compartment was started.
1957	Sinkholes began to appear in the Venterspost Compartment; more and more developed over the next four years.
1960	A major dewatering programme was started in the Oberholzer Compartment; within a short time the Oberholzer Eye had dried up and sinkholes started to develop.
1962	A vertical-sided sinkhole 180 feet in diameter and 100 feet deep collapsed without warning and engulfed the crushing plant of the West Driefontein mine, causing 29 deaths.
1963	Slow subsidence throughout the year saw the floor of the sinkhole known as Schutte's Depression in Carletonville lowered by 20 feet, completely destroying one house.
1964	A sinkhole 200 feet across opened up in the middle of the night in the village of Blyvooruitzicht; a family of five were all killed when their

	house fell 100 feet into the hole. Three more houses fell in as the sides of the hole slumped in shortly afterwards.
1966	The largest sinkhole of all (400 feet across and 170 feet deep) caved in just outside the town of Carletonville. There was no loss of life.
1967	A sinkhole opened up in an empty school playing-field in the town of Westonaria.
1968	The West Driefontein mine received a sudden inrush of water which broke through from the Bank Compartment.
1969	Dewatering of the Bank Compartment was started.
1972	The village of Bank was evacuated and abandoned as numerous sinkholes developed, together with major ground fractures along the edges of subsidence zones.

In total, hundreds of sinkholes developed in these few years. Though some old, natural sinkholes do occur in the region, the sequence of events clearly indicates the relationship between the sinkholes and the mine dewatering. Most of the collapses were directly due to the lowering of the water-table as water was drained from the mines, and the periodic influences of muddy water into the mines emphasised the connection with sediment disturbance at the surface. In addition to the naturally developed sinkholes which pre-date the mine dewatering, there are four different types of sinkholes which have formed in the Wonderfontein Valley.

The broad shallow subsidence depressions which develop over a period of years form one distinct type – the 1963 Schutte's Depression is an example. The total movement may be more than 20 feet, but as it is so slow damage to buildings is often negligible, except to those on the edge of the depression where earth cracks tend to develop. This type of subsidence does not involve the dolomite but is merely due to compaction of the clays and unconsolidated sediments which overlie it. It therefore tends to take place where broad but deep depressions occur in the buried sediment–limestone interface. The compaction itself is due to the loss of water pressure as drainage takes place, and there is clearly some relationship with fissuring in the dolomite – indeed the very large collapse hole which developed in 1966 in Carletonville lay at the end of a marked linear depression of the compaction subsidence type.

The large collapse subsidences are also related to the shape of the dolomite–sediment interface. They are essentially due to the washing down of sediment into the dolomite fissures as downward drainage is improved through the lowering of the water-table. As the lower layers of sediment are washed down, the upper layers tend to bridge across the resultant void – for a limited time only. It is the failure of the bridged material which accounts for the development of vertical-sided sinkholes. Small sinks are related to individual fissures in the dolomite, and it appears that the eight very large sinkholes which developed in the Oberholzer Compartment were probably formed over a buried surface of dolomite which was eroded into pinnacles, so that, on drawdown, sediment could bridge across a large area using the pinnacles as supports; collapse into multiple cavities could then take place. These large sinkholes are related to the dolomite–sediment interface, occurring where deep narrow valleys are cut into the buried surface; they can also develop along the steep-edge zones of broader 'buried valleys' – as shown by the 1966 Carletonville collapse. Such sinkholes are also related to the drop in the water-table, as the eight big holes all followed a water-table lowering of 500 feet, and even small holes of this type occur mainly where the water level has fallen 50 feet or more.

A third type of sinkhole development has been recognised, in which a purely natural sinkhole has developed and has then been filled in by natural accumulation of debris. A recollapse is then triggered by the lowering of the water-table. Such a two-phase subsidence could have taken place in many cases; it has been specifically recognised where Quaternary-filled sinkholes have collapsed in the Karoo sediments – which are generally regarded as not being prone to sinkhole development at present. The holes in the school playing-fields at Westonaria were of this type. Finally, there have been many instances of small sinkholes developing around houses and roads due to increased drainage around them on to the land. This results in more washing down of sediment into the dolomite, but is unrelated to the mine dewatering.

The causes of the subsidences were clear enough, yet at the same time the dewatering projects had been initiated for economic reasons dictated by the patterns of mining. With hindsight and taking into account the extent and cost of the damage due to subsidence, maybe the mining companies would consider that dewatering was not the best course. But, once the programme had been initiated, the problem was to try to foretell which areas were likely to subside. A far-reaching geophysical programme was started in the early 1960s in an attempt to predict future collapses, but it reached the conclusion that direct prediction of sinkhole appearances was beyond the capabilities of available techniques. It was only possible to evaluate the potential danger on a regional basis and so provide some guidelines as to which areas were likely to suffer subsidences. This evaluation was based on the nature and thickness of the sediment and on the amount of water-table lowering. Well records provided the latter data; an excessive drop in water level led to the designation of an area as potentially unsafe. The sediment thicknesses were estimated by a combination of gravity measurements and borehole drilling, from which the relief of the top of the dolomite could be mapped and examined for danger zones, such as very deep or pinnacled areas. Gravity measurement stations were sited every 50 or 100 feet in the town and every 300 feet in open country. Boreholes were used as a control on the geophysical calculations and were spaced about a mile apart. The programme had some success since areas prone to large-scale subsidence could be identified, but the sensitivity of gravity measurement is not adequate to detect small-scale features associated with smaller potential subsidences. The large scale of the Wonderfontein Valley sinkholes did therefore make them a little easier to predict. The 1967 sinkholes at Westonaria had been predicted by the gravity survey, and the playing-fields had been declared unsafe and kept empty before the collapses took place. The technique was thus a step forward in identifying areas of potential ground failure.

When the crusher at West Driefontein disappeared downwards in 1962 there was obvious concern about the safety of the new plant being built nearby. Drillholes were sunk and a cavity was found and filled before construction proceeded any further. This exercise was very expensive but represented a saving on the possible loss of the new works. Of course, such an intensive programme of drilling is prohibitively expensive over large areas, leaving only the gravity surveys and the well records to give some indication of ground safety to the planners of the area's development.

Collapse and subsidence over mine workings

Collapse of mine workings can result in a double catastrophe, affecting both the miners working underground and the people and property on the affected land directly above. Although roof falls do occur and represent a major hazard, the collapse of working mines is very seldom on a large enough scale to result in surface subsidence. On the other hand, abandoned mines commonly collapse, and can represent a major threat to buildings and activity above.

Mines are normally worked so that enough of the mineral or rock is left behind in the form of pillars to support the roof, but there is an obvious temptation to the miners to remove as much of the pillars as possible just before the mine is abandoned. The slow processes of rock decay and breakdown then leave a time-lag before pillar and roof failure takes place. This process of 'robbing the pillars' was particularly common in the past. The town of Scranton, Pennsylvania, suffered extensive damage soon after the turn of the century due to undermining at a depth of only 70 feet for anthracite. Inadequate pillars were left, so that soon after the workings were abandoned the roof collapsed over large areas. Numerous buildings in the town were severely damaged and the fact that the inadequate pillars offered some support at regular intervals resulted in the town's main street ending up like a roller-coaster, with dips of 5 feet or more between each pillar. Bad roof conditions in poorly consolidated rocks can make roof collapse almost inevitable after a certain time, even with the most reasonable of mining practices. The old ironstone mines at Nettleton in eastern England are roofed by weak clays and sands, and even narrow driveways have now collapsed and conical depressions have appeared in the fields.

The other great hazard of old mines is the way in which shafts were abandoned. Up until the start of the century mine shafts were rarely filled in when they fell into disuse. Instead, a framework, usually of timber and boards, was laid across the top of the shaft and covered with a few feet of soil. Once the mines were forgotten the timbers beneath the surface would slowly decay, creating a very serious hazard. In 1892 at Lindale railway yards, near Barrow-in-Furness, Cumbria, an old iron mine shaft opened up underneath a railway engine. The driver just had time to jump clear before the engine disappeared. At Abram, near Wigan, Lancashire, an old coal mine shaft had been filled and capped before railway yards were built over it. The fill was inadequate and compacted, and in 1945 the capping failed, engulfing thirteen coal wagons, an engine and the driver. The town of Wilkes-Barre in Pennsylvania is underlain by many old coal mines, and in 1968 the capping of an old shaft beneath a main road failed; the slow break-up of the road asphalt gave a motorist time to escape but his car was lost down a hole 30 feet across. Around Matlock in the English Pennines old lead mines riddle the wooded hills and it is not uncommon for a walker to fall down a shaft when the rotten wood coverings give way.

The problem with these old mine shafts is locating them; once found they can easily be filled or capped with concrete. Drilling boreholes in order to locate old shafts is an exceptionally expensive operation even on a small construction site, because the small size of shafts necessitates a close spacing of boreholes. Their limited size also makes shafts difficult to locate by geophysical means, though the National Coal Board of Britain has had some success using sensitive proton magnetometers. These detect differences in the magnetic properties between the

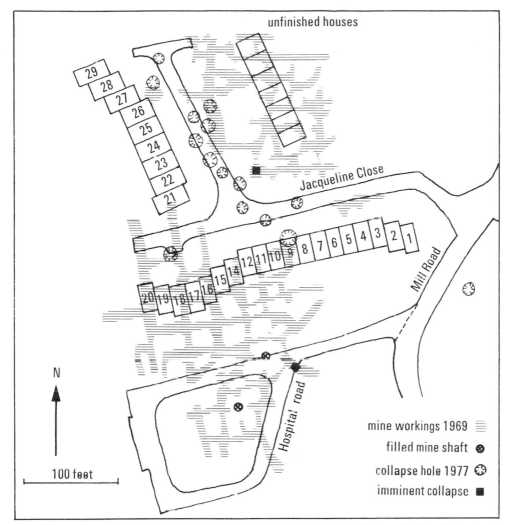

Jacqueline Close, in Bury St Edmunds, with the many collapse holes which had developed by 1977 due to drainage into the underlying old chalk mines.

surrounding rocks and the debris used to fill the shafts, but although they can indicate the location of old shafts they are not reliable enough to make boreholes unnecessary. Unfortunately it is only since 1872 that the surveying and registering of mine workings has been compulsory in Britain, and workings from before that date are rarely traceable. Where no signs exist on the surface, local information is sometimes the best guide to the sites of old mines. In 1964 a group of houses were built on Jacqueline Close on the fringe of Bury St Edmunds in Suffolk. The underlying rock is chalk and no site investigations were carried out, even though it was later discovered that two local men had worked as boys in chalk mines directly beneath the site. But there were no maps of the mines, and no one asked around among the local people. Drainage from the houses was into soakaways set 20 feet down into the chalk, and these let water seep down into the old mines 30-50 feet

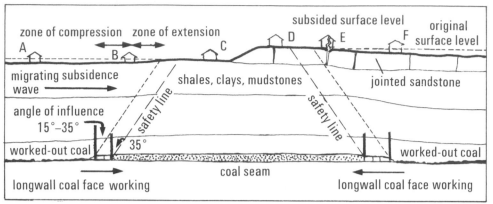

Subsidence due to longwall coal mining. House A has suffered minor damage in the past. House B is currently tilted, as it lies on the subsidence wave. House C will suffer minor damage in the future. House D will suffer major damage as it is on a joint in the sandstone. House E is being torn apart, for a similar reason. House F has suffered negligible damage in the past because it lies on a natural raft.

below ground. The drainage water turned the chalk into a slurry, which then flowed into the mine workings, creating pipe cavities up to the surface. In December 1968 the front drive of 9 Jacqueline Close disappeared down one of these pipes – 15 feet across and 60 feet deep. When exploration revealed the extent of the mines, the four-year-old houses were condemned as unsafe and the residents were forced to move out as more and more collapses opened up under the drains – all because the building company, the planning authorities, and the local residents never talked to each other until it was too late.

There is one special type of mine subsidence which is planned. Conventional methods of horizontal mining, in which galleries are mined between pillars left for roof support, are not economically feasible for the extraction of the very thin beds which make up a large proportion of the world's coal seams. Consequently most modern coal mines are worked by the highly mechanised method of longwall retreat mining, whereby a cutting machine takes the coal out along the whole length of the face (200 feet or more). Mobile supports hold up the roof in the working area at the face, but behind that the roof is allowed to collapse progressively. This invariably results in subsidence of the surface, and a certain amount of damage to roads and buildings is accepted as one of the costs of this method of mining. Monitoring and research over many years means that patterns of subsidence are now fairly well understood and normally predictable. In practice, longwall retreat mining results in a subsidence wave which sweeps across the surface, creating first tension, then tilting, followed by compression and finally settlement at a new lower level. If the subsidence wave is steep the tension may cause buildings to crack, and the compression may create buckled walls; the tilting is less of a problem as it normally readjusts and eliminates itself. Damage to buildings in the urban areas which overlie so many coal mines throughout the world is reasonably predictable and its cost is acceptable to the mining companies.

Where buildings and installations on the surface are of very high value it may not be economically viable to mine beneath and damage them. Instead, a pillar of coal can be left to support them. This may well have to be of considerable size, depending upon the angle of influence – which determines the area affected by subsidence other than that directly above it. A safe working figure for the angle of influence depends on the nature of the rocks between the coal seam and the surface – in Britain it is normally taken as $35°$ from the vertical, while in the regions of softer rocks in Holland $45°$ is more practicable. This often means that, particularly over deep mines, massive pillars must be left. Britain's new coalfield at Selby in east Yorkshire is crossed by the London to Edinburgh high-speed railway, and a pillar to support this would need to be a mile wide. This amount of coal is too valuable to leave behind, so in this case the cheapest alternative is to re-route the railway round the edge of the coalfield. The Selby coalfield faces another problem since it is crossed by the River Ouse which has a very low gradient. The total amount of subsidence can usually be reckoned as 90 per cent of the thickness of the removed seam, or rather less if some waste rock is packed back into the mined area. On this reckoning, extraction of the 10-foot-thick Barnsley seam will drop the River Ouse area below sea level, with the possibility of extensive flooding. Consequently, the construction of land drainage systems and extensive dykes along the river is creating yet more cost for the Selby mining venture – though in this case the cost was anticipated.

The subsidence wave described above can only develop as gentle curves in adequately flexible rocks such as clays or shales. More brittle rocks such as sandstone or limestone (or faulted rocks) fracture instead of bending, and the subsidence takes place in a sequence of irregular steps. A house suffers severe damage if it is built across the edge of two blocks of rock which subside independently, even if by the same overall amount. At the Sigma Colliery in South Africa, a thick bed of dolerite above the coal seam fractured irregularly and caused severe localised subsidence damage. The Hucknall and Mansfield region in England's Nottinghamshire coalfield has particular problems because the surface rock there is a jointed bed of strong Magnesian Limestone. Any building which happens to straddle a joint in the limestone suffers repeated damage as the succession of coal seams are worked out from deep underneath. A house at Hucknall had to be demolished only recently when one side of it dropped badly, where its foundation was separated by a fault from the rest of the building. A new house has since been built on the site, based on a rigid concrete raft. Predictions of ground movement, essential in the planning of new construction works, depend in this case on locating the major existing fractures in the limestone. This is made difficult by the surface veneer of flexible boulder clay, but air photograph studies have had some success in finding fractures – notably the big gulls, which are the fractures formed along the valley sides where the limestone breaks due to inadequate support by the plastic clay beneath it. The recognition of the importance of these fractured rocks has played a major part in the reduction of subsidence damage, which was sometimes so severe in the early years of the mining industry.

The future

In various parts of the world and at various times in the future, roads and fields, houses and people are going to be lost due to sudden ground subsidence. For any particular person the chances of instant death in this way are very remote, but they do exist. And the fate of some houses and roads is already sealed. After some of these future subsidences surprise will be expressed, because they will have been virtually unpredictable – so they can be counted as just bad luck. But after others it will be perfectly clear that enough was known beforehand to have enabled them to be avoided or prevented; by then it will be too late, and property and lives will have been needlessly lost.

This gloomy prophecy is made because, although prediction methods exist, people cannot be bothered to spend the time looking into possibilities which are, in general terms, as remote as catastrophic subsidences. More importantly, nobody takes responsibility for such investigations; no authority can be called responsible for the planning which will avoid such hazards. Planned subsidence by Britain's National Coal Board is now well regulated and controlled by their engineers, and is not a significant danger; compaction on large building sites is the responsibility of the resident engineer. But abandoned mines and isolated solution cavities are no one's direct responsibility, so they are ignored – even when the facts are available for anyone to see and interpret.

At Venterspost in South Africa ground movement has been monitored on benchmarks for many years because of the major sinkhole collapses which have made the region famous. In some cases ground surveying can reveal movements which predict a sudden collapse. In 1973 a sinkhole developed overnight, at the cost of both property and lives. Only afterwards was the survey information plotted out from the monitoring scheme – and it was seen that the collapse could have been predicted. Why had the survey data not been drawn up when it had been obtained? Because no one was responsible?

The kitchen floor of a house in Chesterfield, Derbyshire, collapsed into an old mine working in 1977. The working was in a coal seam only a few feet down, for the coal was very nearly at outcrop and had been worked out maybe a hundred years before. These old shallow workings are not uncommon, and when Coal Board engineers arrived for the routine job of resupporting the house they claimed that they knew of many such workings in the area and it was no surprise to them. But in that case, why had the houses been built there? Because no one checked the records?

In 1959 the Town Council of Bury St Edmunds, in Suffolk, refused to buy a parcel of land offered to them 'because of rumours of liability to subsidence'. But in 1964 the council granted planning permission for houses on this land, with no mention of the possibility of ground instability. In 1966 the same council refused a mortgage to the prospective buyer of one of these houses on Jacqueline Close, 'because there were underground workings on the site'. The builders, Tricord Developments Ltd, had boreholes drilled to 20 feet depth, even though a geologist had predicted that the mines were 40 feet down. Armed with the report on the boreholes (which predictably had found no mine workings), the council gave permission for more houses to be built. In 1967 the first of the collapse sinkholes developed in Jacqueline Close. Then events speeded up. More collapses occurred; Tricord Developments went into liquidation; the council declared the houses unfit; the Borough Engineer retired prematurely; and the council claimed that it had no power to spend public money on rehousing the residents of Jacqueline Close. So a couple of dozen families continue to pay mortgages on derelict houses. Why did neither the council, nor the builders, nor the developers check the rumours (true as it turned out) of mines on the site? Because no one really thought about subsidence, and no one accepted the responsibility for so checking?

UNDER GROUND

In 1924 the Tanna Tunnel was being driven through a high ridge south-west of Tokyo in Japan. By 10 February of that year the western heading was 6900 feet in from daylight and at that point was 500 feet below ground-level. Then, without any warning, the rock at the tunnel face collapsed, and was replaced by a torrent of water and mud. Sixteen construction workers were drowned or buried as this wave of destruction swept into the tunnel.

The Tanna Tunnel achieved notoriety because of the appallingly bad ground through which it was built. A complex interbedded series of highly permeable volcanic ashes, laced with faults and pockets of clay, presented a tunneller's nightmare: the inrush of 1924 was just one of the many problems met underground in that one tunnel. Weak rocks saturated with water result in collapse and flooding the two great threats to underground workers. It is probably true that tunnellers and miners depend more than anyone else for their safety on the nature and properties of rocks, and furthermore on their ability to predict what lies ahead. As in most other situations in engineering today, almost any problem can be satisfactorily overcome on the one proviso that the problem is known. In the case of tunnelling or mining this means knowing just what rock is going to be revealed when the next section is cut or blasted out, and the sufficiently accurate prediction of geological structures far below ground surface is always difficult, sometimes almost impossible. It is a reflection of these difficulties that so many tunnels or mine headings are now preceded by long probing boreholes along the axis of the working.

Most obvious of the many hazards which await a miner or tunneller is roof collapse. But in fact most rocks, given reasonably favourable geological structure, are very strong and quite capable of spanning large voids with little or no support. This is not to claim that rocks do not fail and collapse underground, but an even greater danger is presented by water. Either on its own, flooding into workings with terrifying speed, or mixed at high pressure with unconsolidated sediment and flowing as a liquid, water is a permanent threat in an underground environment.

The hazards of underground water

With the ever-present threat of water immediately overhead, tunnelling beneath a river, through soft saturated riverbed sediments, represents a formidable problem. The first river crossing by tunnel was begun by the great engineer Marc Brunel and his famous son Isambard, beneath the Thames at London in 1825. On the advice of geologists who had put down many trial borings the tunnel was driven only 14 feet below the riverbed where a strong clay was predicted. But the three-dimensional pattern of the sediments of a riverbed is almost invariably very complex and rarely predictable from the evidence of scattered boreholes. As tunnelling proceeded all sorts of weak, mobile and saturated sediments were encountered, and progress was only made possible at all by the tunnelling shield specially designed for this tunnel. Two years later the first heading was 300 feet out under the river when water pressure burst through the weak mud seal and a great flood swept into the tunnel through a hole scoured out from the riverbed. With the tunnel flooded to tide-level the only means of sealing the hole was from the outside, and, incredibly, this was successfully done by throwing hundreds of tons of clay bags on to the riverbed from a chain of barges. The seal was judged adequate when the tunnel could be pumped dry, and then work began again. The whole process was repeated when the river broke through yet again, but eventually the tunnel was completed under conditions which would not be contemplated today. In later times the problems of water flowing through highly permeable sediment into sub-river tunnels have been partly overcome by using compressed air in the tunnel, and keeping the water out by matching its pressure. The early tunnels under the Hudson at New York and beneath the Clyde at Glasgow were excavated in this manner, though it was shown how critical was the balance of pressures – too little and the river 'blew' into the tunnel, too much and the tunnel air 'blew' out to the river. By far the safest method of tunnelling beneath rivers is to go deep enough to stay in solid rock; the famous Mersey Tunnel at Liverpool was thus bored the whole way in solid sandstone, and the river muds were diligently avoided.

Even in consolidated rock, water is a problem underground – and it is particularly dangerous where fault zones of broken rock can conduct enormous flows of water. The Seikan Tunnel, currently being bored between the Japanese islands of Honshu and Hokkaido, must rank as one of the most challenging projects of all. It will be 34 miles long, passing beneath a sea channel 450 feet deep, and is situated in a faulted complex of igneous and sedimentary rocks. In May 1976 water broke into the tunnel at a depth of 650 feet below sea-level. With an initial flow of over 20 cusecs the inrush flooded two miles of tunnel before the drainage systems could master it and it was weeks before the heading was again dry. Faults present two kinds of water hazard underground. They may act as channels for water if they contain zones of broken rock, or they may act as hydrological barriers where they contain sheets of gouge – fine clay-like material where rock has been ground to a powder by the fault movement. The worst of both worlds was found in the San Jacinto Tunnel in California. Rock just above the inclined fault planes was found to be heavily fractured and highly permeable, and the faults themselves contained layers of impermeable gouge. Tunnelling through the faults from beneath therefore resulted in disastrous surges of water as the gouge barriers were breached, whereas approaches from the upper side involved much more manageable steady drainage.

Certain rocks have very high permeabilities and are capable of transmitting vast flows of water. Deep below ground, where encountered by mining or tunnelling operations, they are normally saturated with water under high pressure. Sandstones, limestones, volcanic ashes and lavas are the most permeable rocks which consistently provide the most water. In addition sandstone can provide more serious problems where it is only poorly cemented. In 1959, drilling of the Awali Tunnel in the Lebanon ran into a steeply inclined bed of sandstone; the result was flooding and silting of over a mile and a half of the tunnel. Surface geological investigation had determined the presence of the sandstone but had given no indication of the properties of the rock under the pressures found in the tunnel more than 2000 feet below the ground. The steep hydraulic gradients induced by the artificial drainage into the tunnel heading had combined with the low cohesion of the sandstone to permit piping and cavitation, which was in turn responsible for the magnitude of the water flow into the tunnel. Once this was finally appreciated, the tunnel was rerouted for over a mile, to minimise the passage through the troublesome sandstone.

Limestone is another highly permeable rock, though its permeability is of a completely different type from that of sandstone. With limestone the rock itself is commonly almost impermeable, yet it has the ability to transmit vast flows of water through solutional openings – caves – within it. The problems are complicated by the completely unpredictable patterns of such water-bearing caves. The Severn Tunnel was built to carry the mainline railway from England to Wales, and part of its course lay through massive Carboniferous Limestone. In 1879 the heading on the Welsh side, which was then well beneath dry land, ran into a flooded cave right at the top of the limestone. The resulting flood completely filled the tunnel, but fortunately there was no loss of life. It appears that one cave passage carried the drainage of a large area of land out to a submarine spring in the Severn estuary, and its flow was unceasing; only after extensive extra shafts and levels had been cut to allow drainage and pumping was the Severn Tunnel completed. In the Jura mountains of Switzerland, the Grenchenberg Tunnel met similar problems with water where it traversed two thin bands of highly fissured limestone. In one heading the inflow of water was so great that all work had to be stopped for two months, until the flow had decreased to a more manageable size.

It is not only tunnellers who meet underground problems in limestone. Around the world there are numerous mines which have been developed to exploit the rich mineral deposits which so often occur in limestone. The great Morococha copper mines in Peru and the lead mines of Halkyn Mountain in Wales are just two that have had serious water problems, made more difficult by great inrushes from flooded limestone caves. But the greatest of all mine floodings took place in the world's biggest gold mine in South Africa.

The West Driefontein gold mine, currently the largest in the world, lies in the heart of the rich Rand goldfield near Johannesburg, in the Wonderfontein Valley mentioned in the previous chapter. The gold is mined from conglomerate beds, known as reefs, which occur in a thick sequence of quartzites; the quartzites and conglomerates are completely impermeable. But the gold beds are found only at considerable depths, and between them and the surface are about 3000 feet of dolomites, which are highly fissured, cavernous and indeed excellent aquifers. Complicating this pattern of groundwater hydrology are a series of vertical syenite dykes which cut right through the dolomites, quartzites and gold reefs. They are impermeable, and very efficiently divide the dolomite groundwater resources into watertight 'compartments'.

Most of the workings in the West Driefontein mine are under the dyke-bounded section of dolomites known as the Oberholzer compartment, and to improve both efficiency and safety in the mine this compartment was long ago dried out by a

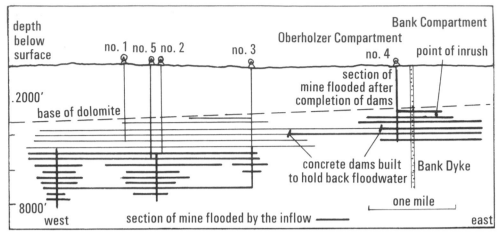

depth below surface

no. 1 no. 5 no. 2   no. 3

Bank Compartment

Oberholzer Compartment

no. 4   point of inrush

2000'

base of dolomite

section of mine flooded after completion of dams

concrete dams built to hold back floodwater   Bank Dyke

8000'

west   section of mine flooded by the inflow ———   east

one mile

A section across the West Driefontein mine shows the vast extent of the workings which were flooded in 1968 before emergency dams could be built.

programme of massive pumping. In 1964 West Driefontein extended eastwards, which meant driving galleries through the Bank dyke and working the gold reefs underneath the adjacent Bank compartment. The dolomites of the Bank compartment had not been dewatered, but the mine workings were only in the impermeable quartzites below, and while a certain amount of leakage into the mine was to be expected this could easily be dealt with by the installed pumping equipment. In addition West Driefontein was equipped with a vast amount of extra pumping plant and an ingenious series of drainage routes, which could divert excess water into old workings acting as temporary reservoirs. One purpose of these arrangements was to overcome any erratic inrushes of water which were experienced periodically, and more of which were anticipated.

This was the situation until 26 October 1968. Then at nine o'clock on that morning a fissure opened up in the roof of the workings underneath the Bank compartment, and a torrent of water poured in. But this was no ordinary inrush, of the sort that had been anticipated. The flow of water was 160 cusecs from this one fissure – six times the normal flow of water from all the other leakages in the whole mine put together. More importantly the total water input into the mine was now about half as much again as the total pumping capacity. The outcome was all too obvious, but by a swift, efficient and courageous evacuation up the shafts all the 13,500 men working in the mine at the time of the inrush reached the surface safely.

Then, as the mine slowly started to fill with water, its rescue was planned in a race against time. Adequate extra pumping plant could not be installed fast enough, so the only alternative was to contain the flood. Fortunately all the water flowed into the main part of the mine along just two galleries feeding from the eastern end of the workings where the inrush was. The flood rivers in both these galleries were 3-4 feet deep, but in each case there were loop passages which permitted concrete dams to be built. It was twenty-six days of frantic effort and brilliant engineering in appalling conditions before the dams were sealed and the flood was stemmed. By then the mine contained floodwater 2500 feet deep, but the higher levels and the crucial pumping stations were saved. While the eastern section of the mine was temporarily abandoned to the waters, the main section of West Driefontein was steadily pumped dry and brought back into production.

The source of the inrush was clearly the saturated dolomites overlying the mine, and the combination of the 2800 foot head of water and the cavernous nature of the dolomites accounted for the magnitude of the flood. But the water had also broken down through about 100 feet of impermeable quartzite which separated the mine from the dolomite. The development of the mine involved cutting large gently inclined slopes – cavities from which the gold-bearing ore had been extracted – and this naturally involved some disturbance of the roof rock. Though supports were left in (or put in) to stop the roof collapsing, a certain amount of movement between the blocks of rock in the mine roof was inevitable. A major fault passed through the mined gold ores and the overlying dolomites in the vicinity of the point of inrush. This would have had a twofold effect – cave development in the dolomite would have concentrated on the fault line, ensuring a good supply of water right down, and a localised zone of joints and faults would have facilitated movement of the mine roof. A slight earth tremor the night before the inrush may also have helped, but it is easy enough to see how a fissure could have developed to breach the impermeable barrier between the saturated dolomite and the mine.

The question then arises as to whether the flooding was predictable. The pessimist would claim that mining beneath flooded cavernous dolomite made it inevitable, but this is rather unfair. With impermeable quartzite in the roof, mining could have proceeded for years with no more than minor leakages. Unfortunately the science of rock mechanics has not yet developed to the stage where a useful quantitative estimate of the chances involved could have been given to the mine engineers. While the strengths of individual rocks can be measured, there is so far no reliable way of predicting the stability of the thousands of joints which occur hidden in rocks deep below the surface. The mine only had experience and 'rule of thumb' on which to base its planning; a chance was taken, but in this case it was the wrong one. The ultimate solution was of course to dewater the dolomites of the Bank compartment – an expensive operation. Since the flooding this has been done, because, with the fissure established into the mine, there was no alternative.

The threat of buried valleys

'Rockhead' is the term used by miners and engineers to describe the underground boundary between the solid, consolidated rocks, and the overlying unconsolidated sediments. The rockhead may lie at or just below the surface, beneath a thin layer of soil, or it may lie at considerable depth. In the latter case it presents an awful threat to miners and tunnellers. Accidentally driving a tunnel or mine heading from good solid rock through the rockhead means breaking into soft, loose, mobile sediments, normally sand or clay, saturated with water at high pressure. This is usually catastrophic.

The problem for miners and tunnellers alike is knowing just where the rockhead is at any particular point. If the rockhead is relatively flat and uniform it poses little problem, but it can have a very complex shape. It does after all represent a buried topography – it was the shape of the land before it was buried by the sediments which now overlie it. Understanding and predicting the shape of the rockhead therefore depends on a knowledge of past landform processes which in turn are dependent on earth movements and climatic changes. The many glaciations and other climatic changes within the Ice Ages of the last few million years make such prediction all the more difficult. Obviously the greatest hazards are presented to miners and tunnellers where the rockhead locally dips down to greater depth. This frequently happens where an ancient valley has been completely filled with sediment, and such buried valleys may give little immediate surface indication of their shape.

The Weissentstein Tunnel was cut through a ridge in the Swiss Jura Mountains in 1907. At one point it passed under a shallow valley and an estimate of sediment thickness in the valley floor had been made. The tunnel was designed to go beneath these sediments, but no account had been taken of the buried valley which lay hidden there, and when the tunnel ran into it there were considerable difficulties in supporting the wet sediment. Buried valleys can reach depths well below sea-level, where normal valley erosion took place when sea-levels during the Ice Ages were far lower than they are today. The subsequent rise in sea-level has been matched by sediment accumulating in the old valley. Beneath the River Tyne at Newcastle, in England, there is a 130-foot-deep sediment-filled valley which had to be carefully avoided by the numerous shallow coal mines that worked the area many years ago.

Buried valleys are even more difficult to locate, where they do not follow the pattern of the modern valleys – and after all there is no reason why they should. When the Waggital water tunnel was driven beneath the Schwendibach valley in Switzerland, a considerable depth of sediment was anticipated. Consequently a trial pit was excavated in the valley floor, above the tunnel line, and the rockhead was discovered at a depth of 40 feet. The tunnel was projected at a depth of 100 feet so boring went ahead; but 50 yards further north the working ran into the offset buried valley which just reached to the depth of the tunnel.

The deepest and most dangerous buried valleys are found in glaciated regions. This is because glaciers, being solid enough, can move uphill, and so can overdeepen a particular part of a valley. When the glaciers then retreat, water-borne sediments accumulate in and fill up these overdeepened sections. This is a major problem to tunnel engineers, because so much of Europe and North America was glaciated during the Ice Ages. At Coleman, in the Canadian Rockies, coal miners found a buried valley full of sediment which extended nearly 300 feet deep beneath the Crowsnest River. The builders of the famous St Gotthard Tunnel through the Swiss Alps came close to disaster when they passed underneath the Andermatt valley at a depth of 1050 feet nearly two miles from the northern portal. In the 1870s they had no knowledge of the buried valley which lay there and was only discovered by drilling boreholes seventy years later. The Andermatt buried valley is 920 feet deep, and its saturated sands and clays extend to within 130 feet of the tunnel.

While a careful consideration of past and present geomorphology can give some indication of the possible presence of a buried valley, it cannot be precise enough for safe underground tunnelling. Consequently any hint of the presence of a buried valley must be followed up by adequate geological exploration. Boreholes or trial pits are the most accurate way of locating the rockhead, but if a large area has to be investigated, drilling enough boreholes can be very expensive. Nowadays seismic geophysics is frequently used with considerable success. In this technique shock waves are passed through the ground: their speed is basically a function of the rigidity of the rock, or sediment, so that as the waves are refractured or reflected by different layers, the subsurface geology can be deduced by timing the waves' return to the surface. Fortunately the rockhead, bounding soft sediment and solid rock, is easily determined in this way, though problems can arise with deep narrow buried valleys which may give false seismic signals from their sides instead of their floor. This is thought to have happened at Mauvoisin in Switzerland, where an access tunnel was being drilled under the valley at a dam site. A buried gorge was known to exist from the geophysical investigations, but the heading broke unexpectedly into the side of the alluvium-filled gorge where it was not expected, and in the subsequent inrush of water and sand, four engineers were killed. The consequences of inadequate exploration of buried valleys can be only too disastrous.

The Lötschberg Tunnel, in Switzerland, earned its place in the annals of engineering disasters from the moment its construction proceeded without adequate consideration of the geological situation. The tunnel was designed to carry a mainline railway for more than 9 miles through the Bernese Alps, from Kandersteg on the north side to Goppenstein in the south. Both tunnel portals lie at floor level in spectacular glaciated valleys surrounded by some of Switzerland's finest scenery. At the Kandersteg end the valley has a long profile which is clearly stepped – a feature common to so many glaciated valleys. The railway enters the tunnel at the foot of one of these steps, and, almost immediately above the portal, the valley floor rises nearly 600 feet. But upstream the valley divides, and one branch, the Gasterntal, passes over the line of the tunnel.

The engineers who worked on the planning stages of the tunnel during the last few years of the nineteenth century envisaged few geological problems. From the Kandersteg end, the tunnel was expected to pass through limestones beneath the Fisistock peak and then into good granite under the Balmhorn mountain; but there were some doubts expressed about the conditions underneath the Gasterntal. The tunnel would lie 610 feet beneath the ground, which in the valley consisted of soft sediments. However, geological advisers predicted that the sediment was only 200 feet deep at most, and that it offered 'not the slightest risk' to the tunnel. Plans for the tunnel therefore progressed. Then an independent geologist claimed that the sediments could be as much as 650 feet deep, in which case part of the tunnel would have to be cut through them, and he suggested that a trial shaft should be sunk in the Gasterntal floor. But by then the project was gathering momentum; somehow this geological report was ignored and in October 1906 the driving of the Lötschberg Tunnel began.

Nearly two years later the Kandersteg heading had reached a length of 8775 feet. The predicted 'danger zone' under the north wall of the Gasterntal had been passed and the tunnelling was now well under the valley. At 2:30 am on 24 July 1908 another round of charges was fired in the normal way. But the result was an enormous avalanche of boulders, mud, water and sand which poured into the tunnel. Twenty-five workmen were killed as the debris flowed down the heading and filled 4300 feet of the tunnel. Up above in the Gasterntal, a great vortex had developed in the riverbed, in the centre of a circle of cracked ground 480 feet across – a typical subsidence depression.

Very little information was ever released about the details of the disaster and

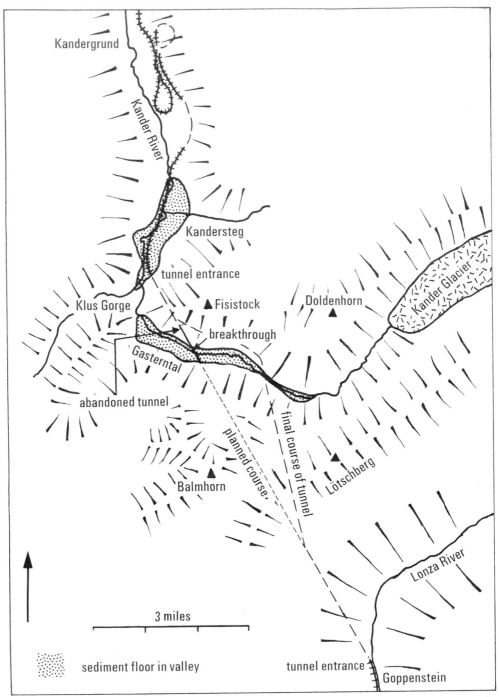

Kandergrund

Kander River

Kandersteg

tunnel entrance

▲ Fisistock

Doldenhorn ▲

Kander Glacier

Klus Gorge

breakthrough

Gasterntal

abandoned tunnel

planned course

final course of tunnel

Balmhorn ▲

Lötschberg ▲

Lonza River

3 miles

sediment floor in valley

tunnel entrance

Goppenstein

The Lötschberg railway tunnel, with the courses of both the doomed first attempt and the successfully completed route beneath the Gasterntal.

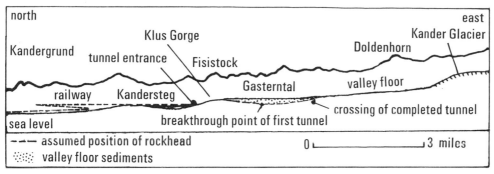

*The long profile of the Kander Valley and Gasterntal shows how slight is the reverse
gradient which led to the deep sediment fill broken into by the first Lötschberg tunnel.*

events immediately afterwards. It was, however, quite clear that the tunnel heading
had broken through into the side of the very deep sediment-filled Gasterntal. There
was a suggestion that the rock 20 feet back from the fateful breakthrough had shown
signs of 'dislocation' associated with the impending change in conditions, but it is
probable that any such structures in the rock were independent of the Gasterntal
sediments. There was no sign of weathered rock at the approach to the sediment-
filled valley, and the last shotholes drilled had all been dry; there seems to have been
no direct warning of the disaster. Exploration holes later sunk into the Gasterntal
floor reached a depth of 720 feet, but the findings were not announced. Meanwhile,
the tunnel still had to be completed. Working through the water-saturated valley
sediments would have been possible only when they had been adequately stabilised
by either grout injection or freezing. Both methods were considered to be very
difficult in this particular case, and the sediment in the tunnel itself could not be
cleared because of its continual movement under pressure. And so the sediment-
filled heading was blocked off by a concrete plug (4830 feet of tunnel being
adandoned), and a new line was followed which took the tunnel round three curves
so that it passed under the Gasterntal further upstream where a safe 495 feet of rock
separated the tunnel and the sediment. In 1913, the Lötschberg Tunnel, over 9
miles long, was opened to rail traffic.

The Lötschberg disaster should never have happened. The Gasterntal is a perfect
example of a deep glaciated valley with a sediment floor, and in such valleys the
depths of the sediment are totally unpredictable. Stepped and locally reversed
gradients are typical features of Alpine glaciated valleys, and either lakes or thick
accumulations of soft unconsolidated sediment must always develop behind these
gradient reversals when the Ice Age glaciers retreat to leave normal river drainage
in the valleys. Both the Gasterntal and the valley in which lies the village of
Kandersteg are outstanding examples of such sediment-filled glacial basins. Solid
rock is exposed in the Klus gorge downstream of the Gasterntal. But for the tunnel to
meet the sediment as it did required a reverse gradient of no more than one in ten on
the rockhead in the buried valley floor, and there are many cases in Switzerland
alone where much steeper slopes than that have been scoured by glaciers moving
uphill under their own pressure. The signs were there, but both the engineers and
the 'geological advisers' ignored them.

143

In fact, no geologist could have predicted accurately the depth of the Gasterntal sediments. But any competent geologist, such as the one who was ignored before the disaster, should have said that the sediments *could* be as deep as the tunnel. An exploratory hole in the valley floor should have been an essential part of the design stage planning. It might have been worth taking the financial risk of having to divert the tunnel line (as was eventually done) and dispensing with a rather deep exploration beneath the Gasterntal floor, as long as safety was assured by continually placing long probing boreholes in advance of the tunnel heading. Then, at least, twenty-five lives would have been saved. As it turned out, a hole drilled in the valley floor, before construction began, would have been the cheapest solution of all. If the tunnel were being cut today geophysics might be used to investigate the sediment depths, but the narrowness of the Gasterntal might still leave the interpretations open to error; the moral of the Lötschberg story is that there can be no subsitute for at least one borehole.

The problems of difficult rock structures

In rock conditions which can be described as 'geologically reasonably uniform' the driving of a tunnel or mine heading need involve no special difficulty or hazard from ground failure. Whether the rock be strong or weak, the principles of rock mechanics can be applied, and by a mathematical approach a suitable method of excavation may be selected. However, in so many cases a tunnel has to be driven through rocks of varying properties and complex structure, which will make the tunnelling project difficult – that is, time-consuming and expensive – if the geological conditions are investigated and duly allowed for. If on the other hand the geology is not adequately understood, tunnelling or mining in difficult ground can lead to disaster.

In 1948 a partial collapse occurred in the Kvineshei railway tunnel in Norway, eight years after it had been completed. A tall pipe-like cavity had developed by progressive collapse in the roof of the tunnel; the void was up to 20 feet in diameter and reached a height of just over 100 feet. It had formed along the intersection of two faults. Faults are a perpetual problem to engineers, because they are so unpredictable in pattern and are almost invariably planes of weakness. As they develop by movement between two blocks of rock they commonly contain zones of broken rock known as breccia, or sheets of fine-ground rock known as gouge, and the latter may contain very weak clay minerals. In the Kvineshei collapse one fracture had a breccia poorly cemented with soluble calcite, and the other contained a gouge of montmorillonite – a clay mineral renowned for its swelling properties when in contact with water. As is usual the rock was heavily fractured near the faults; water from the calcited fault then caused the montmorillonite to expand and eventually the pressure and weight of unsupported rock was too much for the unreinforced lining of the tunnel.

Unlined pressure tunnels in hydro-electric schemes are particularly prone to rock failure when in use, due to the enormous hydrostatic forces imposed on the rocks and also to the pumping effect from changes in pressure caused by different use of the water energy. The Kemano Tunnel on the west coast of Canada failed in 1956 two years after it had been put into service. The tunnel had become nearly blocked from collapse debris falling from a great upward developing cavern over 70 feet across in the tunnel roof. This cavern had formed along a fault containing no more than two inches of gouge, though the rock for a few feet on each side of the fault had been weakened by its alteration to chlorite – a very weak hydrated mineral. The soft altered rock had been washed out, and then the unsupported rock on either side had progressively collapsed. Dewatering the tunnel, clearing the debris and placing a massive concrete arch through the cavern cost $2 million – very much more than the cost of a short length of concrete lining across the fault zone if the situation had been recognised during the initial construction. A thin protective lining of concrete had been placed across faults intersected in the Lemonthyme Tunnel, in Tasmania, when it was built in the 1960s. But it too failed in 1969 after only five months of use. Again faults were the problem, but in this case two faults cut through the phyllites and schists only 10 feet apart, and on each there were easily sheared zones of crushed phyllite. Without support across the fault planes the block of rock between the faults had weighed too heavily on the tunnel's thin lining, and collapse was inevitable. The repair work again involved much more massive steel and concrete support through the zone of poor rock.

A study of geological catastrophes in tunnels can supply many individual examples, but there is one tunnel which exemplifies almost every variation of geological hazard. This is the Tanna Tunnel in Japan, which because of the incredibly difficult geological conditions took sixteen years to build – even though it is only 5 miles long – at the expense of over seventy lives. Started in 1918 and completed in 1934, the Tanna Tunnel carries the mainline railway from Tokyo to Kobe through Takiji Peak on the Izu peninsula. The problems in the construction of the tunnel arose from the structurally complex, heavily faulted series of permeable volcanic ashes which had to be driven through. Many of the volcanic ashes were so permeable and poorly consolidated that they behaved more like a liquid than a solid, and in addition some clay beds had strong swelling properties. Twice the tunnel heading failed due to the swelling pressures, and in one case the entire face crew were killed by the inrush of clay. Even the stronger beds of rock were heavily faulted, and in 1921 a fault zone with a thick layer of gouge was responsible for the collapse of a 150 foot long section of the tunnel. Sixteen workers were killed in this one fall, and seventeen more were trapped for a week behind the heap of fallen rock before they could be dug out.

Water was always a problem in the Tanna Tunnel, and the problem reached its height in 1924. The western heading had a major flood of cold water (as described at the start of this chapter), due to the extremely high permeability of the volcanic rocks. But in the same year the eastern heading met hot water issuing at high pressure from a zone of fault breccias. Tunnels normally only meet significantly hot water at great depths: the Simplon Tunnel in Switzerland is the best-known example, in which water temperatures reached 133°F where the tunnel was 7000 feet below the surface. The Tanna Tunnel was nowhere near this depth, but being in a relatively more active volcanic region, the streams of geothermal water were met at far shallower levels. The 1000-foot-long section of tunnel through the faulted zone containing hot water took three and a half years to cut. The volcanic activity of Japan is just one reflection of the country's location on an unstable part of the Earth's crust; this same instability is responsible for earthquakes, and it put the final twist in the tale of the Tanna Tunnel. By 1930 the work was approaching completion when a relatively minor earthquake shook the region, but the vibrations were enough to disturb the weak volcanic ashes around the tunnel and a roof fall buried five workers. Two were dug out alive, but the other three added their names to the long toll of the Tanna Tunnel.

Volcanic ash was also the cause of a fatal collapse in the Wilson Tunnel on the island of Oahu in the Hawaii group. This tunnel was built in 1954 to carry the main road north out of Honolulu, and for most of its length it was cut in volcanic lava which proved to be an almost ideal tunnelling medium. The tunnel was driven from the northern end only, and as it approached the southern end it ran out of the lava into a soft clay-like bed of volcanic ash and disintegrated lava. The contractor unwisely continued to use a full-face method of excavation with roof supports which, though more than adequate in the lava, were not enough in the clay. The result was a series of roof falls in the tunnel where the clay ran in and left subsidence pits on the surface about 100 feet above. Two falls occurred in July 1954 and blocked the heading, but fortunately without any casualties among the men. Then in August, while work to clear the fallen debris was proceeding, a third fall occurred and five workmen lost their lives. From then on, tunnelling through both the fallen ground and the remainder of the undisturbed clay was by way of small multiple headings, and with this method there were no further collapses. Unstable roof conditions are almost to be expected in a material as weak as the Wilson Tunnel clays, but are not so easily anticipated in older, tougher, well-compacted rocks. The Skogn Tunnel, a water tunnel in central Norway, was cut in old metamorphic rocks, but it too failed. It was realised, too late, that the rocks had decayed just enough for some of the minerals to alter to a montmorillonite clay – and the slippery flakes of this mineral dispersed through the rock had weakened it enough to cause the failure.

In some situations ground movement is inevitable, regardless of rock type, and what is more it may be almost impossible to resist. When rocks are buried at great depth they are compressed due to the enormous confining pressures. When some of this pressure is released, in one direction, by the excavation of a tunnel or mine there is bound to be a tendency for the rock to move into the created void. At shallow depths the amount of pressure released is enough to cause movement in weak clays, but strong rocks such as granite remain firm. However, at depths of many thousands of feet the pressures are high enough to deform any rock. Switzerland's Simplon Tunnel reaches a depth of around 7000 feet below the mountain ridge, and in one particular zone there were serious problems with the slow but extremely powerful creep of the walls into the tunnel working. At the even greater depths of the South African gold mines, the walls do not gently deform but instead explode into the mine openings. These rock bursts, as they are called, normally occur some time after the mine gallery has been cut – the elasticity of the rock permitting a slow creep before the elastic limit is passed and the rock breaks out. A second variety of inevitable rock movement also takes place in mines, where ore deposits are mined out leaving great open cavities, or stopes, with pillars and supports which are only designed to be adequate for a limited length of time. It is unnecessary and ecomically undesirable to leave enough pillars of ore behind to make the stopes permanently stable when they need never be revisited after being mined out. The delayed action of rock movement allows time for perfectly safe mining to be followed by progressive collapse of the abandoned stopes, and in most circum-

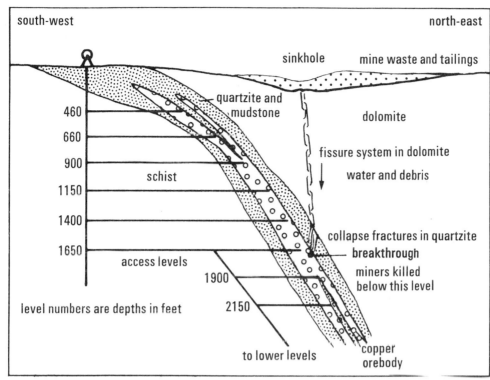

south-west

north-east

sinkhole   mine waste and tailings

quartzite and
mudstone

460   dolomite

660

900   fissure system in dolomite

schist   water and debris

1150

1400

1650   collapse fractures in quartzite

access levels   breakthrough

                1900   miners killed
                                         below this level

level numbers are depths in feet   2150

                                         copper
to lower levels   orebody

*A cross-section through the Mufulira mine, with the implied position of the enormous
collapse sinkhole which led to the disaster of 1970.*

stances such collapse is no cause for concern. On the other hand, if the collapse
works upwards into a different type of rock the results can be catastrophic – as they
were at the Mufulira copper mine.

Mufulira lies in Zambia's very rich 'copper belt', and since 1933 the mine has
been working a thick inclined bed of high-grade copper ore. The orebody dips
steeply to the north-east and is up to 120 feet thick. As is normal practice the access
galleries in the mine and all the surface installations are in and on the undisturbed
ground on the footwall side of the orebody. As the orebody is extracted, large
inclined stopes are left to collapse, and this results in progressive collapse working up
through the hanging-wall rocks until the ground surface also subsides. The crushing
and ore-processing plant at the mine produces an enormous amount of waste,
mainly in the form of a fine slime, and over the years this has been dumped out
above the hanging-wall side of the mine. This had the dual advantage of keeping
the waste away from the installations on the footwall side, and also filling in some
swampy ground which was a malarial threat when the mine opened. As the hanging
wall of the mine continued to subside, lakes developed on the surface and these too
were filled in with the mine tailings, and by 1956 this fine debris filled a basin 40 feet
deep.

In normal conditions this practice of dumping the tailings on the hanging wall
would have been safe enough. As the collapse took place into the mine, the roof
rocks would develop fractures towards the surface, but due to the increase in bulk of

broken rock these fractures would diminish in size away from the mine openings; with mine workings at a depth of 1000 feet or more, as at Mufulira, any fractures that opened to the surface would be so narrow that they would rapidly become sealed by the sediment that was washed in. But conditions were not normal at Mufulira. Immediately above the orebody there is a thin zone of quartzites, but above that, massive dolomites extend all the way to the surface.

The first indications of trouble appeared towards the end of 1968 when a sinkhole, 200 feet in diameter, developed in the blanket of tailings. There must have been a sizeable cavity developing below to absorb this quantity of lost material, but no undue concern was expressed and the sinkhole was filled in with more tailings. Then, in April 1970, mud issued from a roof fissure in the mine at a depth of 1750 feet; no tailings could be identified in this mud but there were fragments of soil – clearly indicating an open connection to the surface. Fissures and caverns must have been developing in the breaking hanging-wall rocks on a large scale to permit flow of sediment to such a depth, but the scale of the fissuring and the danger it presented were not fully appreciated. Through the summer of that year, more mud extrusions were found in the mine, and more sinkholes developed in the tailings above. But the sinkholes were just filled in, and work continued below.

On 25 September 1970 there was a massive and catastrophic inrush. A torrent of water, mud, mine tailings and debris cascaded into the mine through a roof break at a level 1750 feet below the surface. The material was so saturated with water it was highly mobile, and it flowed through the mine workings and cascaded down to the lower levels. There was extensive damage on all levels below that of the inrush, and the lowermost galleries in the mine, more than 2650 feet below ground, were filled to the roof with water and sediment. Eighty-nine miners lost their lives, drowned or buried in the fluid avalanche. On the surface above, a sinkhole 1000 feet across and 50 feet deep developed in the great beds of tailings dumped there from the mine plant.

It is quite clear what happened at Mufulira. The mine tailings leaked down into the mine via fissures in the collapsing hanging-wall rocks. The surprising aspect is the enormous scale of the event, and it is this which turned a fairly ordinary mud leakage into a catastrophic inrush. This is where the hanging-wall geology becomes significant. The dolomites, which occupy most of the thickness from surface to mine, must have been highly fissured by natural solution – they should best be described as cavernous. The size of the surface sinkhole showed that 25 million cubic feet of tailings disappeared underground, but only 11 million cubic feet could be accounted for as having entered the mine workings. Even after allowing for some compaction there was an enormous volume of sediment which had just been lost into the fissures in the dolomite, and such highly cavernous rocks transmit water or sediment all too easily.

It was anticipated that the progressive roof collapse of the mined-out workings at Mufulira would result in the thorough break-up of the thin zone of quartzites just above the orebody. If non-cavernous rocks had extended to the surface the collapse would have progressively diminished upwards, so that there would have been no danger from the tailings dumped above. But the dolomites were extremely cavernous. Before the disaster it was not known that the dolomites contained any sizeable voids, but even without any positive evidence it must always be accepted that dolomites can be cavernous, merely because they are soluble in groundwater.

Even when the sinkholes and small inrushes appeared, no heed was taken of the warning they offered. The dumping of the tailings contributed little to the disaster, because subsidence would have taken place anyway on the surface, thus allowing a lake to form, and the inrush would then have been of water instead of a mixture of water and mud. With a potentially cavernous rock such as dolomite in the roof the method of mining at Mufulira should have been either one that did not involve subsequent roof collapse, or one that allowed abandoned collapsing sections of the mine to be permanently sealed off by concrete plugs in the access galleries. The alternative was to gamble on the size of any inrush, and with cavernous rocks above, that must be a bad risk – as events proved.

The special problems of coal mining

Coal mining has a special place in the industrial world, first because of the enormous size and economic importance of the industry, and secondly because of the many dangers to which coal miners are exposed. Coal occupies the lion's share of the world's miners, and it is therefore doubly unfortunate that, in general terms, the mining of coal is probably more hazardous than the mining of any other mineral. This is in no way a reflection on the methods and safety standards of the industry, but is due to certain features of the geological situations in which coal is found – in particular its association with explosive and poisonous gases, and its occurrence in sequences of structurally weak sedimentary rocks.

Coal is formed by the bacterial decay of rotten vegetation, and one of the many by-products of this process is the formation of various gases, notably the highly inflammable methane. In many cases of coal formation the gases escape and are lost, but in some instances the methane is trapped in any porous rocks – often the coal itself or sandstone and possibly under high pressure. This pressurised gas is only released when it can flow into the openings of a coal mine, where it then carries the double risk of being both poisonous and, when mixed with air, explosive. Some coal seams have a reputation for being very 'gassy', while others present almost no gas hazard. While it is simple to measure the amounts of gas issuing from any coal seam, it is not generally possible to determine why a certain seam is gassy, and therefore geological considerations unfortunately cannot be used to predict the gas hazards of coal workings.

Coal mining is not the only underground activity in which explosive gas can be a danger. Ordinary tunnelling in coal-bearing rocks may encounter gas, but having only a single heading and quickly lining it with concrete does almost eliminate the dangers. In addition, gas is associated with oil, also formed by the decay of organic debris – but in this case mostly animal remains, rather than the plant remains which form coal. The San Fernando water tunnel near Los Angeles, California, was being cut in 1971 through very porous sandstones containing both oil and natural gas. A number of small explosions occurred and then a larger one which killed sixteen men; it was typical of gas explosions in that some died in the initial blast, some in the fire which burned immediately afterwards, and yet others were suffocated in the lethal mixture of gases produced.

Another explosive hazard in coal mines is provided by airborne coal dust, which, mixed with the right amount of air, becomes as dangerous as dynamite. A coal dust explosion in April 1942 in China's Honkeiko Colliery claimed the record for underground catastrophes when 1572 miners died. To a certain extent the dangers of coal dust can be minimised by careful working and mixing with inert limestone dust, but if gas is present in a coal seam there is no way of keeping it out of the workings. The only treatment is the very careful planning of adequate ventilation systems and escape routes for both the gases and the miners; and indeed the great progress made in this field has greatly reduced the accident rate, from the appalling regularity of explosions taking enormous numbers of lives in the last century, to the much rarer and smaller explosions in modern mines. While ventilation can easily dispose of regular and predictable gas seepages, it is the isolated 'outbursts' of pockets of pressurised gas, where the gas literally explodes from the coal seams, which still provide a threat. In 1971 an outburst at Cynheidre Colliery in Wales killed six miners. Even viewed in retrospect it was not geologically predicatable; only very extensive boreholes or excessive ventilation capacity stood any chance of mininising the effects of the gas, and even then it is doubtful if the lives could have been saved.

Mining out large areas in horizontal or gently inclined coal seams must inevitably introduce a certain amount of danger of rock collapse when the rocks are as structurally weak as many of those adjacent to coal seams. Coal is always found in sequences of sedimentary rocks – normally a mixture of very weak shale, and sandstone which is strong enough only if unjointed. Both roofs of shale or sandstone, and supporting pillars of coal, are so weak that some danger is involved if any coal is to be mined at all. The rocks may fail in one of three ways: the coal pillars may collapse, the roof may fall in between supports, or the floor may break upwards due to relief of weight between the pillars. Though large-scale collapses are now hopefully a feature of the past, due to the improvement of safety standards, small rock falls will probably never be eliminated – in Britain alone they still claim an average of thirteen lives every year.

In the year 1837 the Workington Colliery in north-west England was extracting coal from seams underneath the seabed. The roof of the workings was left supported by pillars of coal, and to form these pillars about 35 per cent of the coal was left in place. In the aims of economical mining, the mine manager at the time ordered the 'robbing of the pillars' – an exercise in brinkmanship where the pillars are thinned down to their minimum. But at Workington he estimated wrongly, and on 28 July the inevitable happened: some of the coal pillars failed, the roof collapsed, the breakdown of the roof rocks formed fissures up to the seabed, and the sea poured in. Up above a whirlpool in the sea was observed from the shore, and down below twenty-seven men and boys were drowned. This disaster should never have happened, because safe pillar sizes are reasonably determined as a function of the strength of coal and the depth of rock cover. Modern developments in rock mechanics have assisted in this field, and current practice, leaving probably 70 per cent of the coal untouched where pillar and stall coal mining is carried out, has virtually eliminated the hazard,

In contrast, small-scale roof collapses are almost impossible to predict – even where the 'small scale' is big enough to crush a man to death. Geological study can usually only lead to generalisations. Experience in both North America and Europe has demonstrated the importance of both joint densities and changes in type in the roof rocks for predicting the probabilities of collapse. A thin bed of shale forming a seam roof just below a massive sandstone commonly results in the shale falling away from the sandstone. Fracture zones in sandstones give bad roof conditions, and ironstone nodules easily drop out of weak shales. All are generalities; it is only the alert eye of the miner, the foreman or the mine geologist which can assess individual cases, but the assessment can only be helped by understanding the many geological factors involved.

If gas and rock are the two great hazards of coal mining, water is the third. The high permeability of so many of the rocks – notably the sandstones – associated with coal seams, makes water almost inevitable in a coal mine. Even from the most highly porous sandstones, the rates of water inflow could rarely constitute a hazard to life, though they can be an economic menace in terms of interruptions to working and also of the necessity for continuous pumping. When a mine is abandoned and the pumping ceases, the same permeability of the sandstone results in a rapid flooding of old mine workings up to the level of the local water-table. With successive generations of mines closely spaced to gain maximum extraction of the coal, the danger of driving a heading into old workings is all too apparent.

An inrush of water at the Lofthouse Colliery in Yorkshire caused the death of seven miners in 1973. The disaster was entirely due to the main workings meeting the flooded galleries of an abandoned adjacent mine, and it happened because a map of the old mines was not clearly understood; the existence of the threat was not known at Lofthouse. One of the basic rules of any geological investigation – check the available data – had not been adequately carried out. The fact that the map of the old mine was reinterpreted during the inquiry shows that a more thorough consideration of the old records could have avoided the loss of seven lives.

Far worse was the tragedy at Chasnala Colliery in Bihar, India, when 372 miners lost their lives in a huge flooding at the end of 1975. The coal seam at Chasnala is steeply inclined, and water from a huge flooded opencast mine broke through into a heading at a depth of 550 feet in the underground mine. The scale of the inrush gave little chance for the miners in the main workings, mostly at a depth of 1000 feet. In this case the opencast mine was known, and a zone of coal was left in place to act as a barrier between the water and the working mine below. Either the barrier was not thick enough in terms of the strength of the coal, or the coal was more weathered and broken than was expected, or maybe the old opencast mine was deeper than thought. Whatever the reason for the flood, the cause was an inadequate knowledge of the precise conditions above the mine, and beneath flooding workings the consequences of such ignorance can be catastrophic.

It is perhaps arguable that the disasters at Chasnala and Lofthouse were not geological in nature. There is obviously overlap between the responsibilities of the geologists, mine engineers, managers and surveyors, and it is very difficult to attach blame in such cases. In 1970 water from a surface pond broke into the Zielonka Colliery in Poland, and five miners died in the flood. As a result of this and the subsequent inquiry, the mine geologist, foreman, chief engineer and manager were all jailed. Admittedly the legal systems of the Eastern European countries do have a rather harsher attitude than is general in the West, but in this case the court obviously thought that if responsibilities had been shouldered at Zeilonka the tragedy need not have occurred. Certainly the possibility exists that catastrophes of this nature can be avoided.

In 1938 an exploration borehole revealed a thick coal seam – the Knockshinnoch

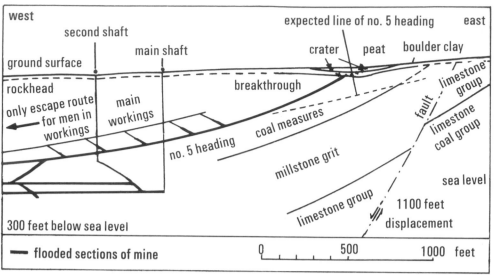

Knockshinnoch Castle Colliery and the fateful No. 5 heading which, through misinterpretation of the geology, broke through to the surface deposits.

Main Coal – in an undeveloped section of the New Cumnock coalfield on the northern fringe of the southern uplands of Scotland. As a result of this, the Knockshinnoch Castle Colliery went into production in 1942. The two shafts of the colliery were close together and from them ran roadways which were cut in barren rock to act as the main underground transport routes. From these, access was gained to the various coal workings. The seams all dipped roughly to the north, and future progress in the mine could be made at greater depths in that direction. To the west lay an older abandoned mine, and a zone of faults bordered the workings to the east. In the years up to 1950 the main coal working was up the dip towards the south and south-east. The method of working was 'stoop and room', whereby galleries 18 feet wide were driven in a gridiron pattern with centres 100 feet apart. By this means one-third of the coal was extracted, leaving two-thirds to support the roof. The headings were 6 feet high and a layer of coal was left in the roof to support a rather weak shale immediately above. With the normal use of pit-props, roof collapse was not a problem. In 1950 the workings centred around the main access route of No. 5 Heading which ran obliquely up the dip aiming for a major fault to the south; the only way out of these workings was back down to the level of the transport roadways of the West Mine and thence to the foot of the shaft.

Typically for the coalfields in this part of Scotland, the geology of the mine was not simple. Little underground exploration had been carried out, and due to an almost continuous cover of superficial deposits there are practically no surface exposures of the coal-bearing rocks, which together account for the late discovery of so rich a seam. The geological maps showed outcrops of boulder clay, alluvium, peat, gravel and some Coal Measures in the immediate vicinity of the mine, but almost nothing was known about the thickness of the superficial deposits. The coal seam was broken by a few small faults and had a northerly dip which was becoming steeper towards the south. A major fault was known to exist further to the south; it was known to have a large displacement (over 1000 feet) and was expected to terminate the coal field in that direction. However, the details of the geology beyond the limits of working were open to conjecture, and the advancement of the No. 5 Heading was partly for the purpose of exploring towards the south-east.

It was expected that the Knockshinnoch Main Seam would end its usefulness where it met the zone of broken ground along this major fault. By projecting the dip of the coal at the time, the Coal Board's Sub-Area Planning Department had, in April 1950, estimated that this would occur about 100 feet below ground. But further south the dip became even steeper, and it soon became obvious to those at the mine that the heading in the coal seam was going to meet the surface before it arrived at the fault zone. It was even thought by some of the management how useful this would be in terms of access and ventilation to that end of the colliery.

On 30 August 1950 a shot fired at the face of No. 5 Heading revealed a bed of stones and sand. The rockhead had been met, and a trickle of water started to run from these superficial sediments into the mine. This caused no concern; extra props were placed to support the end of the mine roof, the heading was temporarily left alone – and nothing changed for a week. Meanwhile the surveyors had found that the roof of the breakthrough point was 38 feet below the ground surface. On the morning of 7 September, after a night of very heavy rain, the flow of water into the mine was seen to have increased. The roof props had been footed only on loose rock debris, and this was soon scoured away by the increased water. Some of the props fell; then in the early evening there was a more extensive roof fall at the heading, and at the same time a shallow depression formed in the field above. Plans were made to fence off the depression in the field, but down below the miners continued to work.

At 7:30 in the evening a 'terrific roar' was heard in the mine, and a great mass of saturated peat broke into the mine at the No. 5 Heading. A treacly river of black sludge flowed down the heading and spread out into the workings. Its downward rush took it into all the openings on the downwards-sloping, northern side of the heading, so that the sludge very soon filled all the galleries giving access to the foot of the shaft; the peat eventually rose to a depth of 16 feet within the main shaft. Although it was fluid enough to reach into all the downhill extremeties of the mine, the sludge was fortunately too viscous to flow more than a few yards uphill from the No. 5 Heading. Eleven men who had been working in rooms just off the top end of No. 5 Heading all died in the inrush. Two more men, who had been working the conveyor belts at the lower end of No. 5, were trapped and eventually died a lingering death. Six men escaped up the shaft in good time, but 116 more were in the main workings mostly on the updip side of No. 5 Heading at the time of the inrush. They could only escape uphill and then along to the western end of the mine, where they were then cut off by the peat sludge filling all the galleries between them and the shaft.

By great good fortune the men were trapped in the section of the mine which at one point approached to within just 24 feet of a drive in the abandoned Bank Colliery to the West. A complicated but well-executed and very dramatic rescue effort lasted for two days. A tunnel was broken out between the two mines, and an escape route through over a mile of gas-filled passages saw all the 116 men safely out to the surface. The high drama and complete success of this rescue rather stole the limelight, but it was nonetheless a catastrophe – for the thirteen men who died, and for the mine, now half-full of sludge.

It is clear enough what happened at Knockshinnoch. The mine heading broke through the rockhead into 38 feet of superficial deposits. As revealed in the side of the sinkhole which developed above the breakthrough point, these unconsolidated sediments consisted of a lower layer of sandy boulder clay, followed by a thin bed of lacustrine mud and topped with 12 feet of peat. The top couple of feet of peat formed a partly dried crust, but most of it was a saturated, semi-liquid sludge. When the mine first broke through from below, the boulder clay and mud held firm, but after a week's delay there was a massive subsidence, causing the inrush in the mine and the simultanous formation of a collapse crater 400 feet in diameter in the field above. The collapse and inrush was triggered by a failure of the thin zone of weak rock, probably weathered so near to the surface, which roofed the mine. With the rock falling away from underneath, the boulder clay and mud broke up and let the semi-liquid peat flow down into the mine. But the fate of the mine had been sealed since the heading first arrived at the rockhead.

In the case of Knockshinnoch it is more significant to ask not how, but why the disaster happened. In many geological situations it is perfectly safe to drive an upward mine tunnel out to the surface, so this aspect of mining practice was not to blame. On the other hand the driving of a heading into the underside of a bed of semi-liquid peat should never have been allowed to happen. The inquiry held after the Knockshinnoch accident found that the immediate cause was a lack of communication. The Sub-Area Planning Department, located in offices not at the mine, had the geological map of the area and therefore knew of the peat deposit; the planners expected the coal seam to continue to the fault and not to the surface, so they directed that the No. 5 Heading should proceed. The mine management did not have a geological map, but they did know that the heading would meet the surface and not the fault; with the plans from the Sub-Area offices clearly dictating a continuation on No. 5 Heading the mine officials saw no reason to curtail its progress.

Both groups of officials made fundamental errors in terms of geological considerations. The Planning Department based their plans on a prediction of a uniform dip of the coal seam over a distance of over 1000 feet, from the position of the heading in April 1950 to the expected intersection of the coal and the fault zone. The planners ignored the possibility of fault drag, where the beds of rock are bent due to a drag effect as they are moved against a fault plane; with a fault as large as that known to exist just south of Knockshinnoch, fault drag could reasonably have been expected to be significant and to cause the coal seam to rise more steeply to the south. What is more, the structure of the coal seam was projected for an excessive distance in an area known to be structurally complex, where other folds or faults could easily occur inside a distance of 1000 feet. As the planners predicted that the seam would terminate at the fault over 100 feet down, they regarded the superficial deposits as irrelevant to their considerations. But this irrelevance was dependent on the falsely assumed accuracy of their predictions. They ignored the possibility that an error in their predictions could, and in fact did, make the nature and distribution of the superficial deposits highly relevant. The planners rested on a false sense of security, inadequately founded on their over-frail assumptions.

At the other end of the communications gap, the mine management, knowing as they did that the No. 5 Heading was not following its predicted course, just watched it rise towards the surface. Geological considerations were not the mine manager's direct responsibility, but it was quite apparent that the surface deposits could have been almost anything, and that a possibility of danger therefore existed. There was no geological map kept at the mine, but the glacial history of the area was all too easily apparent. The whole of Scotland was glaciated in the Ice Ages, Knockshinnoch lies at the northern end of a fine glaciated valley, Glen Afton, and nearly everywhere around the mine the rockhead is obscured by unknown thicknesses of boulder clay. Under these conditions the surface deposits are unpredictable, and the destination of No. 5 Heading should have been carefully checked. The farmer who owned the field above the heading knew of the peat; he knew how soft the ground was, he had seen the rushes on the wet patch of ground, and he had seen peat in the edges of the ditches around the field. But no one asked the farmer.

Even when the heading broke through the rockhead at the considerable depth of 38 feet, nobody considered the possibility of a post-glacial hollow being filled, not just with boulder clay, but with dangerously mobile sediments such as muds or saturated peat. The surveyors, checking the surface level after the breakthrough, found the ground 'a wee bit soggy', but still nobody either looked at the geological map or dug a hole just with a spade to find out what was there. Instead the hole in the rockhead was left open, work continued in the mine, and disaster was imminent.

One of the recommendations of the Knockshinnoch accident inquiry was that no working should approach within 150 feet of the surface without the geology being investigated by boring or other approved means. The other means might well include a seismic refraction survey, which could very easily determine the geography of the rockhead in such a case. In addition they recommended that an early part of the investigations should include some simple consideration of the geological possibilities. If only someone at Knockshinnoch who knew of the position of the No. 5 Heading had given some thought to the geological situation, disaster could have been averted. If only someone had spent a few minutes walking over the field and looking in the ditches, or had glanced at the geological map, or chatted to the farmer, thirteen lives would not have been lost.

The conclusion of the Knockshinnoch story must not begin 'if only'. If it is to mean anything, it must be the underlining of the fundamental rules of geological investigation. Reading the map, checking all possible sources of information, looking at the ground, and then considering the possibilities, are the first steps in solving any geological problem. Understanding sub-surface geology is generally a complex process; it may be nearly impossible without dozens of boreholes, but there are often plenty of bits of evidence. It is like completing a jig-saw: fit the pieces of evidence incorrectly or ignore one piece, and the picture cannot be completed. And in the worlds of engineering and planning, an incomplete picture of the geology leads so often to catastrophe.

The future

Lötschberg and Knockshinnoch showed the results of ignoring geology. They are in the past. Seikan is in the future. This incredible Japanese submarine tunnel is not completed, so it cannot yet be quoted as an example of a successful tunnel project. Indeed, there have been some flooding problems already. On the other hand,

Seikan is in a class of its own. It has already penetrated far more difficult ground than that which caused the disasters of Knockshinnoch and Lötschberg. And when it is completed it will stand as a monument to the appalling ground conditions that can be overcome by current civil engineering practice.

Present progress at Seikan suggests it will be finished. The venture is based on twenty-five years of geological investigations, together with probing boreholes which keep a cautious minimum of 1000 feet in advance of the tunnel headings. And if Seikan can be completed successfully, almost any other underground project should be a routine operation as long as adequate attention is given to the geology. Conversely, any future mining or tunnelling project where ground problems turn into a disaster could be ascribed to geological incompetence. But will the lessons of the past be learned, or will man again ignore the geology and bring about yet more catastrophes?

BIBLIOGRAPHY

EARTHQUAKES

Bolt, B. A., Horn, W. L., Macdonald, G. A., Scott, R. F., 1975, Geological Hazards; Springer-Verlag, New York.

Eiby, G. A., 1967, Earthquakes; F. Muller, London.

Heck, N. H., 1936, Earthquakes; Oxford University Press.

Lane, F. W., 1945, The Elements Rage; Country Life, London.

Oakeshott, G. B., 1976, Volcanoes and Earthquakes, Geologic Violence; McGraw-Hill, New York.

Richter, C. F., 1958, Elementary Seismology; W. H. Freeman, San Francisco.

(*These references include many case studies of individual earthquakes described throughout the chapter.*)

Link, M. C., 1960, Exploring the drowned city of Port Royal; National Geographic Magazine *117*, 151–64.

Faults and earthquakes

Bolt, B. A., 1970, Causes of earthquakes; 21–45 in Earthquake Engineering, Wiegel, R. L. (ed.), Prentice-Hall, New Jersey..

Brander, J., 1976, Turkey's earthquake; New Scientist *72*, 537.

Side-effects: landslides, subsidence and tsunamis

Eckel, E. B., 1970, The Alaska earthquake, March 27 1964: lessons and conclusions; U.S. Geol. Surv. Prof. Paper, 546.

Hansen, W. R., 1974, Some engineering geologic effects of the 1964 Alaska earthquake; 193–210, in La Géologie de l'Ingénieur, Calembert, L. (ed.), Soc. Géol. de Belgique.

Miller, R. D. and Dobrovolny, E., 1959, Surficial geology of Anchorage and vicinity. Alaska; U.S. Geol. Surv. Bull., 1093.

Clapperton, C. M. and Hamilton, P., 1971, Peru beneath its eternal threat; Geographical Magazine *43*, 632–9.

Ericksen, G. E. and Plafker, G., 1970, Preliminary report on the geologic events associated with the May 31, 1970, Peru earthquake; U.S. Geol. Surv. Circ., 639.

Wiegel, R. L., 1970, Tsunamis; 253–306, in Earthquake Engineering, Wiegel, R. L. (ed.), Prentice-Hall, New Jersey.

Bernstein, J., 1954, Tsunamis; Scient. Amer. *191*, 60–4.

Earthquake belts and stable areas

Anderson, D. L., 1971, The San Andreas Fault; Scient. Amer. *225*, 53–68.

Iacopi, R., 1971, Earthquake Country; Lane Books, California.

Greensfeider, R., 1971, Seismologic and crustal movement investigations of the San Fernando earthquake; Calif. Geol. (Apr-May), 62–6.

The prediction and inducement of earthquakes

Pakiser, L. C., Eaton, J. P., Healy, J. H., Raleigh, C. B., 1969, Earthquake Prediction and Control; Science *166*, 1467–73.

Press, F., 1975, Earthquake Prediction; Scient. Amer. *232*, 14–23.

Rikitake, T., 1976, Earthquake Prediction; Elsevier, Amsterdam.

Whitcomb, J. H., Garmany, J. D., Anderson, D. L., 1973, Earthquake Prediction: Variation of Seismic Velocities before the San Francisco Earthquake; Science *180*, 632–5.

Earthquake protection and zoning

Kunze, W. E., Fintel, M., Amrhein, J. E., 1963, Skopje earthquake damage; Civ. Eng. *33*, 56–9.

Nichols, D. R. and Buchanan-Banks, J. M., 1974, Seismic Hazards and Land-Use Planning; U.S. Geol. Surv. Circ., 690.

Borcherdt, R. D. (ed.), 1975, Basis for reduction of earthquake hazards, San Francisco Bay Region, California; U.S. Geol. Surv. Prof. Paper, 941-A.

VOLCANOES

Bolt, B. A., Horn, W. L., Macdonald, G. A., Scott, R. F., 1975, Geological Hazards; Springer-Verlag, New York.

Francis, P., 1976, Volcanoes; Penguin Books, London.

Macdonald, G. A., 1972, Volcanoes; Prentice-Hall, New York.

Rittmann, A. and L., 1976, Volcanoes; Orbis, London.

Wilcoxson, K., 1967, Volcanoes; Cassel, London.

(*The above works contain extended case histories of many of the examples cited in the chapter without reference below.*)

The nature of volcanic activity

Foshag, W. F. and Jernaro Gonzalez, R., 1950, Birth and development of Paricutin Volcano; U. S. Geol. Surv. Bull., 965-D.

Bardarson, H. R., 1972, Ice and Fire; H. R. Bardarson, Reykjavik.

Thorarinsson, S., 1970, The Lakagigar eruption of 1783; Bull. volcan. Series 2, *33*, 910–27.

Booth, B., 1974, Persistent Etna; Geog. Mag. *46*, 415–17.

Volcanic violence

Edey, A. M., 1975, Lost World of the Aegean; Time Life International, Amsterdam.

Minimising volcanic damage

Clapperton, C. M., 1973, Eruption of Helgefell; Geog. Mag. *45*, 482–6.

Clapperton, C. M., 1973, Dying fire of a new volcano; Geog. Mag. *45*, 623–7.

Embleton, C., 1970, Iceland: country of sagas and volcanoes; Geog. Mag. *42*, 333–42.

Williams, R. S. and Moore, J. G., 1973, Iceland chills a lava flow; Geotimes *18*(8), 14–17.

Mason, A. C. and Foster, H. L., 1953, Diversion of Lava flows at Oshima, Japan; Am. Journ. Sci. *251*, 249 58.

Murton, B. J. and Shimabukuro, S., 1974, Human adjustment to volcanic hazard in Puna District, Hawaii; 151–9, in White, G. F. (ed.), Natural Hazards, Oxford University Press.

Prediction of volcanic disasters

Crandell, D. R. and Mullineaux, D. R., 1975, Technique and Rationale of Volcanic Hazards Appraisals in the Cascade Range, Northwestern United States; Environmental Geology *1*, 23–32.

Booth, B., 1976, Predicting eruptions; New Scientist *71*, 526–8.

Shimozuru, D., 1971, A seismological approach to the prediction of volcanic eruptions; in The surveillance and prediction of volcanic activity, UNESCO Publication Earth Sciences *8*, 19–45.

LANDSLIDES

Bolt, B. A., Horn, W. L., Macdonald, G. A., Scott, R. F., 1975, Geological Hazards; Springer Verlag, New York.

Brunsden, D., 1971, Ever-moving hillsides; Geog. Mag. *43*, 759–64.

Leggett, R. F., 1962, Geology and engineering; McGraw-Hill, New York.

Morton, D. M. and Streitz, R., 1967, Landslides; Mineral Information Service *20*, 123–40.

Sharpe, C. F. S., 1968, Landslides and their related phenomena; Cooper Square, New York.

Terzaghi, K., 1950, Mechanics of landslides; 83–124, in Application of geology to engineering practice, Berkey Volume, Geol. Soc. Amer.

Zaruba, Q. and Mencl, V., 1969, Landslides and their control; Elsevier, Amsterdam.

Mathews, W. H. and McTaggart, K. C., 1969, The Hope Landslide, British Columbia; Proc. Geol. Assoc. Canada *20*, 65–75.

Voight, B., 1977, Rockslides and Avalanches; Elsevier, Amsterdam.

Rockfalls

Watson, R. A. and Wright, H. E., 1969, The Saidmarreh Landslide, Iran; Geol. Soc. Amer. Spec. Paper *123*, 115–39.

Shreve, R. L., 1968, Leakage and fluidization in air-layer lubricated avalanches; Geol. Soc. Amer. Bull. *79*, 653–8.

Hsu, K. J., 1975, Catastrophic debris streams (Sturzstroms) generated by rockfalls; Geol. Soc. Amer. Bull. *86*, 129–40.

Shreve, R. L., 1968, The Blackhawk Landslides; Geol. Soc. Amer. Spec. Paper, 108.

Barney, K. R., 1960, Madison Canyon Slide; Civil Engineering (Aug), 72–5.

Daly, R. A., Miller, W. G. and Rice, G. S., 1912, Report of the commission appointed to investigate Turtle Mountain, Frank, Alberta; Nat. Museum of Canada Memoir, 27.

Rockslides

Taylor, F. M., 1966, A landslide at Matlock, Derbyshire, 1966; Mercian Geol. *1*, 351–5.

Drouhin, G., Gautier, M. and Dervieux, F. 1948 Slide and subsidence of the hills of St. Raphael – Telemly; Proc. Second Int. Conf. Soil Mech. and Found. Eng. *5*, 104–6.

Alden, W. C., 1928, Landslide and flood at Gros Ventre, Wyoming; Amer. Inst. Min. and Met. Eng. *76*, 347–58.

Water in landslides

Jaeger, C., 1969, The stability of partly immerged fissured rock masses and the Vajont rock slide; Civ. Eng. and Public Works Rev. *6*, 1204–7.

Jaeger, C., 1972, Rock mechanics and engineering; Cambridge University Press.

Kiersch, G. A., 1964, Vaiont Reservoir disaster; Civil Engineering *34*, 32–9.

Muller, L., 1964, The rock slide in the Vajont Valley; Journ. Int. Soc. Rock Mech. *2*, 148–212.

Earthslides

Barton, M. E., 1973, The degradation of the Barton Clay Cliffs of Hampshire; Quart. Journ. Eng. Geol. *6*, 423–40.

Sullivan, R., 1975, Geological hazards along the coast south of San Francisco; Calif. Geol. (Feb), 27–36.

Walcott, C. D. (ed.), 1924, Report of the committee of the National Academy of Sciences on the Panama Canal slides; Mem. Nat. Acad. Sci., 18.

Attewell, P. B. and Farmer, I. W., 1976, Principles of engineering geology; Chapman and Hall, London.

Chandler, R. J., 1970, The degradation of Lias clay slopes in an area of the east Midlands; Quart. Journ. Eng. Geol. *2*, 161–81.

Skempton, A. W., 1964, Long-term stability of clay slopes; Geotechnique *14*, 75–101.

Flow slides

Crawford, C. B. and Eden, W. J., 1963, Nicolet landslide of November 1955, Quebec, Canada; Eng. Geol. Case Histories, Geol. Soc. Amer. *4*, 45–50.

Holmsen, P. 1953, Landslips in Norwegian quick-clays; Geotechnique *3*, 187–94.

Tavenas, F., Chagnon, J. Y. and La Rochelle, P., 1971, The Saint-Jean-Vianney landslide: observations and eyewitness accounts; Can. Geotech. Journ. *8*, 463–78.

Kerr, P. F., 1963, Quick clay; Sci. Am. *309*, 132–41.

Skempton, A. W. and Northey, R. D., 1952, The sensitivity of clays; Geotechnique *3*, 30–53.

Campbell, R. H., 1975, Soil slips, debris flows and rainstorms in the Santa Monica Mountains and vicinity, Southern California; U.S. Geol. Soc. Prof. Paper, 851.

Casagrande, A., 1965, Role of the calculated risk in earthwork and foundation engineering; Proc. Amer. Soc. Civ. Eng., Journ. Soil. Mech. Div. *91* (SM4), 1–40.

Aberfan Tribunal, 1967, Report of the Tribunal appointed to inquire into the disaster at Aberfan; HMSO, London.

Aberfan Tribunal, 1969, A selection of technical reports submitted to the Aberfan Tribunal; HMSO, London.

Anderson, J. G. C. and Trigg, C. F., 1976, Case-histories in engineering geology; Elek Science, London.

Knox, G., 1927, Landslides in South Wales valleys; Proc. S. Wales. Inst. Eng. *43*, 161–247.

Powell, D. L. J., 1939, The sliding of colliery rubbish tips; Powell Duffryn Company (reprinted in Aberfan Tribunal, 1967).

Watkins, G. L., 1959, The stability of colliery spoilbanks; Colliery Engineering (Nov).

Bishop, A. W., 1973, The stability of tips and spoil heaps; Quart. Journ. Eng. Geol. *6*, 335–76.

Landslide prediction and control

Stevenson, P. C., 1975, A predictive landslip survey and its social impact; Proc. 2nd. Aust. N.Z. Conf. Geomech. Brisbane, Inst. Eng. Australia, 10–15.

Franklin, J. A. and Denton, P. E., 1973, The monitoring of rock slopes; Quart. Journ. Eng. Geol. *6*, 259–86.

Woods, H. D., 1958, Causes of the Sear's Point landslide, Sonoma County, California; Eng. Geol. Case Histories, Geol. Soc. Amer. *2*, 41–3.

Wood, A. M. M., 1955, Folkestone Warren landslips: investigations 1948–1950; Proc. Inst. Civ. Eng. *4* (II), 410–28.

Hutchinson, J. N., 1969, A reconsideration of the coastal landslides at Folkestone Warren, Kent; Geotechnique *19*, 6–38.

Viner-Brady, N. E. V., 1955, Folkestone Warren landslips: remedial measures 1948–1954; Proc. Inst. Civ. Eng. *4* (II), 429–41.

WATER

International Commission on Large Dams, 1973, Lessons from dam incidents; ICOLD, Paris.

O'Connor, R., 1957, Johnstown – the day the dam broke; London.

Flood plain inundation

Hoyt, W. G. and Langbein W. B., 1955, Floods; Princeton University Press, Princeton, N. J.

Newson, M. D., 1975, Flooding and flood hazard; Oxford University Press.

Legget, R. F., 1962, Geology and engineering; McGraw-Hill, New York.

Baker, V. R., 1976, Hydrogeomorphic methods for the regional evaluation of flood hazards; Environmental Geology *1*, 261–82.

Harding, D. M. and Parker, D. J., 1974, Flood hazard at Shrewsbury, United Kingdom; 43–52, in White G. F. (ed.), Natural Hazards, Oxford University Press.

Kidson, C., 1953, The Exmoor storm and the Lynmouth floods; Geography *38*, 1–9.

Cressey, G. B., 1955, Land of the 500 Million; McGraw-Hill, New York.

Todd, O. J., 1936, A Runaway River Controlled; Engineering News-Record *116*, 735–8.

Todd O. J., 1942, Taming Flood Dragons along China's Hwang Ho; Nat. Geog. Mag. *81*, 205–34.

Hazards of water management

Dresch, J., 1973, On the fringes of drought and despair; Geog. Mag. *45*, 786–7.

Chappell, J. E., 1974, Passing the Colorado salt; Geog. Mag. *46*, 569–74.

Squire, R., 1964, Caves in the Tralee area, Co. Kerry, Eire; Proc. Univ. Bristol Spel. Soc. *10*, 139–48.

Aley, T., 1972, Groundwater contamination from sinkhole dumps; Caves and Karst *14*, 17–23.

Quinlan, J. F. and Rowe, D. R., 1977, Hydrology and water quality in the Central Kentucky Karst, Phase 1; Research Report 101, Univ. Kentucky Water Resources Research Institute.

Geological problems in dam foundations

Guthrie Brown J., 1964, Discussion on dam disasters; Proc. Inst. Civ. Eng. *27*, 366–8.

International Commission on Large Dams, 1973, Lessons from dam incidents; ICOLD, Paris.

Smith, N., 1971, A history of dams; Peter Davies, London.

Walters, R. C. S., 1971, Dam geology; Butterworth, London.

Knill, J. L., 1974, The application of engineering geology to the construction of dams in the United Kingdom; 113–47 in La Géologie de l'Ingénieur, Calembert, L.(ed.), Soc. Géol. de Belgique.

Ransome, F. L., 1928, Geology of the St. Francis dam-site; Econ. Geol. *23*, 553–63.

Clements, T., 1966, St. Francis Dam Failure of 1928; 89–91, in Lung, R. and Proctor, R. (eds), Engineering Geology in Southern California; Assoc. Eng. Geol. Arcadia. Calif.

Outland, C. F., 1963, Man-made Disaster, the story of the St. Francis Dam; A. H. Clark Co., Glendale, California.

Jessup, W. E., 1964, Baldwin Hills Dam failure; Civil Engineering (Feb), 62–4.

James, L. B., 1968, Failure of Baldwin Hills Reservoir, Los Angeles, California; Engineering Geology Case Histories, Geol. Soc. Amer. *6*, 1–11.

Hamilton, D. H. and Meehan, R. L., 1971, Ground Rupture in the Baldwin Hills; Science *172*, 333–44.

Jaeger, C., 1963, The Malpasset Report; Water Power *15*, 55–61.

Jaeger, C., 1972, Rock mechanics and engineering; Cambridge University Press.

Appleton, B., 1977, All BuRec designs to get independent check (Results of inquiry into Teton Dam failure); New Civil Engineer (13 Jan), 8–9.

SUBSIDENCE

Allen, A. S., 1969, Geologic settings of subsidence; Reviews in Engineering Geology, Geol. Soc. Amer. *2*, 305–42.

Bolt, V. A., Horn, W. L., Macdonald, G. A., Scott, R. F., 1975, Geological Hazards; Spinger-Verlag, New York.

Legget, R. F., 1973, Cities and Geology; McGraw-Hill, New York.

Subsidence due to solutional removal of rock

Brune G., 1965, Anhydrite and gypsum problems in engineering geology; Eng. Geol. *2*, 26–38.

Srikantic, S. V. and Bhargava, O.N., 1972, Subsidence sinkhole at Runjh (Himachal Pradesh, India); Eng. Geol. *6*, 191 201.

Christiansen, E.A., 1971, Geology of the Crater Lake Collapse Structure in Southeastern Saskatchewan; Can. Journ. Earth Sci. *8*, 1505–13.

De Mille, G., Shouldice, J. R., Nelson, H. W., 1964, Collapse structures related to evaporites of the Prairie Formation, Saskatchewan; Geol. Soc. Amer. Bull. *75*, 307–16.

Bell, F. G., 1975, Salt and subsidence in Cheshire, England; Eng. Geol. *9*, 237–47.

Calvert, A. F., 1915, Salt in Cheshire; Spon, London.

Evans, W. B., Wilson, A. A., Taylor, B. J., Price, D., 1968, Geology of the country around Macclesfield, Congleton, Crewe and Middlewich; HMSO, London.

Wallwork, K. L., 1960, Some problems of subsidence and land use in the Mid-Cheshire industrial area; Geog. Journ. *126*, 191–9.

Subsidence on unconsolidated sediments

Prokopovitch, N. P., 1972, Land Subsidence and Population Growth; Proc. 24th Int. Geol. Cong. (Montreal) *13*, 44–54.

Peck, R. B. and Bryant, F. G., 1953, The bearing-capacity failure of the Transcona elevator; Geotechnique *3*, 201–14.

Mann, A., 1975, The inclination that defies explanation; Telegraph Mag. *537*, 9–10.

Spencer, C. B., 1953, Leaning Tower of Pisa; Eng. News-Record (2 Apr), 40–3.

Mitchell, J. K., Vivatrat, V., Lambe, T.W., 1977, Foundation performance of Tower of Pisa; Proc. Amer. Soc. Civ. Eng., Journ. Geotech. Eng. Div. *103* (GT3), 227–49.

Subsidence due to withdrawal of ground fluids

Poland, J. F., Lofgren, B. E., Ireland, R.L., Pugh, R. G., 1975, Land subsidence in the San Joacquin Valley, California, as of 1972; U.S. Geol. Surv. Prof. Paper 437-H, 86.

Marsden, S. S. and Davis, S. N., 1967, Geological Subsidence; Scient. Amer. *206*, 93–100.

Davis, G. H., Small, J. B., Courts, H. B., 1963, Land subsidence related to decline of artesian pressure in the Ocala Limestone at Savannah, Georgia; Eng. Geol. Case Histories, Geol. Soc. Amer. *4*, 1–8.

Cooke, R. U. and Doornkamp, J. C., 1974, Geomorphology in Environmental Management; Oxford University Press.

Berghinz, C., 1971, Venice is sinking into the sea; Civil Eng., Am. Soc. Civ. Eng. (Mar), 67–71.

O'Riordan, N. J., 1975, The Venetian ideal; Geog, Mag. *47*, 419–26.

Ricceri, G. and Butterfield, R., 1974, An analysis of compressibility data from a deep borehole in Venice; Geotechnique *24*, 175–92.

Loehnberg, A., 1958, Aspects of the sinking of Mexico City and proposed countermeasures; Amer. Water Works Assoc. Journ. *50*, 432–40

Poland, J. F. and Davis, G. H., 1969, Land subsidence due to withdrawal of fluids; Reviews in Eng. Geol., Geol. Soc. Amer. *2*, 187–246.

Thornley, J. H., Spencer, C. B., Albin, P., 1955, Mexico's Palace of Fine Arts settles ten feet; Civ. Eng. (June), 50–4.

Subsidence and collapse on cavernous limestone

Sowers, G. F., 1975, Failures in limestones in humid subtropics; Proc. Amer. Soc. Civ. Eng. Journ. Geotech. Eng. Div. *101* (GT8), 771–87.

Tratman, E. K. (ed.), 1963, Report on the investigations of Pen Park Hole, Bristol; Cave Res. Gp. Gt. Brit. Publication 12.

Kleywegt, R. J. and Enslin, J. F., 1975, The application of the gravity method to the problem of ground settlement and sinkhole formation in dolomite on the Far West Rand, South Africa; Proc. Hannover Symposium on Sinkholes and Subsidence, Int. Ass. Eng. Geol. Paper T3–0.

Early, K. R. and Dyer, K. R., 1964, The use of a resistivity survey on a foundation site underlain by karst dolomite; Geotechnique *14*, 341–8.

Coker, A. E., Marshall, R., Thomson, N. S., 1969, Application of computer processed multispectral data to the discrimination of land collapse (sinkhole) prone areas in Florida; Proc. 6th Int. Symp. on Remote sensing of Environment, Ann Arbor, Michigan *1*, 65–77.

Kennedy, J. M., 1968, A microwave radiometric study of buried karst topography; Geol. Soc. Amer. Bull. *79*, 735–42.

Newton, J. G. and Hyde, L. W., 1971, Sinkhole problem in and near Roberts Industrial Subdivision, Birmingham, Alabama; Geol. Surv. Alabama, Circular 68.

Foose, R. M., 1969, Mine dewatering and recharge in carbonate rocks near Hershey, Pennsylvania; Eng. Geol. Case Histories, Geol. Soc. Amer. *7*, 45–60.

Van Horn, F. B., 1910, A Cave-In Caused by an Underground Stream at Staunton, Virginia; Engineering News *64*, 238–9.

North, F. J., 1952, Some geological aspects of subsidence not related to mining; Proc. S. Wales Inst. Eng. *68*, 127–58.

Aley, T. J., Williams, J. H., Massello, J. W., 1972, Groundwater Contamination and Sinkhole Collapse induced by leaky impoundments in soluble rock terrain; Eng. Geol. Series, Missouri Geol. Surv., 5.

Bezuidenhout, C. A. and Enslin, J. F., 1970, Surface subsidence and sinkholes in the dolomitic areas of the Far West Rand, Transvaal, Republic of South Africa; in Land Subsidence, Publication no. 88, Assoc. Internal. Hydrol. Scient., UNESCO. *2*, 482–95.

Brink, A. B. A. and Partridge, T. C., 1965, Transvaal Karst: Some Considerations of Development and Morphology with Special Reference to Sinkholes and Subsidences on the Far West Rand; South African Geog. Journ. *47*, 11–34.

Foose, R. M., 1967, Sinkhole Formation by Groundwater Removal: Far West Rand, South Africa; Science *157*, 1045–8.

Collapse and subsidence over mine workings
Anon, 1916, More Mine Cave-Ins Threaten Parts of Scranton; Eng. News *76*, 280–2.
Dean, J. W., 1967, Old Mine Shafts and their Hazards; Min. Eng. *126*, 368–80.
Lee, A. J., 1966, The Effect of Faulting on Mining Subsidence; Min. Eng. *125*, 735–45.
Orchard, R. J., 1973, Some Aspects of Subsidence in the U.K.; Proc. Fourth Ann. Symp. Illawarra, Austral. Inst. Min. Met. Paper 3.

UNDER GROUND

Beaver, P., 1972, History of tunnels; P. Davies, London.
Jacobs, J. D., 1975, Some tunnel failures and what they have taught; in Hazards in tunnelling and on falsework, Institute of Civil Engineers, London, 37–46.
Sandström, G. A., 1963, The history of tunnelling; Barrie and Rockcliffe, London.

The hazards of underground water
Hayward, D., 1977, Tale of a tunnel (Seikan Tunnel); New Civil Engineer (19 May), 29–37.
Cousens, R. R. M. and Garrett, W. S., 1970, The flooding at West Driefontein mine, South Africa; Proc. 9th Commonwealth Cong. Min. Met. *1*, 931–87.

The threat of buried valleys
Sandström, G. A., 1963, Trouble in Lötschberg; 330–9, in The history of tunnelling, Barrie and Rockcliffe, London.

The problems of difficult rock structures
Spooner, J. (ed.), 1971, Mufulira interim report; Min. Journ. *276*, 122.

The special problems of coal mining
Marshall, J. S., 1971, Outburst of coal and firedamp at Cynheidre/Pentremaur Colliery Carmarthenshire, Report; HMSO, London.
Duckham, H. and B., 1973, Great pit disasters; David and Charles, Newton Abbot.
Overbey, W. K., Komar, C.A., Pasini, J., 1973, Predicting probable roof fall areas in advance of mining by geological analysis; U.S. Bur. Mines Tech. Proj. Report, 70.
Bryan, A., 1951, Accident at Knockshinnoch Castle Colliery Ayrshire, Report; HMSO, London.

GLOSSARY

adit – roughly horizontal mined passage, in many cases specifically for the purpose of drainage

aftershock – minor earth tremor following in the wake of a larger earthquake

alluvium – river-deposited sediment which may be clay, silt, sand or gravel

andesite – type of volcanic lava with an intermediate silica content

anhydrite – natural mineral with composition of calcium sulphate

anticline – any type of fold in rocks which rises in the centre, i.e. an upfold

aquifer – rock which contains large amounts of groundwater

artesian head – natural pressure in groundwater which causes it to rise above ground level from a well

basalt – very fluid type of volcanic lava with a low silica content

bentonite – type of clay containing a high proportion of the mineral montmorillonite

biotite – silicate mineral with an easily sheared platey structure

brining – method of salt mining which involves pumping salty water out of permeable salt-bearing rocks

calcite – mineral with composition of calcium carbonate, the main component of limestone

caldera – large crater formed by collapse at the summit of a volcano

camber fold – gentle type of fold where beds of rock slope towards valleys, formed by compaction and plastic deformation of underlying weak rocks

compaction – loss of volume occurring in sediments due to the weight of overlying sediments or structures

conglomerate – sedimentary rock with rounded cobble-sized fragments

cusec – abbreviated form of the unit of flow 'cubic foot per second'

dacite – type of volcanic lava with high silica content

doline – closed hollow, normally in limestone regions, which having underground drainage does not fill with water

dolomite – mineral with composition of calcium magnesium carbonate; also rock consisting largely of the mineral dolomite, very similar in appearance and properties to limestone

earthquake belts – zones on the Earth's surface, mostly along plate boundaries, in which earthquakes are particularly common

epicentre – point on the surface directly above the focus, or point of origin, of an earthquake

felsite – medium-grained, light-coloured igneous rock

foreshock – minor earth tremor which may or may not precede an earthquake

fumarole – hot spring or steam vent of volcanic origin

geyser – large, spectacular type of fumarole which may fountain volcanic water high into the air

glaciofluvial – descriptive of processes involving meltwater rivers on or below glaciers

gneiss – generally strong crystalline metamorphic rock characterised by the presence of foliation, a mineral orientation which may create a shear weakness in the rock

gouge – ground-up powdered rock formed along some faults

granite – coarse-grained, light-coloured, silicon-rich igneous rock

greenschist – variety of schist containing significant proportion of green silicate minerals

ground waves – earthquake vibrations visible as actual wave motions in the ground

grout – chemical or cement mixture injected into rocks by engineers to render the ground either more stable or more impermeable

groyne – artificial barrier built across a foreshore or beach, in order to minimise erosion and sediment transport by wave action

head – general term for unsorted surface deposits largely of solifluction origin

hydrocompaction – type of sediment compaction caused by the addition of water

hydrostatic head – pressure in water due purely to its depth or head

igneous rock – type of rock formed from crystalli-

166

sation of a molten, liquid magma

ignimbrite – type of volcanic ash which is still hot when it lands on the ground and therefore welds itself into a solid rock

lacustrine clay – clay deposited in a lake

lapilli – volcanic tephra, the size of coarse sand

lava – molten rock, or magma, which emerges from a volcano

loess – very fine-grained, wind-deposited silt sediment

levee – natural or artificial bank formed along the margin of a river or its floodplain

magma – molten rock

marl – calcareous variety of clay

metamorphic rock – type of rock transformed by considerable heat and/or pressure (without completely melting) deep inside the Earth

montmorillonite – variety of clay mineral with a hollow structure, capable of holding extremely large proportions of water

moraine – sheet or bank of glacially deposited, unsorted debris or sediment

pegmatite – very coarse-grained igneous rock normally occurring only in thin sheets

periglacial – descriptive of very cold, but not glacial, environments, normally with permafrost, in which solifluction and landslides are common

permafrost – permanently frozen layer in the ground, beneath a surface layer which freezes each winter but melts each summer

phyllite – fine-grained, easily sheared metamorphic rock, intermediate in structure between slate and schist

plate boundaries – mobile, disturbed zones which separate relatively rigid segments of the Earth's crust known as plates

quartzite – very tough crystalline rock formed largely of the mineral quartz

rhyolite – very viscous type of volcanic lava with a high silica content

rock salt – natural mineral with composition of salt, or sodium chloride

rockhead – boundary surface between unconsolidated superficial sediments and underlying solid rock

schist – metamorphic rock consisting mostly of platey minerals such as chlorate and biotite, which shears very easily along the mineral alignment

schistosity – parallel orientation of platey minerals in a schist causing easy splitting and shearing

seatearth – leached sandstone, siltstone or clay immediately underlying a coal seam

sedimentary rock – type of rock formed by lithification or solidification of sediments accumulated on the Earth's surface

sensitive clay – clay which will distort and even liquefy as it loses strength on disturbance or vibration

seismograph – instrument used to detect minute ground vibrations

sericite – weak, easily sheared, clay-like mineral commonly formed as alteration product in igneous and metamorphic rocks

sinkhole – hole in the ground, normally in limestone country, which absorbs a stream, or merely a doline or hollow with underground drainage

slickenside – scratch mark on a fault plane formed by blocks of rock moving against each other

solifluction – slow but persistent downslope mass movement of soil and surface sediment saturated with water but not capable of liquid flow

stope – mined-out cavity, normally steeply inclined, with pillars of rock left in to keep the walls from collapsing inwards

stratimorph – topographic feature whose shape is determined by the form of the strata, or beds of rocks

tailings – very fine-grained slurry, the waste product of modern mineral-processing plants

tectonic – descriptive of any feature or process relating to large-scale movements of the Earth's crust

tephra – fragmental debris produced by a volcano, including volcanic ash, lapilli, tuff and volcanic bombs

thrust fault – type of fault involving more horizontal than vertical movement of rocks

tiltmeter – instrument used to detect very slight changes in inclination of the ground surface

tsunami – large sea wave generated by actual movement of the sea or ocean bed, associated with earthquakes or volcanic eruptions

tuff – volcanic tephra, the size of very fine grains of sand

unconsolidated sediment – loose, friable sediment such as sand and clay which has not been lithified or solidified

underpinning – engineering technique of placing foundations under an existing inadequately supported building or structure

unloading joint – rock fracture developed close to and parallel to its surface, due to relief movement when weight of overlying rocks is removed

INDEX

Individual catastrophes described at greater length are in **bold** type